"*Sunday Best* is a beautiful cookbook that invites you to create special moments with those you love through food. This vibrant collection delivers a deep sense of home, family, history, and the feeling that no matter how different we may look, we can all relate to gathering around the table to honor the little victories we achieve every day."
—**MARCUS SAMUELSSON**, chef, author, and restaurateur

"*Sunday Best* is far more than cookbook, it's a spiritual state of mind and a cause for celebration! Chef Adrienne channels so much joy and care into her delicious recipes, you can feel the warmth and knowledge on every page. With her debut cookbook, she gives us the excuse we need these days to dress up, roll up our sleeves, and get cooking."
—**GAIL SIMMONS**, food expert, TV host, and author of *Bringing It Home: Favorite Recipes from a Life of Adventurous Eating*

"Adrienne's *Sunday Best* is a collection of memorable soul food recipes at their best. Just reading the book makes me smile as there are so many relatable cultural moments that take me back to the big family dinners of my childhood. The tips throughout are invaluable and will completely up your cooking game for eternity."
—**CARLA HALL**, chef, cookbook author, and TV host

"A celebration of Adrienne's cooking that pays homage to her roots and fine dining techniques, *Sunday Best* reminds us how sharing a meal can bring people together."
—**ERIC RIPERT**, chef

Sunday Best

Sunday Best

COOKING UP THE WEEKEND SPIRIT EVERY DAY

ADRIENNE CHEATHAM

with Sarah Zorn

photographs by Kelly Marshall

Clarkson Potter/Publishers
New York

dedicated to

Big Sister, Mrs. Ruby Cannon-Cheatham, the heart and soul of our family.

Stephen, Susan, Jack, Jacqui, and Ira, who have been helping me write this book for years without any of us knowing it.

And for my family, the ones I share blood with and the people I've shared meals with. Your love is in these pages and I'm grateful that the joy we've shared can be shared with others.

Contents

Introduction   11

Morning Love: Breakfast   21

Flaky Layered Biscuits with Sausage Gravy   23
Pecan Five-Spice Sticky Buns   25
Buttermilk and Corn Flour Pancakes with Warm Peach Compote   29
Challah French Toast Waffles   31
Overnight Grits with Fried Eggs and Mushroom Ragout   33
Tater Tot Waffles with Candied Bacon   37
Kick the Can Salmon Croquettes   38
Toasted American Cheese "Parachutes"   42
Cornbread Toad-in-the-Hole with Crab and Andouille   45
Big Easy Eggs Sardou   47
Green Tomato Shakshuka   51
Grand Slam Breakfast Tarts   52

All-Day Grazing: Snacks   55

Hanky-Pankies (Cheesy Porky Caraway Bites)   56
Butter Bean Hummus   60
Pimento Cheese–Stuffed Celery   61
Spicy-Sweet-Crispy Candied Chicken Wings   63
Pickled Shrimp Escabeche   66
Oven-Fried Okra Chips   67
Cornbread Gougères   70
Fried Olives with Anchovy Dip   71
Mango Tajín Gazpacho Shooters   73
Best-*Ever* Hush Puppies   74
Berbere-Spiced Mini Lamb Meatballs   77
Crunchy Hoppin' John Bhel Puri   80
Third Coast Shrimp Toast   83

That Special Touch: Sauces   85

Buttermilk Vinaigrette   86
Cha-Cha (Tabletop Pepper Sauce)   88
Turnip-Top Pesto   91
Fermented Pepper Sauce (Cha-Cha's Cousin)   92
Mustard-Green Chimichurri   94
Charred Green Onion Relish   96
Red Miso BBQ Sauce   98
Smoky Red Gravy   99
Beer-Apple Jus   100
Bacon-Miso Sauce   102
Country Gravy (aka the Southern Mother Sauce)   108
Poor Man's Remoulade   109

Remaking the Dinner Plate: Protein, Starch, and Veg   111

PROTEIN

Brioche-Crusted Salmon   114
Stout-and-Soy-Roasted Chicken   117
Humboldt Park Fried Chicken   118
Braised Turkey Necks   121
Red Miso BBQ Quail   123
Grilled Skirt Steak with Mustard-Green Chimichurri   124
Cheerwine-Braised Oxtail   127
Smothered Pork Chops with Smoky Red Gravy   130
Herb-and-Mustard-Slathered Veal Chops   133
Slow-Cooked Ham Hocks   134
Roasted Catfish with Herby Yogurt   137

STARCH

Sky-High Popovers 140

Pilsen Red Beans and Rice 141

Sour Cream Cornbread 144

Hominy Tabbouleh 145

Barley Grits with Roasted Grapes
and Almonds 147

Split Pea Salad with Warm
Bacon-Sherry Vinaigrette 150

Sweet Potato Gnocchi with
Bacon-Miso Sauce 152

Mashed Parsnips 156

Trinity Rice Pilaf 157

Turnip Latkes 159

VEG

Collard Green Kimchi 161

Red Cabbage and Beet Slaw 165

Blistered Green Beans with
Crushed Peanuts and Soy 166

Charred Okra with Roasted Tomatoes 167

Elote Macque Choux 168

Grilled Green Tomato Salad with
Buttermilk Vinaigrette and Pepitas 171

Collard Green Salad with
Sesame Vinaigrette 172

Brussels Sprouts with
Brown Butter and Hazelnuts 174

Bourbon-and-Brown-Sugar-Glazed
Root Vegetables 175

Spicy and Crispy Whole-Roasted
Cauliflower 177

Green Cabbage Gratin 178

Pure Sunday Vibes: Family-Style Feasts 181

Slow-Roasted Pork Shoulder (Pernil) 182

Black Garlic Roasted Leg of Lamb 183

Pecan-Crusted Pork Rib Roast 187

Mississippi Pot Roast 189

Roger's Park Meat and Potatoes 190

Slow-Roasted Harissa Short Ribs 192

Chicken and Cornbread Dumplings 195

Mom's Stuffed Shells with Smoky Red Gravy 197

Grandma Lydia's Shrimp Creole 202

Controversial Gumbo 204

Boudin-Stuffed Calamari 208

Tasty Transformations: Leftovers Reimagined 213

Cornbread (or Biscuit) Panzanella 214

Overnight Grits Arancini 217

Cast-Iron Deep-Dish Pizza 219

Crustless Kitchen-Sink Quiche 223

Pan-Fried Spaghetti Rösti 226

Louisiana Yaka Mein 227

Seven-Layer Salad 231

Green Tomato Chili 233

Coconut Curry Stew 234

Anything Can Pickle 235

Creamy Vegan Pasta 241

My Goodies: Sweets and Desserts 243

No-Churn Strawberry
Shortcake Ice Cream 244

Sweet Tea Granita 247

The Best Baked Apples 248

Yuzu Banana Pudding 251

Buttermilk Brûlée with
Pickled Blueberry Compote 252

Chocolate-Bourbon Pecan Pie 254

Sugar-and-Spice-Dusted Calas
(aka Rice Beignets) 256

Roasted White Chocolate Crepe Cake
with Hazelnuts and Pecans 259

Salted Vanilla-Coconut Rice Pudding 261

Apple Pie for Uncle George 267

Sugared Biscuits and Chocolate Gravy 269

Roasted Pineapple Cornmeal Cake 273

Acknowledgments 277

Index 283

Introduction

In the Black community, you typically have a set of clothes that are reserved for church. Your nicest dress, your socks with the fold-over lace on them, a pair of conservative heels. It's a practice that extends all the way back to the days of slavery. There were laws preventing Black people from congregating in groups of more than two or three. The only time they were really allowed to gather was at the plantation church house on Sundays. So they'd shine up their shoes, dust off their pants, and wear the best of what they had. And this continued through—and in many places, well after—segregation. Since their nicest clothes were generally their church clothes, people would put on their "Sunday best" just to go to town, because they wanted to look respectable so that they would be seen as acceptable. It was a way of saying "take me seriously" to anyone who didn't accept Black people as equal.

Even today, those who cook African American food—which is to say, Southern and soul food—have had to push back against similar prejudices, demanding respect for a cuisine that's seen as just humble and homespun. By highlighting the subtleties, nuance, and cultural influences from the diverse groups that have had a hand in the pot, I've made it my mission to dress Southern food up in its own Sunday best. Whether by showcasing clever techniques, incorporating unexpected ingredients, or adding a bit of finesse through enticing finishing touches or thoughtful plating, I want to show that this food deserves a place at the table and in the narrative of serious cuisine. And that, like all other cuisines that began with humble, country cooking, it too can grow and evolve.

The concept of Sunday Best also encapsulates the value I place on feeding people. Think about it: for most of us, the very first meals we ever ate were prepared by our parents, which makes cooking a primary and fundamental way of expressing care and love. So to me, feeding others isn't a labor or chore but a privilege. It's an honor to nurture both body and soul. I make a point of reminding myself of that every time I step into the kitchen. Not just at work, but at home, and not just one day a week, but every day. I believe that Sunday Best represents an ideal that most of us share, or at least strive for. Regardless of whether it involves dressing up for church, it refers to putting on not only your best clothes but also your best attitude. It's when you cook your best food, for the people you care about most. And it's when you take the time to amplify and glorify who you are, as friends, as a community, and as a family.

When you rewind to my childhood, you'll discover why I come by my affinity for the Sunday Best approach to cooking so naturally. Growing up, I had three grandmothers: my mom's mom, Patricia, and two on my dad's side. There was his mother, Ceola, and his father's wife, Emmer. And then there was his father's sister Ruby—we call her Big Sister—who was actually more of a close friend and grandmother figure to me, even though she lived way out in Mississippi, instead of near us in Chicago. So yes, growing up, I had three or four grandmothers, and it never occurred to me that it was unusual. Who doesn't have three or four? Not to mention a divorced dad, Jack (who is Black); my mom, Susan (who is white); all their siblings and half siblings; and my very own sister, Jacqui—all of whom came together to eat and celebrate on Sundays despite divorces and differences and even a little bit of prejudice too.

My mom and my dad, two very different people, met in 1975 while working at the Oscar Mayer plant in Chicago. They only really knew each other by sight until the night they decided to go out drinking with a bunch of coworkers, several of whom were Black. They chose a bar near my mom's Irish Catholic neighborhood on the North Side, and the manager refused to admit those "n-words." Well, my mother wasn't having that. She got into a big argument with the manager, telling him that if he didn't let them in, well, the white members of the group would also go and spend their money elsewhere. For a pair of rebellious twenty-year-olds in 1970s Chicago, it turns out that adversity was all they needed to form a romantic bond.

Needless to say, when my mom started dating my dad, nobody's family members were very excited about it on either side—especially a couple of my mom's macho brothers, then in their teens, and her father, who was a bit of an Archie Bunker type. But he was also a good person, and a good Catholic, which he liked to say meant that you respect and embrace people. In fact, when the city had desegregated the schools in his neighborhood, there was one Black student in the elementary class and my grandfather told his own children that they were going to invite him over to do his homework and have dinner once in a while. Because we're good Catholics.

So when Mom brought home Dad to meet the family, well, that really tested my grandfather's "good Catholics" theory. Add to that the fact that he was a World War II marine veteran, while my father, upon being drafted for the Vietnam War,

"For a pair of rebellious 20-year-olds in 1970s Chicago, it turns out that adversity was all they needed to form a romantic bond. "

had written a conscientious objector dissertation based on Black Panther Party principles. My grandfather asked for a copy of the paper, and after he read it he was like, "Well, you're smart. I'd never looked at things from this perspective. You just barely got the right to vote and still don't have full rights and aren't accepted as a full citizen. So it would be crazy to ask you to go to the front lines and fight for a country that hasn't fought for you."

My grandfather was as open-minded as he could be, and he and my dad became great friends. My mom's siblings ended up embracing my dad as well, and he stayed one of the family long after my parents divorced. (He once even brought my grandfather flowers when they went out to dinner, which of course prompted my grandfather to insist to the waitress that they weren't gay.) My mom and dad split when I was ten, and frankly, I don't know how they even stayed together that long. But when they made the announcement, my grandfather sat them down. He said, "You have kids to raise. I don't care if you can't work things out as adults, but you're not going to mess with your children. It doesn't matter if you two are together or not, but you're going to raise this family like a family."

So even though he didn't live with us anymore, my dad still took my sister and me for breakfast at Valois or Salonica every Sunday morning. And each Sunday night, the four of us would pile into the car and drive to the North Side for dinner at my maternal grandparents' house. Still very much a family.

My mom had gone back to work when I was about five as a host at a diner and bar called Mellow Yellow in our neighborhood. Jacqui and I practically grew up at Mellow Yellow. Every day after school, we'd walk straight to the restaurant and wait for Mom to finish her shift. We'd sit in the nonsmoking section and do our homework, and the bartender, Ernie, would make us Shirley Temples and milkshakes. If my father wasn't working the overnight shift or a double at the Oscar Mayer plant, sometimes he'd meet us there too.

So to me, restaurants were where family was, and I came to learn that the camaraderie that develops among restaurant staff makes them seem like family as well. If the bathroom needed to be mopped and all the waiters were on the floor, my mom would say that the girls would do it because that's what people have kids for, right? Even when she didn't work there anymore, she'd go back to help sometimes if she knew they were short-staffed. Or if a busser called out, it didn't matter if I wanted to hang out at the mall on the weekend. She'd inform the restaurant that if they gave me twenty bucks, I'd be there for the whole day.

I was really sick as a kid, which made me incredibly socially awkward. I have eczema, and every time I caught strep throat it turned into what is now known as MRSA (methicillin-resistant *Staphylococcus aureus*). It left me with scars that made it look like I had been in a fire. I wore turtlenecks in the summer, or two layers of stockings under shorts, and told myself no one noticed, despite the stares. But no one stared at me at the restaurant. No one cared. If anything, my mom had shared more with her coworkers about my condition than she had with me. So the restaurant became my safe space. I was more comfortable being there than in the real world, around people I didn't know how to communicate with.

Toward the end of high school, I told my parents I wanted to go to a four-year culinary school and become a chef. My father had the Southern Black response to that announcement, which was that he didn't fight for civil rights for me to essentially go become a servant. I assured him it wasn't anything like that, that I wanted to work in Michelin-starred restaurants. He was like, "I don't know what the hell that means, but I got two master's degrees so you can become a burger flipper?" My mom had a more practical response, which was that she had seen too many of her friends burn out in the restaurant business with nothing to fall back on. She urged me to go to college first and develop another skill set. If I wanted to become a chef after that, fine. I'd be on my own financially, but she wouldn't be upset at me for it.

I followed my sister to Florida A&M University, where we shared an off-campus apartment. Jacqui ended up involving me in the weekend dinner parties she regularly held with her friends. They had been potluck sorts of affairs to start, and being that FAMU was a historically Black university in the South, that meant that the spread generally consisted of collard greens, mac and cheese, and other Southern-style dishes built to feed a lot of people on the cheap. But then my mom gave us a Walmart card, telling us that it was okay to buy a few extra groceries every once in a while to feed our friends. Since we were fortunate enough to not be super poor anymore, we could take care of other people.

With this extra help, we started a tradition called Cheatham Soul Food Sundays and did all the cooking ourselves. We still made the kind of food all of us had grown up on, but we started playing around with it. We threw Chicago-style fish fries, for instance—essentially cornmeal-coated catfish served along with big pots of spaghetti, a common combination in neighborhoods on the South Side of Chicago. And there were always collards, but they'd be tweaked somehow. In fact, my sister's close friend Melissa developed a recipe with chicken and stewed tomatoes in it to please her friends who didn't eat pork. I thought it was blasphemous and refused to try it for years!

After I graduated, I told my mom that I was sorry, but I still wanted to go to culinary school. I moved to New York City to attend the Institute of Culinary Education. When it came time for my internship, I was referred to Le Bernardin by another classmate. I was offered a full-time job there one year later, in 2007, and ended up working my way up to executive sous-chef over the span of eight years.

Among many, many other lessons, Le Bernardin's chef and co-owner, Eric Ripert, taught me how to define what my vision was, stick with it, and use that vision to hone my food. He also opened my eyes to the fact that I could incorporate other cuisines and ingredients from around the world into my food, as long as I did so with purpose and respect. And he helped me to see that cultural crossover has shaped cuisines for hundreds of years.

Take the South, where African slaves built the cuisine of America. Since they worked the fields and the kitchens, everything passed through their hands. They learned to nixtamalize corn from Indigenous Americans. They picked up on French and Spanish techniques and influences from those who had colonized the land. They came to know tomatoes and peppers when they fled to Mexico seeking freedom. Every time cultures crossed, each group took something of the other with them. So with this in mind, I learned to develop dishes that tell a story about me and the way I see the world. I found that I could use ingredients like grits or collard greens as a jumping-off point to track my own family journey from the fields of Mississippi, to Chicago, to fine-dining restaurants in New York—and beyond!

It was upon accompanying Eric to an industry event in the Cayman Islands that I met Marcus Samuelsson. This was exciting, as I'd long been a regular at his restaurant Red Rooster in my adopted home of Harlem. Sometime after the event, he saw me sitting at the bar, remembered me, and offered me a job. I was hesitant because I absolutely loved working for Eric (not to mention being able to say I was executive sous chef at such a prestigious restaurant as Le Bernardin!). But I also knew I'd probably never progress past that point, since the guys in the positions above me had been there for twenty-five years, and would likely remain until they retired. If I wanted the chance to actually be in charge of a kitchen, that opportunity lay with Marcus.

It was fascinating, observing the dichotomy between these two great chefs. With Eric, the question was always: What can we take away? What needs to be here to enhance, and what doesn't? With Marcus, it was: What can we add? What can we do to make this more special, to add a new dimension, to make this more exciting and attention grabbing? Eric likes subtlety, to hide nuance, unexpected flavors, and texture in an otherwise beautifully unassuming plate, while Marcus wants to catch your eye and hit you in the face with intense flavor.

The result, naturally, is that I fall somewhere in the middle of the two of them. I appreciate the beauty in what can at first glance look like simplicity, but I also know how to put on a show. It may sound funny, but defining your style as a chef is sort of like putting together your Sunday Best look. You can wear an elegant sheath with kitten heels and a little hat, or you can choose an eye-catching low-cut dress and stilettos. They both suit the occasion, but what you wear speaks directly to you, to what makes you feel, well, your best. My chef mentors taught me that there's no right or wrong when it comes to defining your style, but once you determine what it is, you wear it with confidence and run with it!

It was a few years later, during a short in-between-restaurants "find myself" time, when I got a call about auditioning for Bravo's cooking competition show,

> "So with this in mind, I learned to develop dishes that tell a story about me and the way I see the world."

Top Chef. I'd never actually watched any episodes before, and obviously, I went in entirely too naive! During the show's crazy challenges, it's easiest to default to stuff you already know, so in the earliest episodes, most of my dishes were variations on things I'd done at Red Rooster or Le Bernardin. The problem was that I adapted them in ways that didn't make sense, for situations in which they didn't belong. And since they weren't my recipes, I wasn't behind them the way I should have been. They weren't me.

The judges taught me that I needed to stop overthinking things and just make delicious food. Just make *my* food. Once I was able to clear my head of all manner of self-imposed mental hurdles, I found I could tap into my own culinary perspective. That's when the game literally changed for me. Instead of giving the judges dishes they'd seen before, and seen done better, I began cooking the food that was personal and unique to me—essentially, regional Southern cooking married with fine-dining techniques. Instead of thinking about the guidelines of the challenge first and then cobbling together something to fit those guidelines, I started by asking myself, "What do I love to eat and cook? And what can I do to make it reflective of regional Southern cuisine?" The results included sea urchin with spoonbread and buttermilk dashi, blackened octopus with squid ink grits, and yuzu banana pudding. Clearly, those dishes resonated—enough with the judges to propel me to the finale, and enough with me that I could finally make a break from my mentors and plot my own course.

Following the show, I spent a lot of time reflecting on how I wanted to express who I am, and what I'm about, through food. I kept coming back to the idea of Sunday Best, and it served as the inspiration for my pop-up series by the same name. Everything had really clicked into place in my mind by the end of *Top Chef*, and I harnessed that momentum in order to bring people together over dishes like Red Miso BBQ Quail (page 123) and Collard Green Kimchi (page 161). Because in addition to speaking to my mission to "dress up" what's seen as humble Southern fare, I loved the idea of using Sunday as a medium to find kinship with cultures other than my own.

Across religions and cultures, almost every family I know has a Sunday ritual. And since it's such a universal connector, it generally involves food! Sunday is the last opportunity to chill before getting up early for work or school on Monday. You assemble in a safe place with the people you love and abandon the midweek formality of a pork chop and a scoop of mashed potatoes on each plate. Meals are served family style, the kids run in and out of the kitchen, and someone sneaks a piece of crispy skin off the chicken. Maybe some of the details differ from household to household, but the overall feel of camaraderie and togetherness is always the same.

There are countless ways in which the Sunday Best spirit has enhanced and informed my life. It's a way of being and thinking and cooking that I want to continue to embrace and to share throughout my life. It's about taking something that's simple and unassuming and showing how special it is. It's about remembering that no matter how busy or difficult life gets, you can always focus on the love and positivity that come from feeding yourself and the people around you. Because Sunday Best is honoring the beauty of what you can accomplish and create when your mind is in a place of celebrating and appreciating everything.

how to "sunday best" your every day

GOOD THINGS HAPPEN IN THREES: The difference between the way restaurant chefs and home cooks make a meal comes down to three main things: higher heat, constant tasting, and seasoning along the way while cooking. Using higher heat in the oven is like searing a chicken breast in cast iron instead of poaching it; the heat caramelizes the liquid and amino acids on the exterior much faster, giving you deeper flavor and little bits that just verge on blistering (which means much more intense flavor). So instead of cooking at 350°F, crank your oven up to 425°F the next time you're roasting a chicken or lightly oiled vegetables. Restaurant cooks get familiar with the subtle changes that happen in food by constantly tasting (using disposable tasting spoons). We know when something will need a pinch of sugar to offset bitterness, or a splash of water when a braise, stew, or sauce is becoming too concentrated, before it's too late. So taste often and adjust your seasoning accordingly. Professional cooks also know that every component has to bring something to the party; each time you add an ingredient to a dish, you have to either season it before it goes in or add a pinch of salt along with it. Everything contains water, and that water will dilute the flavor of whatever it's been added to if it doesn't bring its own seasoning. You also want salt to work its way into your ingredients while cooking, so seasoning only at the start and very end is never enough.

READ THROUGH YOUR RECIPES: Before you cook, scan the recipe to get a feel for what you'll be doing when and what equipment you need. Chefs call this *mise en place*—putting everything in its place—which essentially consists of gathering chopped and measured ingredients (some of which can be combined) in little bowls. Not that you need to be that fussy about it. But having your meat ready and seasoned before the pan starts smoking, or knowing you have to have a splash of wine on hand to keep the sauce from overreducing, will do amazing things for your flow and help you become a more confident cook.

UPGRADE YOUR PLATES: Who said your wedding china needs to be saved for anniversaries? And why does your grandmother's silver only get pulled out for Thanksgiving? If you're going to have to wash dishes anyway, they might as well be pretty ones that put you in a romantic, festive, or (fill-in-the-blank) mood.

GET COMFORTABLE RIFFING: Sure, it's important to follow certain steps or preparations in a recipe to the letter. But the more you cook, the more you realize how much room there is to play. So while yes, I've taken great pains to develop these dishes for you, nothing would make me happier than if you discovered ways to make them your own. Do you prefer tilapia to catfish? Have at it. Hate cilantro? That's what parsley is for. Prefer well-done steak to medium rare? Well . . . that one's on you.

REINVENT YOUR ROTATION: We all have go-to dishes that we're so familiar with, they're practically part of our muscle memory—which is why we tend to make them again and again and again. Being comfy with what you cook is great, but building familiarity has to start somewhere. So how about choosing one new recipe to try each week, then try it again, then try it again (maybe, this time, with cilantro). Before you know it, this dish will also be part of your muscle memory, and ready to officially add to your renewed and revived meal rotation!

PLAY SUPERMARKET SWAP: One of the easiest ways to get out of a rut is to identify something you love, then replace it with something that's ever so slightly different. Do you tend to gravitate toward spinach? Next time, why not grab Swiss chard? Do you dig Caesar salad? Try making a dressing with a dash or two of fish sauce. Do you always default to potatoes? There are so many cool starchy tubers out there, from plantains to batata to yucca.

GO BIG WITH GARNISHES: I'm not talking about the 1970s trend of putting a sprig of curly parsley and a lemon wedge in the center of the plate (or adding bell peppers for "color"). There are so many small touches that can ramp up the elegance factor of a dish without actively interfering with the flavor, from a drizzle of oil, to a sprinkle of finishing salt, to a handful of microgreens, to a smattering of (chopped, flat-leaf) parsley.

ADD A PERSONAL TOUCH: This may be a dangerous admission for a professional chef. But—when it comes to what I serve at home, at least—I'm totally cool with taking credit for store-bought stuff, as long as some sort of stamp is added to make it better (and yours). That can be as easy as adding onions and garlic sautéed in olive oil to a bag of precooked grains, or rubbing butter and paprika on the skin of a rotisserie chicken and popping it on a lower rack under the broiler for a second to crisp it up.

'TIS THE SEASON: Seasoning meat (and fish) with salt ahead of time makes a huge difference, especially with large or thicker cuts. Salt draws out moisture from the meat and gets absorbed into the cells (like a delicious exchange program), working its way through. While this is happening, the lean muscle proteins are also broken down, making them more tender and juicy. It's fine to salt a piece of fish one to two hours before cooking, steak or chicken a few hours ahead, or a large roast the night before and keep it in the refrigerator. You'll just be replacing water content with seasoning, and your meat will be more delicious and tender than if you'd salted it right before cooking.

REFINE YOUR GRIND: I generally go with freshly ground black pepper in my recipes, but you'll find that on occasion, I call for cracked pepper. It's not a deal breaker if you don't have a mortar and pestle or one of those grinders where you can adjust the texture by loosening a screw. But know that I reference cracked pepper for a reason, since the crunch, spice, and bite are great at cutting through anything that's especially meaty, creamy, or fatty.

PREHEAT YOUR PANS: You'll notice that I often heat my pans before adding fat, which is a total restaurant thing. That's because metal is full of microscopic hills and valleys. So when you pour oil into a cold pan, it immediately seeps into those crevices. If you heat the pan first, however, the metal expands and flattens, so that it elevates the oil instead of absorbing it and creates an actual nonstick surface.

morning love
Breakfast

As a chef, I don't think twice about putting out effort when it comes to other people. But as far as feeding *me* is concerned, well, I'm always cutting corners. And that's especially true of breakfast.

There's a reason it's called the most important meal of the day, though—and it's not solely about consuming energy-giving calories. Breakfast is an exercise in self-care. If you give yourself some TLC at the beginning of the day, it will begin to permeate the rest of it, and you'll think about yourself a little more too. This is why paying attention to breakfast can really set the tone for the whole day. What's a greater act of self-love than taking time to cook for yourself?

For so many of us, weekend breakfast (or brunch) takes on a celebratory feeling because of how little time we devote to our first meal during the week. This was definitely the case in my family. Saturdays and Sundays were when my mom dragged out the old-school waffle iron we loved so much, or when we went to a neighborhood restaurant where I could order steak and eggs. If we were visiting my dad's family in the South, it was the opportunity to pile grits, sausages, and twelve other things on our plates. Otherwise, we pretty much lived on grab-and-go items like muffins, bagels and doughnuts, toaster-friendly hash browns, or an easy treat we called Elephant Ears, made from bits of fried dough.

When I really stop to look back, though, those weekend meals weren't significantly more labor intensive than pouring a bowl of cereal. And humble as they seemed, those weekday dishes had the potential to become something truly special. So with a bit of downsizing and advance planning as far as the former is concerned, and some serious sprucing up of the latter, you can have weekend-worthy dishes at the ready all week round!

Flaky Layered Biscuits
with Sausage Gravy

Although this dough is similar to the one used in your basic roll-and-cut biscuit, I like to use the French laminating technique for mine. By folding the dough over and over on itself, you produce lots of flaky, super-thin layers without much more effort. And the effect is like one of those towering Pillsbury Grands biscuits—except it doesn't come from a can! To reduce your efforts in the morning, prepare the biscuit dough up through the final folding step the day before, and chill overnight.

———————— SERVES 4 (IF YOU'RE A 2-BISCUIT BREAKFASTER!) TO 8 ————————

BISCUITS

2 cups (4 sticks) unsalted butter, frozen

2 cups (280g) all-purpose flour, plus more for dusting

2 cups (240g) Wondra flour (see The Wonders of Wondra for substitutes)

¼ cup (50g) granulated sugar

4 teaspoons baking powder

1 teaspoon baking soda

2½ teaspoons kosher salt

2 cups buttermilk, chilled

2 tablespoons unsalted butter, melted

2 tablespoons honey

SAUSAGE GRAVY

1 tablespoon vegetable oil

12 ounces ground pork

Salt and freshly ground black pepper

1 tablespoon light brown sugar

1 teaspoon dried sage

1 teaspoon dried Italian seasoning blend

1 pinch freshly grated nutmeg

1 tablespoon maple syrup (optional)

¼ teaspoon caraway seeds (optional)

2 tablespoons unsalted butter

¼ cup (30g) Wondra flour

3 cups whole milk, plus more as needed

1. MAKE THE BISCUITS: Grate the butter on the large holes of a box grater or with the shredding disk of a food processor. Transfer to a freezer-safe container and freeze or refrigerate before proceeding.

2. In a large bowl, mix the all-purpose flour, Wondra, granulated sugar, baking powder, baking soda, and salt to combine. Add the frozen butter and toss with your fingers to make sure each piece is coated well (work quickly so that the butter doesn't warm up too much!). With a silicone spatula, fold in the buttermilk until just combined.

3. Turn the dough out onto a lightly floured piece of parchment paper, wax paper, or foil (it will help with moving it around later). Gently press and pat the dough together and roll it out to an even rectangle about 12 × 18 inches.

Transfer the dough on the parchment to a baking sheet and refrigerate for 15 minutes.

4. Slide the parchment paper and dough back onto a flat work surface with the long side closest to you. Lightly dust the top of the dough with a pinch of flour, then fold the two short sides into the center until they are touching (like a set of double doors), and then fold the left side on top of the right (like a closed book).

5. Center the folded dough on your parchment paper and roll the dough out to an 12 × 18-inch rectangle again, rubbing flour on your rolling pin if the dough sticks. Repeat the book folds again, then roll the dough this time to a 12-inch square. Transfer the dough back to a baking sheet and refrigerate for 20 minutes.

(recipe continues)

6. Preheat the oven to 425°F with a rack in the center position. Slide the dough back onto your work surface and use a sharp knife to cut the dough into approximately 2-inch squares. Line the baking sheet with a new piece of parchment paper and line up the biscuit dough squares on the baking sheet, spaced about an inch apart. Return the sheet to the refrigerator and chill the biscuits for another 10 minutes before baking.

7. Place the baking sheet on the center rack and bake for about 20 minutes, rotating once halfway through, until the biscuits are puffed and deeply golden. In a small bowl, mix the melted butter and honey. Remove the biscuits from the oven and brush with the honey butter. Let cool while you make the sausage gravy.

8. MAKE THE SAUSAGE GRAVY: Heat the oil in a large cast-iron skillet over medium-high heat. Add the ground pork and season with a couple of heavy pinches of salt and a generous pinch of pepper. Sear the pork, stirring occasionally and breaking it up with a wooden spoon, until well browned, about 5 minutes. Reduce the heat to low and stir in the brown sugar, sage, Italian seasoning, nutmeg, and maple syrup and caraway (if using). Cook for 2 minutes.

9. Stir in the butter, then sprinkle the Wondra evenly over the top (it should look like a nice snowfall). Stir everything together to create a roux of sorts. The fat in the pan should no longer be visible, and the mixture should take on a light sheen. If liquid fat is still visible, add another teaspoon of Wondra to soak it up.

10. Gradually pour in the milk, stirring constantly and scraping the bottom of the pan; the gravy will loosen and smooth out. Let it come to a low simmer and season with more salt and pepper to taste. If the gravy is thicker than you like, add another splash of milk or water before serving.

11. To serve, split the biscuits and spoon warm gravy on top. Any leftover biscuits can be used to make Panzanella (page 214), and leftover gravy can be stored in an airtight container in the fridge for about 5 days.

KEEP IT SIMPLE

For the gravy, you can use uncooked seasoned sausage or breakfast patties instead of ground pork, and eliminate the spices, sugar, and syrup. Just crumble and cook until brown, then add the butter and flour. If you don't want to go through the motions of making gravy at all, the biscuits are delicious on their own, brushed with a bit of melted butter and honey right after baking.

THE WONDERS OF WONDRA

This "instant" low-protein flour is finely ground, precooked, and dried, so it can quickly dissolve into hot liquids to make sauces or gravies without clumping. If you're not in possession of Wondra, you can make a homemade version by combining 2 cups all-purpose flour with 1 teaspoon of cornstarch, then sifting it a few times to aerate and lighten it up.

Pecan Five-Spice Sticky Buns

These are my ode to those Pillsbury cinnamon rolls, which—no shame—were a beloved staple in my house. Warm, complex Chinese five-spice powder with tingly black pepper really pumps up the volume on the classic cinnamon and adds a touch of adult savor to an otherwise unapologetically kiddie treat. And honestly, your basic iced roll has nothing on the total indulgence of a sticky bun covered with a cascade of caramel-coated pecans.

——— MAKES 10 BUNS ———

DOUGH

1 cup whole milk, lightly warmed (not hot)

2¼ teaspoons (1 packet) instant yeast

1 tablespoon granulated sugar

2 large eggs, beaten

4 tablespoons (½ stick) unsalted butter, melted

½ teaspoon kosher salt

4 cups (560g) all-purpose flour

Toasted sesame oil, for greasing

Vegetable oil, for greasing

STICKY TOPPING

Vegetable oil, for greasing

1½ cups roughly chopped pecans

1 cup (2 sticks) unsalted butter

¾ cup heavy cream

½ cup cane syrup or dark corn syrup

½ cup (packed; 110g) dark brown sugar

¼ teaspoon fine sea salt

1 teaspoon pure vanilla extract

¼ cup bourbon or water

FILLING

6 tablespoons unsalted butter, at room temperature

½ cup (packed; 110g) dark brown sugar

1 teaspoon Chinese five-spice powder

½ teaspoon ground cinnamon

Pinch of kosher salt

1. MAKE THE DOUGH: In a stand mixer fitted with the dough hook attachment, combine the warm milk, yeast, and sugar and mix on low speed until just combined. Let the mixture sit until foamy, about 10 minutes.

2. Return the mixer to low speed and add the eggs, melted butter, salt, and about 3½ cups (490g) of the flour. Mix until a smooth dough forms. If the dough feels wet or sticky, add the remaining ½ cup flour.

3. Grease a large bowl with a drizzle each of the sesame oil and vegetable oil. Place the dough in the bowl and turn it to coat with oil on all sides. Cover the bowl with plastic wrap or a damp towel and let the dough rise in a warm spot until doubled in size, 1 to 1½ hours.

4. MAKE THE STICKY TOPPING: Grease a 10-inch springform pan with oil and line the bottom with parchment paper. Sprinkle the pecans in the pan and shake into an even layer.

5. In a small saucepan over medium heat, melt the butter, then whisk in the cream, syrup, brown sugar, salt, vanilla, and bourbon. Bring to a simmer and cook, whisking constantly, until glossy, about 3 minutes. Pour the sticky glaze over the pecans and set them aside to cool.

6. MAKE THE FILLING: Combine the butter, brown sugar, five-spice powder, cinnamon, and salt in a small bowl and stir with a rubber spatula to blend.

(recipe continues)

7. ASSEMBLE THE BUNS: Turn the dough out onto the counter and roll into a 12 × 16-inch rectangle a little under ½ inch thick. Arrange the dough with a long side closest to you. Spread the filling over the dough, leaving a naked 1-inch border on the far side. Starting from the near side, roll the dough into a tight log and pinch the seam to seal; leave the log seam-side down.

8. Using a sharp knife, cut the log crosswise into 10 pieces. Place the buns, cut-side up, in the springform pan. Cover loosely with plastic wrap and let sit until the buns are almost doubled in size, 45 minutes to 1 hour.

9. Preheat the oven to 350°F with a rack in the center position.

10. Remove the plastic wrap, transfer the springform pan to the oven and bake until the buns are nice and brown and the glaze is bubbly, 30 to 40 minutes. Let cool for a few minutes before carefully inverting the buns onto a serving plate and having at it!

11. Store any leftovers at room temperature in an airtight container for up to 5 days.

EXTRA, EXTRA
Make a double batch of dough (or halve the filling recipe), since any leftover dough can be refrigerated or frozen, then used to create Cast-Iron Deep-Dish Pizza (page 219).

Buttermilk and Corn Flour Pancakes *with* Warm Peach Compote

While waffles were king in my household growing up, pancakes got occasional love too. Since your basic pancake is sort of one-note, I like adding buttermilk for tang and corn flour (not cornmeal, which would make it a johnnycake) for a hint of sweetness, which allows you to ditch syrup for a less sugary-sweet homemade peach compote.

———————————————————— SERVES 4 ————————————————————

PANCAKES

1½ cups (225g) corn flour

½ cup (70g) all-purpose flour

2 tablespoons granulated sugar

2 teaspoons baking powder

1 teaspoon kosher salt

1⅓ cups buttermilk, at room temperature

2 large eggs, at room temperature

1½ teaspoons pure vanilla extract

2 tablespoons unsalted butter, melted, plus more (unmelted) for cooking and serving

PEACH COMPOTE

1 pound ripe peaches (or frozen peach wedges, thawed; avoid canned)

⅓ cup (57g) packed light brown sugar

½ teaspoon ground cinnamon

½ teaspoon ground ginger

½ teaspoon freshly ground nutmeg

2 tablespoons bourbon or water

1. Preheat the oven to 250°F.

2. PREPARE THE PANCAKES: In a large bowl, combine the corn flour, all-purpose flour, granulated sugar, baking powder, and salt. In a separate large bowl, whisk the buttermilk, eggs, vanilla, and melted butter (you don't want the buttermilk and eggs too cold or the melted butter will seize up).

3. Whisk the wet ingredients into the dry, a little at a time, and gently stir until the batter is smooth. It should be on the thicker side; if it is *too* thick, add a splash or two of buttermilk.

4. MAKE THE COMPOTE: Cut the peaches in half and remove the pits. Cut each half into four slices, then cut those slices crosswise into thirds. (This sounds oddly specific, but it should result in uniform pieces, which will ensure even cooking.)

5. In a medium saucepan, combine the brown sugar, cinnamon, ginger, nutmeg, and bourbon. Bring the mixture to a simmer over medium-low heat. When it just begins to bubble, fold in the peaches and continue cooking, stirring occasionally, until the syrup has reduced and thickened enough to coat a spoon, 8 to 10 minutes. Enjoy warm or let cool at room temperature before storing in the refrigerator for up to 8 days.

(recipe continues)

6. MAKE THE PANCAKES: While the compote is simmering, heat a griddle or cast-iron skillet over medium heat. Rub a small piece of butter over the pan to coat it, then ladle about ¼ cup of batter onto the pan to form a circle (it doesn't have to be perfect). Use the ladle to spread the batter out a bit, if needed. The batter should sizzle a little when it hits the pan.

7. Make as many pancakes at a time as you can, leaving enough space between them so that the edges don't run together (if they do, it's not a big deal—just cut them apart).

8. When bubbles start to form around the edges, in about 2 to 3 minutes, flip the pancakes and cook on the other side for 1 minute, or until golden.

9. Transfer the pancakes to a baking sheet and keep them warm in the oven. Repeat the process with remaining batter, buttering the pan as needed between batches.

10. Stack the pancakes on plates, rubbing a pat of butter between each. Serve with the compote (all right, plain old syrup is okay too).

MAKE AHEAD

The peach compote can be made in advance and refrigerated for up to 8 days, which means you can whip up a batch at the start of the week and warm it up as needed. It's great not only on pancakes, but also on Flaky Layered Biscuits (page 23), oatmeal, or a simple slice of toast!

THE DEVIL IS IN THE DETAILS

When it comes to pancakes, you have to butter each one individually. A small, commonsense suggestion, perhaps, but also a bit of a revelation. What's a single pat of cold butter supposed to accomplish sitting on top of a stack?

Challah French Toast Waffles

I've always had a thing for crispy, crunchy textures—which is why I was never much of a fan of French toast, with its gooey, eggy centers. My family's absolute favorite special breakfast item was waffles, which allowed us to play with our old-school iron. This eventually led to a brilliant discovery: pressing French toast preserves its custardy qualities while doubling down on caramelization and adding an incredible all-over crunch.

This technique also proved to be an ingenious time-saver for my mom. Instead of babysitting a pan on the stove, she could pop a couple of slices in the waffle iron, tend to one of the millions of other things she had to do, and come back a few minutes later. I continue to employ this trick when I'm strapped for time but still want to treat myself, and I like to use fluffy challah because it takes only seconds to soak up batter.

SERVES 3

3 large eggs

⅔ cup whole milk

½ teaspoon ground cinnamon

½ teaspoon freshly grated nutmeg

Pinch of kosher salt

1 teaspoon pure vanilla extract (or 1 scraped vanilla bean, if you have it)

1 tablespoon orange zest (optional but awesome)

6 (1-inch-thick) slices semi-stale challah bread

Unsalted butter or nonstick cooking spray, for greasing

1. Preheat a waffle iron according to the manufacturer's directions.

2. In a large bowl, whisk together the eggs, milk, cinnamon, nutmeg, salt, vanilla, and orange zest (if using, which you totally should). One by one, drop each challah slice into the mixture, turning to coat completely. Transfer the soaked bread to a shallow dish and pour any remaining egg mixture over the slices. Let the bread sit for about 10 minutes to soak it all up.

3. Grease the waffle iron on both sides with butter or cooking spray. Place a challah slice in the waffle iron; if your iron comfortably fits multiple slices, go for it. Close the waffle iron and cook for about 5 minutes, until crispy, golden brown, and cooked through.

4. Serve immediately, ideally accompanied by Candied Bacon (page 37).

SIMPLE SWAP

Can't get a hold of challah? Crusty Italian bread is another standout: slice it the night before and let it sit until morning.

the most important meal of the day

No matter how busy my parents were, or how early they left for work, they always made sure that my sister and I had what we needed for breakfast. My mom would cook oatmeal and leave it in bowls for us to microwave. Or she'd make sure we knew where the hash browns were, so we could pop them in the toaster oven. My dad would leave stuff for us to make sandwiches, such as cooked bacon and bread to tuck it in.

It was easy to take those efforts for granted as a kid, not really understanding how broke we were, or how strapped for time my parents were. I definitely knew that I felt taken care of, and cared for. But as an adult—especially one who, I admit it, rarely bothers to treat myself to more than a cup of black coffee—I can look back now and fully appreciate what those acts of love meant. And that they always set the tone for a good day.

And that was during the week. Even before they divorced when I was ten (and continuing for many years after), my parents took a divide-and-conquer approach to the weekend. Saturday was my mom's day. Since my sister and I slept late, she woke up early (typically at 5 a.m.) and had a few blessed hours to herself. She'd work out at the local gym, then pick up doughnuts or a can of Pillsbury cinnamon rolls on her way home. Or she'd have waffle batter made and the iron hot, so she could start cooking the moment we woke up.

Sunday was my dad's day, which was another welcome reprieve for my mom, and an especially special way for my sister and me to stay connected with him after the divorce. He'd take us for a walk by the lakefront, and we'd fill him in on what had happened that week at school. We'd follow it up with breakfast at the Salonica diner, near where we lived in Hyde Park, or at Valois, a cafeteria-style spot where Barack Obama used to go. Then we'd come home and get ready for the rest of the day, which invariably involved shuttling back and forth between various relatives' houses. All four of us together. Every Sunday.

Overnight Grits *with* Fried Eggs and Mushroom Ragout

Most people know that rice has a roughly 1:2 ratio (1 cup rice + 2 cups water = 2 cups cooked rice). But grits are actually 1:4. Meaning the tiniest bit yields four times the amount! Needless to say, grits are an economical way to feed yourself or a crowd. And they don't require a lot of gussying up to be delicious. A bit of butter, salt, and pepper stirred in, paired with a slice of toast on the side, is *amazing*. Or a simple, sustaining mushroom ragout like this one.

Here's the thing to know when preparing grits, though: they're not supposed to be, well, gritty. You know there's a problem if they stick between your teeth! My aunt Dottie in Mississippi taught us a great trick to avoid this grit faux pas: Soak them overnight, just like you would beans. It softens that tough outer hull and ensures you get a perfect cook every time!

--- SERVES 6 TO 8 ---

OVERNIGHT GRITS

2 cups stone-ground white grits (sorry, I can't wrap my mind around yellow grits)

2 cups whole milk, plus more if needed

2 teaspoons kosher salt, plus more to taste

4 tablespoons (½ stick) unsalted butter

Freshly ground black pepper

MUSHROOM RAGOUT

½ cup (18g) dried porcini or other mushrooms

1 pound cremini mushrooms, rinsed and sliced

1 pound white button mushrooms, rinsed and sliced (or you can use wild mushrooms, if desired)

3 tablespoons extra-virgin olive oil

Kosher salt and freshly cracked black pepper

2 tablespoons unsalted butter

1 large garlic clove, finely chopped

2 large shallots, finely chopped

2 or 3 sprigs of thyme, leaves picked

⅓ cup white wine

2 tablespoons cornstarch

FRIED EGGS

Vegetable oil, for frying

2 eggs per person

Kosher salt and freshly ground black pepper

1. MAKE THE OVERNIGHT GRITS: The night before, place the grits in a medium heavy-bottomed pot along with 6 cups of water. Stir once or twice and let the grits settle for a couple of minutes. Use a tea strainer, fine-mesh sieve, or large spoon to skim the surface and remove any floating hulls. Cover the pot with a lid and let it sit on the counter overnight.

2. When you're ready to cook the grits, add the milk to the pot and bring it to a low simmer over medium heat, stirring frequently. Reduce the heat as low as possible and continue cooking, uncovered, stirring occasionally, for about 30 minutes, or until thick and creamy. When stirring, be sure to scrape the bottom and edges of the pot to make sure the grits are not sticking and clumping.

(recipe continues)

3. MAKE THE MUSHROOM RAGOUT: While the grits are cooking, preheat the oven to 400°F and line a baking sheet with aluminum foil. Put the dried porcinis in a medium bowl and cover with 3 cups of very hot water. Let the mushrooms soak for 20 to 30 minutes, until rehydrated and plump.

4. Place the cremini and button mushrooms in a large bowl and toss them with the olive oil, a couple of heavy pinches of salt, and a little pepper. Lay them in a single layer on the prepared baking sheet and roast for 20 minutes, or until the mushrooms have shriveled and caramelized slightly. If they are sticking to the foil, splash a little water onto the sheet to dissolve the fond (the fancy French term for the browned bits). Transfer the mushrooms and their liquid to a bowl and set aside.

5. When the grits have been cooking for just shy of 30 minutes, check them for tenderness. They should be smooth and creamy. If they are still a little al dente, continue cooking on very low heat and add a splash of milk. Once they have reached your desired consistency, stir in the salt; taste and add a little more salt; if needed. Stir in the butter and a little pepper and keep it covered over very low heat until ready to serve.

6. To finish the mushroom ragout, scoop out the rehydrated porcinis (reserving their soaking liquid), place them in cheesecloth or on a kitchen towel, and squeeze them over a small bowl. Save this liquid separately from the soaking liquid. Rinse the porcinis well to make sure no dirt or sand remains. Chop them roughly and add to the bowl of roasted mushrooms.

7. Heat a heavy pot or medium saucepan over medium heat and add the butter, garlic, shallots, and thyme leaves. Cook, stirring occasionally with a wooden spoon, until the shallots and garlic are tender and just beginning to brown at the edges, about 2 minutes. Stir in the mushrooms and cook for 5 minutes, then add the wine. Let the wine simmer until reduced by a little more than half, about 1 minute.

8. Reduce the heat to low, pour the liquid you squeezed from the porcinis into the pot, and simmer with the mushrooms for 10 minutes, stirring occasionally.

9. In a small bowl, stir the cornstarch and ½ cup of the porcini soaking liquid until the cornstarch is dissolved, making sure there are no lumps. Stir the slurry into the pot and simmer until beginning to thicken, 3 to 5 minutes. Taste and adjust the seasoning if necessary. If you like your gravy thicker, dissolve a little more cornstarch in warm water, stir it into the pot, and cook for a few more minutes. If you want it to be thinner, add more of the porcini soaking liquid.

10. Divide the hot grits among serving bowls. Make a well in the center of each bowl and spoon mushroom ragout on top.

11. MAKE THE EGGS: Heat a small skillet over medium heat; add about ½ inch of oil to the pan. Crack two eggs at a time into a small bowl and gently pour them into the pan. Cook, using a spoon to baste the whites with the hot oil (but avoiding the yolks), until the whites are set on top and bubbled and browned at the edges, 4 to 5 minutes. Season with salt and pepper. With a slotted spoon, remove the eggs from the pan, blotting away any extra grease with paper towels, and place on top of the ragout. Spoon a little more ragout on top, if desired. Serve immediately.

MAKE AHEAD

The Mushroom Ragout can be made 3 to 4 days ahead and kept in the refrigerator, then reheated before serving.

Tater Tot Waffles
with Candied Bacon

Potatoes might just be my favorite food. I love them in all forms, especially made into crispy hash browns (or rösti, if you want to be European about it). My mom used to keep a big sleeve of hash browns in the freezer when I was growing up, so my sister and I could just pop them in the toaster oven, wrap them in a paper towel, and eat them on the way to school (we sometimes even used them as "bread" for breakfast sandwiches!).

This recipe combines my love for hash browns—represented by one of the world's greatest inventions, the Tater Tot—*and* my obsession with crispy things and sticking everything I can into the waffle iron. You can even use those crinkle-cut French fries! As long as it's a potato, anything goes.

----------- SERVES 2 TO 4 -----------

CANDIED BACON
1 pound sliced applewood-smoked bacon

¼ cup (packed; 55g) dark brown sugar

¼ teaspoon cracked black pepper

¼ teaspoon ground ginger

TATER TOT WAFFLES
Nonstick cooking spray

1 package frozen Tater Tots, thawed (you can use your favorite brand, as well as any size bag to make as many waffles as you like)

1. Preheat the oven to 375°F.

2. MAKE THE CANDIED BACON: Line a baking sheet with parchment paper and arrange the bacon on it in a single layer.

3. Cook the bacon for 7 minutes. Flip the slices and cook for another 5 minutes.

4. Meanwhile, in a small bowl, combine the brown sugar, pepper, and ginger. Once the bacon has cooked on both sides, sprinkle the brown sugar mixture evenly over the tops of the slices. Reduce the oven temperature to 350°F and continue cooking until the bacon reaches your preferred level of crispiness, 10 to 15 minutes. Drain the slices briefly on a paper-towel-lined plate, but be sure to remove the bacon before the sugar cools and begins sticking to the towels.

5. MAKE THE TATER TOT WAFFLES: Preheat a waffle iron according to the manufacturer's directions.

6. Spray the iron on both sides with cooking spray. Arrange the tots in a tight, even layer in the waffle iron, fitting as many as you can.

7. Close the waffle iron, pressing gently to flatten the tots, and cook until they are nicely browned and crispy all over, about 5 minutes. Serve with the candied bacon.

TIMING TIP
If you're planning ahead, let your tots thaw overnight in the refrigerator. If it's a game-time decision, no worries. Take your tots straight out of the freezer, spread them on a plate or baking sheet, and let them thaw at room temp for 20 minutes before proceeding.

SUNDAY BEST FINESSE
Although Tater Tot Waffles are amazing on their own (served with or without Candied Bacon), they're even better with all manner of toppings. Think smoked salmon and crème fraîche, or Sausage Gravy (page 23) and sautéed peppers. In fact, when entertaining, I often like to cut them into small squares to use as the base of elegant hors d'oeuvres.

Kick the Can Salmon Croquettes

At Le Bernardin, everyone receives a little bowl of salmon rillettes as a treat during lunch. Needless to say, it's very elegant. But the first time I saw the cook making it, it definitely struck me as a nicer version of that stuff that comes out of the can, which is what my cool older cousin, Chelsea, would always use to make *her* salmon croquettes. It's the very first dish she taught me to cook, when I was around twelve years old and I'd go visit her at her apartment. Very much a Southern thing, the preparation generally involves sorting bits of skin and bone from a can of slimy fish. But if you poach your own fresh fillet in white wine and shallots (like they did at Le Bernardin), it makes a world of difference in both flavor and texture.

SERVES 3 TO 6

---

1 cup white wine

1 shallot, chopped small

1 pound skinless salmon fillets, cut into roughly 1-inch pieces

6 saltine crackers

½ medium-size sweet onion (or white or yellow), roughly chopped

¼ green bell pepper, seeded and roughly chopped

3 or 4 sprigs of parsley, with stems, roughly chopped

1 teaspoon vegetable oil, plus more for pan-frying

1 teaspoon Worcestershire sauce

Kosher salt and freshly ground black pepper

1 large egg, beaten

Zest of ½ lemon

1 tablespoon Tabasco sauce or ½ teaspoon fresh lemon juice

1. In a medium saucepan, combine the wine, shallot, and 4 cups of water. Bring to a boil over medium-high heat and cook for 1 minute. While waiting for the water to boil, get a slotted spoon and line a tray with paper towels. Once the salmon goes in, you have to be ready to move quickly!

2. Add the salmon to the pot and stir to make sure the pieces don't stick together. Cook the salmon for about 2 minutes. Remove one piece and pull it apart to test for doneness: the center should be very rare and look like a bull's-eye, with the light pink outside getting dark toward the center. If the dark, rare center is small (about ¼ inch), immediately transfer all the salmon to the paper-towel-lined

tray to drain and cool. If the rare center is large (½ inch or more), let the salmon cook for another 1 to 2 minutes. Just remember that the salmon will continue to cook after you take it out and will get cooked again once in croquette form. If it's cooked all the way through during the poaching step, the end result will be dry.

3. Crush the crackers by hand into a medium bowl. You should have a mix of crumbs and shards, but make sure the bigger pieces are no larger than ⅛ inch.

4. In a small food processor, pulse the onion, bell pepper, and parsley a few times, scraping down the sides if needed, until finely chopped and combined.

5. Heat a cast-iron skillet over medium-low heat. Add 1 teaspoon vegetable oil, followed by the onion mixture. Season with the Worcestershire sauce and salt and pepper to taste and cook, stirring occasionally, until the liquid is almost completely evaporated and the vegetables have that translucent, sweated look, about 4 minutes. Add the mixture to the bowl with the crackers. Wipe out the pan with a paper towel and reserve it for later.

6. Add the cooked salmon, egg, lemon zest, and Tabasco to the bowl and fold to incorporate. You want to break up the salmon while folding so that everything gets seasoned and evenly distributed. Chill for 10 minutes so that the crackers can soak up the excess moisture. The mixture should be just a little moist. Test it by squeezing a small amount in your hand; if it doesn't hold together, add 1 to 2 tablespoons of flour or a couple more crushed crackers.

7. When you're ready to cook, scoop ½-cup portions of the salmon mixture and form them into patties about ½ to ⅔ inch thick and 2 inches across.

8. Heat the reserved pan over medium-high heat and slick the bottom with oil. When the oil is hot but not smoking, place a few of the patties in the pan, making sure not to crowd them. Cook until they form a firm enough crust to flip without breaking up, 2 to 3 minutes. Flip and cook until nicely browned on the other side, 2 to 3 minutes more. Line a plate with paper towels, place the patties on top to drain, and then serve while hot.

MAKE AHEAD
The croquette mixture can be made in advance and refrigerated overnight for cooking the next day.

SUNDAY BEST FINESSE
Poached eggs make a great croquette pairing. Though if I happen to have some caviar on hand, that's how it's going down.

how to "sunday best" breakfast

PRESERVE YOUR FRUIT: Take advantage of any produce you have that's about to go bad by saving it for breakfast. Cook it down into a compote (like the Peach Compote on page 29) or chutney, pickle it for an unexpected addition to oatmeal; serve it alongside sausage, bacon, or ham steak; or cut it up and freeze it for morning smoothies.

CONSIDER CACAO NIBS: Think of them as adult chocolate chips! Scatter them into pancakes for cocoa flavor without excess sweetness, or toss them with granola for a wonderful crunchy texture.

MAKE FOOLPROOF OMELETS: Avoid overbrowned bottoms by using this restaurant method to ensure omelets stay light and fluffy: Preheat the oven to 350°F. Start your omelet in an oven-safe skillet set over medium heat on the stove, gently stirring the surface of the eggs around as you would scrambled eggs, occasionally tapping the bottom of your pan against the cook surface to settle the eggs into any air pockets. When the eggs have cooked about halfway through, put toppings on half of the omelet, then place the pan in the oven for 2 to 3 minutes, or until the eggs are set. Fold the omelet over on itself and plate.

ADD BALANCE TO BREAKFAST SANDWICHES: Breakfast sandwiches are best when you add a little something sweet to cut into all of that salty and savory richness. Drizzle with maple syrup or honey, spread the bread with Peach Compote (page 29) or tomato jam (see below), or stack on a couple of slices of Candied Bacon (page 37)!

TAKE A CHANCE ON TOMATOES: There's a reason they're classified as a fruit! Cherry tomatoes especially can be almost candy-sweet, balanced by a welcome acidity. I love to sauté them whole or simmer them into a jam flavored with sugar, garam masala, star anise, ginger, or cloves. It's terrific for breakfast sandwiches (see above).

SWAP OUT THE SPUDS: If making skillet home fries or shredded hash browns, try combining potatoes (or substituting them completely) with vegetables like parsnips, sweet potatoes, celery root, or carrots for added fun, color, and a mild, earthy sweetness.

BREATHE NEW LIFE INTO BAKED GOODS: Have your biscuits (page 23), croissants, or muffins gone a little stale? Place a damp paper towel on top, let sit for a few minutes, then remove the paper towels and place in a 325°F to 350°F oven for about 5 minutes. It will recrisp the exteriors without drying out the middles.

SAGE ADVICE: Dried sage is responsible for so many of the great flavors you associate with breakfast, especially sausage. Don't eat meat? You can get the same effect by stirring dried sage into scrambled eggs or sautéed mushrooms. And while we're on the subject of spice, pay attention to smoked paprika (awesome with potatoes), as well as poppy seeds, which contribute a lovely nuttiness and bite to everything from quick breads to sliced avocado.

BETTER WITH BUTTERMILK: I love the Southern-style tang that buttermilk brings to basic batter (see Buttermilk and Corn Flour Pancakes, page 29) and dough (Flaky Layered Biscuits, page 23). Don't have any on hand? Create an instant substitute by combining 1 cup of regular milk with 1 tablespoon of white vinegar or lemon juice. Stir and let sit for at least 5 minutes.

PERFECT THE POACH: Poaching eggs may seem entirely too difficult an endeavor when it comes to feeding a crowd, which is why many of us default to scrambling. But as explained in my recipe for Big Easy Eggs Sardou (page 47), poaching is a great do-ahead method to have in your back pocket. Take a cue from restaurants and catering halls by soaking the raw, cracked eggs in vinegar first. You'll get a beautiful teardrop shape every time, instead of a ragged ghost sheet. And if you leave the eggs slightly undercooked when poaching, you can warm them in the oven just before serving.

Toasted American Cheese "Parachutes"

Sunday Best doesn't necessarily mean highbrow. It's all about indulging in celebratory pleasures and tapping into sentimental memories, and parachutes definitely do that for me.

My mom always found creative ways to make magic out of inexpensive, mundane ingredients. That included pointing out how broiling American cheese on bread in our toaster oven produced dramatic, blackened air bubbles, their charred shells veiling molten goodness underneath. So for us, it wasn't just American cheese on Wonder bread—it was an exciting, eagerly anticipated culinary trick.

It's not *quite* as low-end as it sounds. We often used my mom's good sourdough, for instance. Plus, there are ample opportunities for upgrading with the addition of fun condiments—check out some ideas below!

SERVES 2

---

1 tablespoon extra-virgin olive oil

1 small onion, halved and thinly sliced

Kosher salt

1 tablespoon unsalted butter

2 slices country white bread, sourdough, or any good white bread

2 slices American cheese

1. Heat a small skillet over medium heat. Put in the oil, then add the onion. Season with a pinch of salt and cook, stirring frequently, until the onion begins to turn dark brown (about 15 minutes).

2. Add 2 tablespoons water to the pan, scraping up any browned bits stuck to the bottom. Reduce the heat to low and simmer until the water is almost completely evaporated. Stir in the butter and cook until the butter gets a little browned, about 5 minutes. Let cool.

3. Lightly toast the bread (not quite enough to brown, but just to dry the surface a little). Divide the caramelized onions between the pieces of toast and spread evenly.

4. Heat a broiler or toaster oven and line a baking sheet with aluminum foil.

5. Top each piece of toast with a slice of American cheese and place it (cheese-side up, of course) on the baking sheet. Broil 3 to 4 inches from the heat source until the cheese has puffed up and browned, 2 to 4 minutes. Let cool for a moment (the layer of cheese that sticks to the onions will be hot as lava) and enjoy immediately!

KEEP IT SIMPLE
If you don't have time to caramelize the onions for this, use Charred Green Onion Relish (page 96), or any condiment you have in your fridge that goes well with American cheese. Horseradish, sauerkraut, deli-style mustard, and pickled jalapeños all work great!

Cornbread Toad-in-the-Hole
with Crab and Andouille

We used to do a kind of cornbread stack topped with avocado and a fried egg for brunch at Marcus Samuelsson's restaurant Streetbird; it was super messy and indulgent. Since my version uses crab (which makes everyone feel fancy), *this* is a dressed-up version of *that*, and even more playful, since the egg is tucked in the center, toad-in-the-hole style.

SERVES 6

- 6 slices cornbread, about 3 to 4 inches wide and ½ inch thick
- 2 tablespoons unsalted butter
- 6 large eggs
- ½ sweet onion, such as Vidalia, roughly chopped (white or yellow onion will work too)
- ½ green bell pepper, seeded and roughly chopped
- ½ red bell pepper, seeded and roughly chopped
- 1 celery stalk, roughly chopped
- 1 medium garlic clove, sliced
- ½ cup roughly chopped fresh parsley leaves and stems
- Extra-virgin olive oil
- 3 ounces andouille or your favorite smoked sausage (about 1 link), halved lengthwise and thinly sliced
- Kosher salt and freshly ground black pepper
- 1 cup cherry tomatoes, halved
- Worcestershire sauce
- 2 scallions, sliced, white and green parts separated
- 8 ounces picked crabmeat (lump, jumbo lump, Jonah . . . all work great)
- Tabasco sauce, Cha-Cha (page 88), or Fermented Pepper Sauce (page 92)

1. Preheat the oven to 375°F. Line a baking sheet with parchment paper and rub it lightly with a drizzle of oil.

2. Use a small knife or shot glass to cut out the center of each cornbread slice, leaving a ½-inch border around the outside. Save the centers in a zip-top bag for another use.

3. Heat a large nonstick sauté pan over medium heat. Put 1 tablespoon of the butter in the pan and swirl to coat. Lay the cornbread in the pan (work in batches, if needed) and toast the first side for about 4 minutes. Flip the cornbread and add the remaining 1 tablespoon butter to the pan, swirling to distribute the love among the slices. Crack an egg into the hole in each cornbread slice. Reduce the heat to medium-low and cook until the eggs are set on the bottom, 2 to 3 minutes. Use a spatula to carefully transfer the egg-topped cornbread to the prepared baking sheet.

4. In a small food processor, combine the onion, green and red bell peppers, celery, garlic, and parsley and pulse 4 or 5 times, until coarsely chopped, like a Southern-style sofrito.

5. Drizzle a small amount of oil in the pan you used for the cornbread and eggs (why dirty another pan?) and heat over medium heat. Add the andouille and cook until the edges have crisped a little and some of the fat has rendered, 3 to 5 minutes. With a slotted spoon, transfer the andouille to a plate.

6. Add the "sofrito" to the pan and cook for 1 minute, stirring occasionally. Season lightly with salt and pepper, then add the cherry tomatoes. Cook until the tomatoes begin to release liquid, 3 to 5 minutes, then return the sausage to the pan. Add a few dashes of Worcestershire and the scallion whites and reduce the heat to low.

(recipe continues)

Gently fold in the crab until incorporated. Cook until just warmed through, 1 to 2 minutes. Taste and adjust the seasoning, adding a few hits of Tabasco for a little spice and vinegary kick.

7. Place the baking sheet with the cornbread and eggs in the oven and cook for 5 minutes, or until the eggs are done to your liking. Remove from the oven and divide among plates. Spoon the crab-andouille mixture over the top. Garnish with the scallion greens and serve immediately.

CORNBREAD REQUEST

You'll want to purchase (or make) cornbread formed into a tall loaf, not a flat cake, or you won't be able to achieve the kind of slices you need. Also, this is a great way to revive old and stale cornbread (such as leftover Sour Cream Cornbread, page 144, if you portion the batter into loaf pans). There's no need for it to be super moist and fresh.

MAKE AHEAD

You can prepare the recipe up through step 4 ahead of time, refrigerate if holding for more than an hour, and finish in the oven just before serving.

Big Easy Eggs Sardou

Heads up: this breakfast dish calls for multiple components. But the recipes are broken down into easy, approachable steps that will help you manage and master each part. Trust me, this dish is worth the work. Especially since each part allows you to develop and hone really useful skills that you can use time and again (such as poaching perfect eggs or making no-fail hollandaise). If you have someone to cook with, split up the components to divide and conquer!

ARTICHOKE BASE

8 large artichoke bottoms (fresh, frozen, or canned; steamed, thawed, or rinsed, respectively)

1 tablespoon unsalted butter, melted, or olive oil

FOOLPROOF, EASY AF HOLLANDAISE

1 cup (2 sticks) unsalted butter

4 egg yolks

Juice of 1 lemon

Pinch of ground cayenne pepper or dash of Tabasco

Kosher salt and freshly ground pepper

PERFECT EVERY TIME POACHED EGGS

2 cups distilled white vinegar

8 large eggs

CREAMED SPINACH

3 tablespoons unsalted butter

1 garlic clove, grated on a Microplane or finely chopped

½ sweet onion, such as Vidalia, finely chopped (white or yellow works too)

Kosher salt and freshly ground black pepper

3 tablespoons all-purpose flour

3 cups whole milk

2 (10-ounce) packages frozen chopped spinach, thawed, excess liquid squeezed out with a towel

Pinch of freshly grated nutmeg or dash of Tabasco (optional)

1. Preheat the oven to 350°F. Line a baking sheet with aluminum foil.

2. MAKE THE ARTICHOKE BASE: In a large bowl, toss the artichoke bottoms with the butter and arrange in a single layer on the prepared baking sheet. Transfer to the oven and let the artichokes heat through for up to 10 minutes while you prepare the remaining components.

3. MAKE THE HOLLANDAISE: Melt the butter in a small saucepan over low heat, then remove from the heat and let cool to just above room temperature. In a blender, combine the egg yolks, lemon juice, cayenne, and a pinch of salt and pepper and purée on low speed to combine. With the blender running and the lid ajar, slowly pour in the melted butter and gradually increase the speed to medium, blending until the mixture is fully emulsified. Pour the sauce into a heat-safe container with a lid, and place the

container in a small pot with enough water to come halfway up the sides. Keep warm over low heat. Taste and adjust the seasoning before serving.

4. PREPARE THE POACHED EGGS: Pour the vinegar and 1 cup of water into a large, shallow glass baking dish and crack each egg directly into the liquid. Make sure the container is large enough that the eggs are not crowded too tightly. The eggs should be fully covered in the vinegar solution—if the liquid is too shallow, add enough vinegar to just cover the tops of the eggs.

5. Let the eggs soak in the vinegar solution for at least 10 minutes; you will see the egg whites begin to turn slightly opaque around the edges and form a kind of teardrop shape around the yolks. This is when you know you're ready to poach.

(recipe continues)

6. MAKE THE CREAMED SPINACH: While the eggs are soaking, melt the butter in a small saucepan over medium heat. Add the garlic and onion, season with a little salt and pepper, and cook until tender, 2 to 3 minutes. Sprinkle in the flour and stir to coat. Continue to cook until the flour is lightly toasted and just beginning to brown, another 3 minutes.

7. Slowly pour in the milk, whisking vigorously to eliminate all the lumps. Keep whisking occasionally as you bring to a simmer, and cook, whisking, for 3 minutes more before stirring in the spinach. Taste and adjust the seasoning, adding a pinch of nutmeg or dash of Tabasco, if you like. Simmer until the creamed spinach thickens, 4 to 5 minutes. Set aside.

8. POACH THE EGGS: While the spinach is simmering, fill a large shallow pot or deep saucepan with 3 inches of water. Bring to a bare simmer over medium-low heat, then reduce the heat a tad (there should be very few bubbles coming up). Use a large spoon (not slotted) or ladle to gently lift the eggs, one by one, out of the vinegar solution and into the simmering water. (Only poach as many eggs at a time as will fit without crowding; the eggs should be able to float freely in water with at least ½ inch between them.) Cook the eggs until the whites are just set all around but the yolks are still soft to the touch, 2 to 3 minutes.

9. To assemble the dish, place a spoonful of the creamed spinach on each plate and spread it a little (this will keep the artichokes from sliding all over). Top with two artichoke bottoms per plate, then top each artichoke with a large spoonful of creamed spinach. Nestle a poached egg on top of each artichoke–creamed spinach base and drizzle with hollandaise. Crack a little fresh pepper over the top or add a pinch of paprika for color. Serve immediately!

MAKE AHEAD

You can actually poach eggs ahead of time! Place the poached eggs in a baking dish that has been sprayed with nonstick cooking spray (or rubbed with olive oil), add a couple of splashes of water, cover with aluminum foil, and hold at room temperature for up to 3 hours. When ready to serve, place the baking dish in a 350°F oven for 5 minutes to warm just before assembling.

KEEP IT SIMPLE

If you enjoy cleaning and cooking artichokes, please feel free to do so. Otherwise buy them frozen or canned and save yourself the trouble!

Green Tomato Shakshuka

You'll find iterations of this Middle Eastern favorite in French and Italian cuisine as well as Southern—my family frequently made tomato stew and dropped an egg on top. This recipe takes the Southern influence even further with rounds of tangy green tomato—though this time around, they're simmered, not fried.

SERVES 6

6 large green tomatoes (about 3 pounds)

4 medium tomatillos (about ½ pound), peeled and washed (they can be sticky under their husks)

3 tablespoons extra-virgin olive oil, plus a drizzle here and there

Kosher salt and freshly ground black pepper

1 green bell pepper

1 poblano pepper

1 cubanelle, long hot, or banana pepper

1 sweet onion, such as Vidalia, halved and thinly sliced (white or yellow onion works too)

1 celery stalk, thinly sliced on an angle

2 large garlic cloves, halved and thinly sliced

1 teaspoon cumin seeds

1 teaspoon ground coriander

½ teaspoon dried oregano

1 teaspoon sugar

½ cup crumbled feta cheese (optional)

6 large eggs

Chopped fresh cilantro and parsley, for garnish

Crusty sliced bread, such as baguette, for serving

1. Preheat the oven to 375°F.

2. Cut the stems and cores out of the green tomatoes and tomatillos. Cut each tomato in half crosswise and remove the seeds. Chop the tomatoes and tomatillos into ½-inch pieces—don't worry about making it perfect; we're going to crush them anyway—and place in a 9 × 13-inch glass baking dish. Stir in a drizzle of olive oil and season with salt and pepper. Place in the oven and cook until the vegetables have softened and released liquid, 15 to 20 minutes. Set aside to cool; leave the oven on.

3. Meanwhile, cut out the stems and remove the seeds from all three peppers. Cut each into quarters, then slice thinnish. Set aside.

4. Heat a large ovenproof skillet (preferably cast-iron) over medium heat and put in the 3 tablespoons oil. Add the onion and cook, stirring with a wooden spoon, until just beginning to soften, about 4 minutes. Add the celery and garlic, along with the cumin, coriander, and oregano. Season with a pinch of salt and pepper and stir to combine. Continue cooking until the garlic just begins to brown,

about 2 minutes, then add the peppers. If the mixture is getting dry, add another drizzle of olive oil. Cook until the peppers begin to soften, 3 to 5 minutes.

5. Use a fork to crush the roasted green tomatoes and tomatillos, then pour them into the skillet. Add the sugar and adjust the seasoning if needed. Bring the mixture to a simmer and cook for 10 minutes, stirring occasionally. Add a splash of water if it begins to get too dry and stick to the pan.

6. If you like, divide the mixture between individual oven-safe dishes, or keep in the skillet in order to serve family style. Sprinkle feta over the top, if you wish.

7. If using the skillet, make six indentations in the surface of the shakshuka using the back of a spoon. Carefully crack an egg into each well. For individual portions, crack one egg in the center of each dish.

8. Place the pan(s) in the oven and bake until the egg whites are set and the yolks still runny, 5 to 7 minutes. Sprinkle cilantro and parsley over the top and serve immediately, with crusty bread.

Grand Slam Breakfast Tarts

When you work in a restaurant, there's no real opportunity to leave for lunch and dinner breaks, so the kitchen staff puts together "family meals," which everyone enjoys together before the next shift starts. Saturday was always pizza day for Le Bernardin's family meal, because it allowed us to use all the leftover stuff that we had in the walk-in. Since there were a lot of Austrians and Germans on staff, they especially looked forward to my breakfast-y riff on Alsatian tarte flambée (a type of flatbread similar to pizza), with crème fraîche, bacon, and onions, plus my addition of potatoes and eggs. But needless to say—in the spirit of emptying the fridge—you should use this recipe as a jumping-off point, swapping in whatever you have on hand, from leftover roasted vegetables to bits of chopped ham.

_____ MAKES 1 LARGE TART OR 2 SMALLER TARTS _____

1 (½-pound) sheet puff pastry dough, thawed if frozen (there are generally 2 sheets in a 1-pound package)

2 medium Yukon Gold or small Idaho potatoes (about 1 pound), scrubbed

½ cup crème fraîche

¼ cup crumbled cooked bacon (you can use Candied Bacon, page 37)

6 large eggs

1 cup grated Gruyère or Parmesan cheese

Kosher salt and freshly cracked black pepper

2 teaspoons snipped chives or scallions

1. Preheat the oven to 400°F with a rack positioned near the bottom. Line a baking sheet with parchment paper.

2. Unfold the puff pastry and place it on the prepared baking sheet. If your package contains two smaller pieces of puff pastry, place them each on separate baking sheets. Place another piece of parchment on top of the pastry and cover it (them) with another baking tray. This will help the pastry puff evenly. Bake until the pastry is light brown and uniformly puffed, 10 to 15 minutes. Let cool for 10 minutes. Reduce the oven temperature to 375°F.

3. Meanwhile, cook the potatoes until just tender. It doesn't matter how you go about this—baking, steaming, boiling, microwaving—whatever gets them al dente. Once they are cooked and cool enough to handle, slice them into ¼-inch rounds.

4. Spread the crème fraîche over the cooled puff pastry (or divide it between the two pastries), leaving a ½-inch border. Sprinkle the bacon over the top, then arrange the sliced potatoes all around. Strategically crack 6 eggs (or 3 eggs per pastry) between the potato slices, then sprinkle the grated cheese over the top, avoiding the egg yolks as much as possible. Season with salt and pepper and place the pan in the oven, on the rack close to the bottom.

5. Bake the tart(s) for 10 to 12 minutes, until the crust is deeply browned and crisp, the egg whites are cooked (the yolks will be a tiny bit runny in the center), the potatoes are tender, and the cheese is bubbling and browned around the edges.

6. Let cool for 2 minutes before sprinkling with chives. Slice and serve immediately.

all-day grazing
Snacks

My mom's favorite part of a menu has always been the appetizer section, because she likes getting to try a bunch of little things. When she gave up cooking for a certain period of time after she and my dad divorced, she would set out a tray of hummus with crudités, some chips and salsa, and other assorted morsels for dinner. We'd have a bite of this and a nibble of that, and it eventually added up to a complete meal.

My family's longstanding allegiance to appetizers didn't end there. When my mom worked in restaurant distribution as a sales representative for Kraft Foods, my sister and I would tag along on her visits with clients. They'd generally set us up at a table and send us a few snacks to pick at, since it was the easiest and most inexpensive way to keep a couple of kids quiet. And now that I'm a busy adult (not to mention a chef), grazing and noshing—as opposed to sitting down to a full-on dinner—is just the way I eat.

Yet setting out apps isn't merely a low-maintenance way of feeding people. It's also really fun. What would a party be without hors d'oeuvres? They're so flavorful and totally shareable, allowing guests to just grab, gab, and go—all while freeing the host from having to deal with fussy preparations or individual plating. Appetizers are a way of getting the party started, not just revving up your appetite. And if you make them your meal, like my mom did, you'll instantly transform dinner into a festive event!

Hanky-Pankies

(CHEESY PORKY CARAWAY BITES)

So, I thought my family actually invented hanky-pankies. Every Thanksgiving, Easter, First Communion party, or whatever, bringing the hanky-pankies was literally someone's job. But after doing a bit of research in order to find ways to elevate them, I realized that we're not alone. The tradition of celebrating functions with pumpernickel party breads (commonly found in supermarkets, they're those sleeves of mini loaves cut into small squares) topped with a mix of melted Velveeta and sweet Italian sausage sold in a log (family divides are created over whether you toast the bread before or after topping) seems to be pretty wide-spread and runs generations deep.

——————————————— MAKES 32 BITES ———————————————

1 pound ground pork

1 medium shallot, minced

1 tablespoon dried sage, rubbed in your palm to release the oils

½ teaspoon kosher salt

½ teaspoon caraway seeds

½ teaspoon light brown sugar

¼ teaspoon ground allspice

¼ teaspoon freshly ground black pepper

2 tablespoons all-purpose flour

1 cup lager beer

1 cup grated good-quality sharp Cheddar cheese

½ teaspoon (or more, if you like) Tabasco sauce

¼ cup chopped fresh parsley, plus more for garnish

8 slices pumpernickel bread or 16 squares pumpernickel party bread

1. Preheat the oven to 400°F. Line a baking sheet with aluminum foil.

2. Heat a large skillet over medium heat and place the ground pork in the pan. Cook, breaking up the pork with a wooden spoon or heatproof spatula, until the fat is rendered and the meat is beginning to brown, about 5 minutes. Add the shallot, sage, salt, caraway, brown sugar, allspice, and pepper. Reduce the heat a little and cook until the meat is browned and the spices are fragrant, 3 to 5 minutes.

3. Evenly sprinkle the flour over the meat and stir to fully incorporate. Gradually pour in the beer, stirring and scraping up any stuck bits from the pan. Bring to a low simmer and cook until the beer is reduced by half, 3 to 5 minutes. Turn off the heat and add the cheese, stirring and folding to incorporate, creating a thick sauce. Stir in the Tabasco and parsley; taste and adjust the seasoning, if needed. Let the mixture cool for a few minutes.

4. If using full-size pumpernickel bread, working with stacks of four slices, use a serrated knife to trim the crusts off.

5. Divide the pork-cheddar mixture among the pumpernickel slices and spread nearly to the edges. Cut the slices into quarters—or halves if you're using party bread—and arrange on a rack placed over the prepared baking sheet (which makes for easier cleanup).

6. Bake the hanky-pankies until the cheese is bubbly and browned and the bread is toasted, 10 to 15 minutes. Garnish with chopped parsley and arrange on a serving tray. Enjoy immediately.

WASTE NOT WANT NOT
I like to dry my bread scraps in a 325°F oven, then use the food processor to make bread crumbs. Add whatever dried herbs and spices you like!

Butter Bean Hummus

Setting out crudités was a hosting tradition my mom learned from her own mother, who entertained during the 1960s and '70s, when crudités were in fashion. After the divorce (when Mom went on that cooking strike), veggie platters became a real go-to. This was also the '90s, when hummus was experiencing its first wave of popularity in America. So crudités and hummus pretty much passed for supper during a certain stage of my life. And I haven't lost my taste for it.

The process of preparing chickpeas for hummus is pretty similar to the Southern method of cooking up a pot of beans. That's why I like to whip up a dip using butter beans, which are mild, plump, super creamy, and especially luscious when blended. Oh, and if you really want to add some Sunday Best finesse, add a smoked ham bone or turkey wing to the slowly simmering pot.

--------------------- MAKES 2 CUPS ---------------------

2 cups dried large butter beans (ideally soaked in water overnight)

1 medium shallot, halved lengthwise

2 sprigs of thyme

Zest and juice of 1 lemon

¼ cup tahini

1 garlic clove, finely grated

½ teaspoon ground cumin

3 tablespoons extra-virgin olive oil, plus more for serving

Kosher salt and freshly ground black pepper

Smoked paprika, for garnish

1. If you've soaked your butter beans overnight, proceed to the next step. If you haven't, pick through the beans for debris, rinse them, and place them in a large pot with enough water to cover by 1 inch. Cover, bring to a boil over high heat, and cook for 2 minutes. Turn off the heat and let sit at room temperature for 1 hour before draining.

2. Place the shallot and thyme in the pot with the (presoaked or boiled) beans and add enough water to cover by 1 inch. Bring to a simmer and partially cover the pot with a lid, simmering until the beans are completely tender, 60 to 90 minutes, adding water as needed to keep the beans submerged. Remove the lid and let the beans cool to room temperature in the cooking liquid.

3. Drain the beans in a colander (don't rinse them) and discard the shallot and thyme. Place the lemon zest, lemon juice, and tahini in a food processor and process until the tahini is a little fluffy, about 1 minute. Add the beans, garlic, cumin, olive oil, and salt and pepper to taste; process until smooth, 2 to 3 minutes. With the machine running, add 2 tablespoons of cold water and continue to process for another minute or so.

4. Taste the hummus, adjust the seasoning, if needed, and process for another minute to incorporate. Transfer to a container or serving dish, drizzle with a little olive oil, and sprinkle with a dash of paprika.

5. Store any leftovers in an airtight container in the fridge for up to 1 week.

MAKE AHEAD
Beans can be cooked in advance and refrigerated in their liquid overnight.

Pimento Cheese–Stuffed Celery

Cramming things into celery was definitely in vogue in the eighties. I say it's time for a resurgence! When it comes to adding a touch of refinement to humble dishes, it's amazing how big a difference small details can make. Like de-stringing the celery (a trick I learned in the fine-dining world) and using a melon baller to scoop out the insides. The ratio of veg to stuffing becomes a lot more appealing, with the shell of celery acting as an ultra-crisp, refreshing vessel for a scoop of zippy pimento cheese.

MAKES 16 STALKS' WORTH

16 large celery stalks, plus chopped leaves for garnish

8 ounces freshly grated extra-sharp Cheddar cheese (don't use pre-grated for this)

½ small shallot, thinly sliced

½ small garlic clove, crushed

4 ounces cream cheese, softened

¼ cup Blue Plate or other good-quality mayonnaise

½ teaspoon smoked paprika

1 tablespoon Tabasco sauce

Kosher salt and freshly ground black pepper

¼ cup plus 2 tablespoons jarred pimento peppers, drained

2 tablespoons whole-grain mustard (should be chock-full of seeds)

1. Trim the tops of the celery stalks just below the natural crease. Look closely at the top edges—you should see a few small, light dots near the outer curve. Place the blade of a paring knife just behind the dots and peel away the strings from the stalks, just like stringing snow peas.

2. Trim the bottoms of the stalks and use a peeler to peel the celery lengthwise to smooth out the lines and remove the outer skin. Use a small melon baller to scrape out the inner portion and create a little more space to stuff the celery.

3. Place the celery stalks in a bowl or zip-top bag filled with cold water and refrigerate while you make the pimento cheese.

4. Place the Cheddar in a mini food processor. Add the shallot, garlic, cream cheese, and mayonnaise. Process until smooth, 2 to 3 minutes. Add the paprika, Tabasco, a couple of pinches of salt and pepper, and the ¼ cup of the pimento peppers. Continue processing until the ingredients are fully incorporated and mostly smooth (a few chunks of pimento are okay). Taste and adjust the seasoning, if needed. Transfer to a piping bag or a zip-top bag with a ¼-inch opening cut in one corner.

5. Drain the celery stalks and pat dry. Season them lightly with salt and place the stalks, concave-side up, on a cutting board. Finely mince the remaining 2 tablespoons pimento peppers and place them in a small bowl along with the grainy mustard. Stir to combine.

6. Fill each celery stalk with pimento cheese. Cut the stalks into 1-inch pieces and spoon a little of the pimento-mustard mixture on top. Arrange on a plate or serving platter and garnish with celery leaves.

PRO TIP
Use the peeler to create a flat surface down the back of each stalk. This will help the celery stand up on your serving plate and keep it from rolling around.

Spicy-Sweet-Crispy Candied Chicken Wings

I'm more likely to gravitate to wings than to a larger piece of chicken because I love the ratio of crispy skin to meat. I start by using baking soda in the dry rub to begin breaking down the fat, then roast the wings at a low temperature to render said fat, and finally crank the heat up to high to crisp the skin for maximum crunch. To finish, I toss the wings in spicy honey to create a caramelized, almost candy-like coating. Are we drooling yet?

———————————— MAKES AROUND 15 WINGS ————————————

3 pounds chicken wings, drumettes and wingettes separated

1 tablespoon kosher salt

½ teaspoon baking soda

1 teaspoon freshly ground black pepper

1 teaspoon onion powder

1 teaspoon garlic powder

½ teaspoon celery salt

½ cup honey

1 tablespoon Aleppo pepper flakes or other dried red pepper flakes

2 tablespoons Tabasco sauce, Cha-Cha (page 88), or Fermented Pepper Sauce (page 92)

1 tablespoon unsalted butter, at room temperature

Buttermilk Vinaigrette (page 86), for serving

1. Line a baking sheet with aluminum foil.

2. Blot the chicken wings well with paper towels and place them in a large bowl. In a small bowl, combine the salt, baking soda, ½ teaspoon of the black pepper, the onion powder, the garlic powder, and the celery salt. Sprinkle over the wings and toss to distribute.

3. Lay the wings out on a lightly oiled wire rack set over the prepared baking sheet, making sure the wings are not touching. Refrigerate for 20 minutes.

4. Meanwhile, preheat the oven to 300°F. Combine the honey, pepper flakes, remaining ½ teaspoon of black pepper, Tabasco, and butter in a large bowl and stir to combine.

5. Bake the wings for 20 minutes, then raise the oven temperature to 475°F and continue cooking until GBD (golden brown and delicious) and blistered, 25 to 30 minutes more. Remove the tray from the oven and turn the oven off.

6. Transfer the wings to the bowl with the honey mixture and toss to coat evenly. Remove the rack and place the wings directly on the foil-lined sheet, reserving the excess honey mixture in the bottom of the bowl. Place the sheet back in the oven for 5 minutes (yes, the oven that we turned off but that's still warm) to lightly caramelize the honey.

7. Transfer the wings to a serving plate and drizzle with the reserved honey mixture from the bowl. Serve with Buttermilk Vinaigrette, or another dipping sauce if you like.

appetizers for dinner

Post-divorce, my mom's job as a Kraft sales rep went a long way in keeping us fed. Not just because it was a source of income, because goodness knows, there were years that were lean enough to get the lights turned off. But shortly after the split, she declared that since she'd spent the last eighteen years cooking dinner every day, she wasn't going to do it for a long time now. See, my dad was a traditional Southern dude, and he had to have his dinner of protein, starch, and veg, no matter what. I remember how one evening during a heat wave in Chicago, my mom made a big, beautiful, seven-layer salad (inspiration for the one on page 231) instead of turning on the oven, and it was more than substantial enough to fill us up. Except as soon as he'd finished his multiple helpings, my dad asked what the entrée was. Said dinner didn't count if it didn't have meat. She was so pissed. And so my mom swore off the idea of making a "formal" meal the second she could.

Thankfully, no matter how over it she was or how poor we got, my mom could always pull a bag of samples from the Kraft warehouse. She'd put out a hummus platter, a plate of cheese sticks, and some feta triangles and call it a day. Or perhaps some meat taquitos, vegetable egg rolls, and potato-and-pea samosas, so we could have our own all-appetizer version of meat, veg, and starch. It may sound silly, but this international spread was actually my first real exposure to global cuisine! We'd sit at our dining counter, do our homework, and graze. And that's what dinner was Monday to Friday, from the time I was ten years old to when I was about fifteen. Snacks and hors d'oeuvres. And always a salad, of course. An iceberg salad with green goddess dressing, piled in the big wooden bowl.

Pickled Shrimp Escabeche

Pickled shrimp are a really popular and super-easy Southern party food, requiring little more than marinating a mess of shrimp in some plain white vinegar overnight (meaning, if you're making this, you'll want to plan ahead). But I came to appreciate escabeche through my first best friend, Lisa, whose stepfather was from Jamaica. It involves pickling and cooking fish, meat, or vegetables in some form of acid (generally a darker vinegar) loaded with onions, peppers, and spices.

This dish is a marriage between the two. And yes, I'm essentially calling it "pickled pickled shrimp." But the name gives a straightforward snack a sort of sexy, international flair. And an impressive title goes a long way when you're looking to fancify your food!

―――――――――――――――――― MAKES 2 POUNDS OF SHRIMP ――――――――――――――――――

PICKLING LIQUID

1 medium red onion, peeled and halved (leave root ends intact)

6 sprigs of thyme

1 teaspoon whole allspice berries

1 teaspoon whole black peppercorns

1 dried bay leaf

½ green bell pepper, seeded and very thinly sliced

1 garlic clove, halved

1 teaspoon dried red pepper flakes

½ cup malt vinegar

¼ cup white wine vinegar

¾ cup extra-virgin olive oil

Juice of 1 lemon (save the rinds)

SHRIMP POACH

2 pounds jumbo (16/20) shrimp, peeled and deveined

½ cup white wine (optional)

2 dried bay leaves

1 celery stalk, cut in half crosswise

1 tablespoon whole black peppercorns

Kosher salt

1. MAKE THE PICKLING LIQUID: Thinly slice the onion halves, stopping about ½ inch from the root. Set the root ends aside for the shrimp poach. In a medium bowl, combine the sliced onion with the thyme, allspice, peppercorns, bay leaf, bell pepper, garlic, red pepper flakes, malt vinegar, white wine vinegar, olive oil, and lemon juice. Cover and chill.

2. MAKE THE SHRIMP POACH: In a colander, rinse the shrimp under cold water. Fill a large pot with 2 to 3 quarts of water. Add the reserved onion roots and lemon rinds, the wine (if using), the bay leaves, celery, peppercorns, and salt to taste. Bring to a simmer over medium heat. (You just made court bouillon, BTW. Super fancy!)

3. Let the liquid simmer for 4 minutes, then add the shrimp. We want to pull the shrimp out when they're just turning pink, before they're completely cooked, after about 2 minutes. Immediately drain the shrimp in a colander; discard the lemon rinds and onion roots. Add the shrimp to the chilled pickling liquid and stir well. Return the bowl to the refrigerator and chill for 20 to 30 minutes.

4. Transfer the shrimp to mason jars or other nonreactive containers (preferably glass) and pour enough pickling liquid over them to cover. Cover the jar, and refrigerate overnight before serving. Leftovers will keep in the refrigerator for up to 5 days.

SUNDAY BEST FINESSE
I like serving the shrimp in cute mason jars accompanied by butter lettuce cups, so guests can create the perfect bite.

Oven-Fried Okra Chips

Okra can be polarizing because of its slimy texture. But if you cut it lengthwise and roast it at high temperatures until it gets blistered and crunchy, you'll be gifted with pure okra flavor without any of the off-putting goo. It makes an inspired, snacky alternative to chips, especially if you serve it with my Buttermilk Vinaigrette (page 86), which is like ranch dressing with the volume raised. What could be better than that?

--- MAKES 2 CUPS ---

Avocado oil spray (or any other quality cooking spray with a high smoke point), for greasing

½ cup (70g) Wondra or all-purpose flour

¼ cup (35g) fine cornmeal

½ teaspoon kosher salt

½ teaspoon garam masala (curry powder works too)

½ teaspoon smoked paprika

¼ teaspoon granulated garlic

¼ teaspoon onion powder

¼ teaspoon freshly ground black pepper

1 pound whole okra pods, rinsed

1. Preheat the oven to 425°F. Line a baking sheet with foil (matte-side up) and spray it generously with oil.

2. In a large bowl, combine the flour, cornmeal, salt, garam masala, paprika, granulated garlic, onion powder, and pepper, using a whisk or fork to make sure the seasonings are evenly incorporated.

3. Pat the okra dry and slice each pod lengthwise into three pieces. Don't worry about cutting off the stem caps; unless your okra is quite big and mature, they will be tender when cooked. As you're slicing the okra, throw each piece into the bowl with the spiced flour, giving the bowl an occasional shake to coat the slices and keep them from sticking together (this will also help to dry out all that goo). When all the okra is in the bowl, give it a few more tosses to evenly coat.

4. Place the okra on the prepared baking sheet in a single layer, shaking off any excess spice mixture. Generously spray the okra with oil. Bake for 15 minutes, then reduce the heat to 350°F and flip the okra slices. Return the sheet to the oven and continue to bake until the okra is browned all over, about 10 minutes more.

5. Transfer the okra to a paper-towel-lined plate to drain slightly. Enjoy immediately!

PRO TIP
Use a rubber spatula to flip several pieces at a time; a metal spatula is more likely to tear through the foil.

Cornbread Gougères

These fine-dining favorites sound oh so posh, but they're really just cheese puffs. The tastiest possible cheese puffs, of course, made from savory cornmeal-based choux dough, with light and airy centers.

There isn't a better appetizer recipe to have in your back pocket. They come together in minutes, can be made big or small, and can be enjoyed on their own or cut in half and filled with Pimento Cheese (page 61), thinly sliced prosciutto, fried quail eggs, or all of the above!

──────────────── MAKES 25 TO 30 ────────────────

½ cup whole milk

4 tablespoons (½ stick) unsalted butter, cut into small cubes

3 tablespoons sugar

½ teaspoon kosher salt

⅔ cup (85g) all-purpose flour

¼ cup (45g) fine-ground cornmeal

3 large eggs

¼ cup grated Gruyère or Parmesan cheese

Pinch of freshly grated nutmeg

1. Preheat the oven to 375°F. Line two baking sheets with parchment paper.

2. In a large, shallow saucepan, combine the milk, butter, sugar, salt, and ½ cup of water and bring to a low boil over medium heat. Add the flour and cornmeal all at once and stir with a wooden spoon. Cook, stirring constantly, until you have a smooth dough that is starting to dry out and pull away from the pan, 2 to 3 minutes.

3. Transfer the dough to a stand mixer fitted with the paddle attachment (or to a large bowl). On medium-low speed, beat in the eggs one at a time, mixing until fully incorporated before adding the next (if using a bowl, beat with a wooden spoon). Beat in the cheese and nutmeg, then transfer the dough to a piping bag with a ½-inch tip. (You can also use a tablespoon to scoop and shape, but it won't look as pretty.)

4. Pipe the dough into 1-inch mounds on the prepared baking sheets and bake until puffed and lightly browned, rotating the sheets halfway through, 30 to 35 minutes total.

5. Enjoy as is or choose your own adventure when it comes to fillings and toppings (see headnote)!

MAKE AHEAD
The puffs can be prepared to completion and refrigerated for 1 day and baked at 350°F for about 5 minutes to reheat and crisp, or frozen for up to 2 months, and baked at 350°F for around 12 minutes.

Fried Olives
with Anchovy Dip

I was an unusual kid in that I loved olives, although pretty standard in my aversion to anchovies. Thankfully, I eventually saw the light when it came to the latter, as a little bit adds an incredible wallop of umami (as well as a nutty, rather than fishy, quality) to everything it touches.

As for olives, I knew I adored them anyway. But frying them is a revelation. They're warm and briny, crunchy and crispy, and when you dunk them in creamy anchovy dip—well. You're just going to have to try this out and see.

— SERVES 3 OR 4 —

ANCHOVY DIP

3 or 4 anchovy fillets, packed in oil

½ small garlic clove

½ cup mayonnaise

Zest and juice of ½ lemon

¼ teaspoon freshly ground black pepper

FRIED OLIVES

Vegetable oil, for frying

½ cup (70g) all-purpose flour

½ teaspoon smoked paprika

Pinch of ground cayenne pepper

2 cups pitted olives (any color as long as they're not canned)

1 large egg

¼ cup (35g) cornmeal

½ cup fine bread crumbs (seasoned or unseasoned)

1. MAKE THE ANCHOVY DIP: With a chef's knife, chop the anchovies and garlic together on a cutting board. Use the flat side of the blade to press and crush the mixture into a paste. Transfer to a small bowl and add the mayonnaise, lemon zest, lemon juice, and pepper. Stir until well combined, then cover and chill until ready to serve.

2. MAKE THE FRIED OLIVES: Place a medium pot over medium heat and fill with vegetable oil to a depth of 2 to 3 inches. If you have a deep-frying thermometer, attach it to the pot and heat the oil to 375°F. If you don't have a thermometer, look for the oil to start bubbling around the sides and the olives to float immediately when added.

3. In a shallow bowl, combine the flour, paprika, and cayenne. Add the olives, shaking and swirling the bowl to coat well. In another medium bowl, beat the egg. Toss the floured olives in the egg wash to coat.

4. Tap the excess flour out of the first bowl and add the cornmeal and bread crumbs. Using a slotted spoon, lift the olives out of the egg wash and transfer them to the bread crumb bowl, shaking and swirling to coat.

5. Shake the excess bread crumbs from the olives and carefully lower the olives into the oil. Fry until the bread crumbs are golden brown and crispy, 6 to 7 minutes. Drain on a paper-towel-lined plate and serve warm with the anchovy dip.

MAKE AHEAD

The dip can be made up to 3 days ahead and refrigerated, and the olives can be fried earlier in the day before serving, then reheated for 3 to 5 minutes, or until crisp, in a 375°F oven.

SUNDAY BEST

Mango Tajín Gazpacho Shooters

This was the first full recipe of mine that actually made it onto the menu at Le Bernardin. Inspired by the large Mexican American community in Chicago, it drew from my memories of the vendors at the corner selling tropical fruit dusted with spicy and salty Tajín seasoning.

This gazpacho started out as a sauce for a raw fish dish, with a purée of mango, jalapeño, and olive oil, given effervescence with a healthy glug of Champagne. But when the co-owner of the restaurant started asking for a bowl of it so that she could sip it straight up like a soup, it was allowed to stand on its own, and became one of the creations I'm proudest of as a chef. The thing is, it's absolutely foolproof. Mango acts as a natural emulsifier, so the soup has a perfectly silky texture each and every time.

— MAKES 4 CUPS —

1 ripe mango (not too ripe, but definitely not underripe)

¼ cup white balsamic vinegar

1 (½-inch) piece scallion white

1 small jalapeño, seeds and ribs removed, sliced

1 (2-inch) section of cucumber or 1 small Persian cucumber, peeled and chopped

¼ red bell pepper, seeded and sliced

½ teaspoon kosher salt

1 cup good-quality extra-virgin olive oil

Zest of 1 lime

1½ to 2 cups Champagne or other sparkling wine (dry or sweet, depending on your taste, but I recommend a drier Champagne; you can also use club soda)

Tajín seasoning, for serving

1. Use a vegetable peeler to remove the skin and the pale thin layer just under the skin from the mango. With a paring knife, slice the flesh away from the seed; discard the seed (but not before snacking on all of the delicious bits stuck to it).

2. Place the mango flesh in a blender with the vinegar, scallion, jalapeño, cucumber, bell pepper, and salt. Blend on the lowest speed until the mango is broken up (add up to 2 tablespoons of water if needed to keep things moving). With the motor still running, slowly drizzle in the olive oil and blend until emulsified with the mango mixture, gradually turning up the speed as you add more oil. Taste and adjust with more vinegar or salt as needed; if the mango wasn't very sweet, you may want to add 1 teaspoon of sugar. Add the lime zest and purée for just a few seconds to incorporate fully.

3. Just before serving, pour the mango emulsion into a pitcher and add the sparkling wine (start with 1½ cups; if the soup is too thick, add the remaining ½ cup), whisking slowly to thoroughly incorporate.

4. Pour the gazpacho into small cups or shot glasses and sprinkle with a pinch of Tajín.

MAKE AHEAD
The recipe can be prepared through step 2 and kept in a closed container in the refrigerator for up to 2 days before serving.

EXTRA CREDIT IDEA
Serve with a little bowl of Takis or Flamin' Hot Cheetos on the side.

Best-*Ever* Hush Puppies

Hush puppies are a staple of many of the meals my family shared during our annual visits to Mississippi. Fish fries, barbecues, and after-church suppers were all occasions to make large bowls of these crispy, fluffy spheres of goodness. While these hush puppies are amazing on their own, I like to use the batter to coat all manner of things to make hors d'oeuvres, such as small pieces of fish, oysters, figs, or cubed Manchego cheese. Or any of the above wrapped in prosciutto! The possibilities are endless—it usually just depends on what I have in my fridge.

And don't forget about dipping sauces! These puppies pair perfectly with anything, from Charred Green Onion Relish (page 96) to Fermented Pepper Sauce (page 92) to good old Buttermilk Vinaigrette (page 86).

MAKES 24 HUSH PUPPIES

---

2 large eggs, at room temperature

1 cup buttermilk, at room temperature

4 tablespoons (½ stick) unsalted butter, melted

½ teaspoon baking soda

1 teaspoon kosher salt, plus more for seasoning

2 tablespoons sugar

1 cup (140g) medium cornmeal, preferably stone-ground

1 cup (140g) all-purpose flour

1 scallion, white and green parts, thinly sliced

Vegetable oil, for frying

1. In a small bowl, whisk together the eggs, buttermilk, and melted butter. (If your eggs and buttermilk are cold, the butter will seize up. So even if they're not fully at room temp, at least make sure they're not super cold.)

2. In a separate bowl, combine the baking soda, salt, sugar, cornmeal, flour, and scallion. Using a wooden spoon or a spatula, mix the wet ingredients into the dry. Begin with a stirring motion and switch to a folding motion when the mixture becomes thick. Let the batter rest for 10 to 15 minutes.

3. Meanwhile, fill a medium pot or large cast-iron skillet with enough oil to reach a depth of 1 inch, and heat over medium-high heat to 350°F. The oil should be shimmery but not smoking. If you don't have a deep-frying thermometer, test by dropping a tiny bit of batter into the oil: if it quickly browns and floats to the top of the oil, you are ready to fry.

4. Using two spoons (one to scoop tablespoon-size portions from the bowl and the other to scrape them into the oil), shape and drop the hush puppies in batches, adding as many as you can at a time without crowding the pot. Fry, turning the hush puppies with a slotted spoon, until cooked through and golden brown all over, 2 to 3 minutes per side. Adjust the flame as needed if they start browning too quickly (if the oil is too hot, the exterior will brown while the interior remains raw—and no one likes biting into raw hush puppy batter).

5. Drain the hush puppies on a paper-towel-lined plate and season evenly with salt. Serve immediately.

how to "sunday best" snacks

SIZE MATTERS: The number one rule of hors d'oeuvres is that they're bite-size. Beyond that, very little matters. In fact, you could make almost any dish in this book, and as long as you cut it into tiny pieces (and maybe spear it on a stick: see below), it would get devoured at the poshest party.

STICK THE LANDING: Anything is awesome on a stick, from pickled shrimp to a handheld caprese salad of mozzarella balls and cherry tomatoes. Oh, but don't call it a skewer. Call it a *brochette*.

BRING IN UNEXPECTED ELEMENTS: Tiny tweaks pay big dividends when it comes to hors d'oeuvres, whether it's using lamb instead of beef in meatballs or stirring sambal into tomato sauce. Your guests probably won't be able to put their finger on what makes the dish so surprisingly special, and that's all part of the fun.

PRESENTATION IS EVERYTHING: Get creative with your plating: try using mini cast-iron crocks to serve your meatballs, tiny flowerpots for spears of fried okra, or mason jars for pickled shrimp. Or place a layer of thinly sliced cucumbers, translucent wheels of lemon, lines of chives, or fronds of parsley or cilantro underneath your canapés or deviled eggs. Besides the visual wow factor, it will keep them from sliding around.

GILD THE LILY WITH GARNISHES: Garnish is king when it comes to making things look fancy (along with cutting them small, of course). And it could be as simple as topping your bites with a sprinkle of paprika. Or frying up basil, parsley, capers, or even raw grains of rice for a terrific textural contrast. My favorite go-to is using celery leaves. The little cluster you'll find at the core of a celery head is a gold mine. The leaves pack a ton of nice, bright flavor, and they look pretty.

RAID YOUR PANTRY: Canned beans and spices are the cool kid's answer to party mix. Toss your choice of bean (kidney, black-eyed peas, chickpeas, what have you) in a bit of oil and the most interesting seasoning you can find in your cabinet. We're talking Tajín, berbere, cumin, curry, whatever floats your boat. Roast at around 375°F until crunchy, then finish with salt and maybe a little fresh lime zest.

GO A BIT NUTTY: Microplane an almond, pecan, or peanut over your snacks to create an edible snowfall with awesome taste, aroma, and texture.

REVEL IN YOUR LEFTOVERS: Rice. Grits. Mashed Potatoes. Mac and cheese. Any cold, congealed starch can be rolled into balls; dusted in flour, egg, and bread crumbs; and baked or fried to create incredible croquettes (see Overnight Grits Arancini, page 217).

REMEMBER THE RULE OF THREE: If you keep the following ingredients on hand at all times, you'll be ready to play host at a moment's notice. 1. Frozen puff pastry for instantaneous tarts. Just parbake, spread or sprinkle with cheese, finish baking, sprinkle with herbs, cut into squares, and serve. 2. Persian cucumbers for canapés. Just cut into rounds and top with just about anything, from sour cream and smoked salmon to Butter Bean Hummus (page 60). 3. Quail eggs. Either boiled or fried, they make for a garnish that looks as luxe as caviar but is infinitely less expensive.

Berbere-Spiced Mini Lamb Meatballs

Marcus Samuelsson opened up the Horn of Africa to me, with its store of vibrant spices from countries like Ethiopia, Somalia, and Eritrea. The one I came to love most of all is berbere, a blend of chiles, fenugreek, cardamom, coriander, and about ten other things. Which is why it's totally worth it (both financially and time-wise) to just buy a bottle instead of trying to swap in a mix of your own. It's so complex, you can sprinkle it on the simplest proteins or starches and they automatically taste special. But as I discovered upon dining at Abyssinia (the best Ethiopian restaurant in Harlem) for the first time, berbere is pretty much best friends with lamb. It's what makes these bite-size meatballs really pop, along with crunchy pine nuts and sweet raisins.

MAKES 30 MINI MEATBALLS

2 medium red onions, roughly chopped

3 garlic cloves

1 (½-inch) piece fresh ginger, peeled and sliced

1 tablespoon vegetable oil

3 tablespoons berbere spice mix

Kosher salt

¼ cup red wine

1 pound ground lamb

½ cup toasted pine nuts

⅔ cup crumbled feta cheese

1 (14.5-ounce) can crushed tomatoes

¼ cup chopped raisins (or better, whole currants)

1. Place the onions, garlic, and ginger in a food processor and pulse until chopped small but still chunky, 5 or 6 pulses.

2. Heat the oil in a large skillet over medium heat until just beginning to smoke. Add the onion mixture and the berbere, season with a couple of pinches of salt, and stir to incorporate. Cook until the moisture has cooked out and the onions begin to brown in places, about 3 minutes. Add the red wine to the pan, scraping up any browned bits. Reduce the heat to low and simmer until the wine is absorbed/ evaporated and the excess moisture is cooked out, about 3 more minutes. Remove from the heat and let cool to room temperature.

3. Put the ground lamb in a mixing bowl and add half of the cooked onion mixture, leaving the rest of the mixture in the pan. I prefer to use my hands for the next step. With or without gloves is up to you (no judgment), but feel free to use a spoon or spatula instead. Stir the lamb and onion mixture together, add a couple of pinches of salt, and really make sure you get it thoroughly combined. Fold in the crumbled feta.

4. Line a baking sheet with aluminum foil. Scoop the lamb mixture into 1-tablespoon portions and roll them between your palms to make them nice and evenly round (dampen your hands as needed to keep the meat from getting sticky). Place the balls on the foil-lined sheet (I'm kinda OCD about straight lines). It's okay to have them close together or just barely touching. Pop in the refrigerator for 10 minutes.

5. Heat the broiler to high and position an oven rack about

(recipe continues)

2 inches from the heat source. Broil the meatballs until the tops are browned, 5 to 8 minutes. Remove from the oven and set aside.

6. Heat the remaining onion mixture in the pan over medium-high heat and add the tomatoes and raisins. Bring to a simmer, then reduce the heat to low. Pour any juices from the meatball tray into the pan, stir to incorporate, and cook for 5 minutes. Adjust the seasoning to taste.

7. When ready to serve, bring the sauce to a simmer and fold in the meatballs. Add a splash of water if the sauce has gotten too dry, and let everything simmer until the meatballs are heated through, about 10 minutes (longer if they've been refrigerated).

8. To serve, the meatballs can be bathed in the sauce, spiked with toothpicks and placed on a platter, or set up as individual bites on crusty bread or toasted cornbread squares.

SUNDAY BEST FINESSE
If you're getting extra fancy, top each meatball or bread bite with a fried quail egg and a little cilantro.

DOUBLE DUTY DINNER
To turn this party snack into a main meal, shape into 2-tablespoon (or larger) meatballs and serve over Barley Grits (page 147), Mashed Parsnips (page 156), or couscous.

Crunchy Hoppin' John Bhel Puri

This flavorful snack mix is equally inspired by the Southern side dish hoppin' John and the South Asian snack bhel puri, which I learned about from my *Top Chef* castmate Fatima Ali. A combination of puffed rice, vermicelli noodles, spices, and more, it's the perfect canvas for one of my go-to ingredients: oven-roasted black-eyed peas. Supremely crunchy, salty, and savory, I always keep at least a pint container of them on hand in my pantry. Besides playing a starring role in this recipe, they're awesome for adding to salads, soups, or simply eating as is!

MAKES ABOUT 5 CUPS

2 cups cooked black-eyed peas (canned or homemade), drained

¼ cup vegetable oil

1 teaspoon Creole seasoning (I like Tony Chachere's)

1 medium sweet potato, diced small

1 smallish green bell pepper, diced small

2 celery stalks, diced small

½ cup cherry tomatoes, quartered

5 sprigs of cilantro, leaves and stems, chopped (about a scant ¼ cup)

5 sprigs of parsley, leaves and stems, chopped (about a scant ¼ cup)

2 scallions, white and green parts, thinly sliced

2 cups unsweetened puffed rice

¼ cup roasted salted peanuts, lightly crushed

1 cup sev (a thin, crispy noodle found in Indian markets; substitute chow mein noodles in a pinch)

½ teaspoon smoked paprika

¼ teaspoon ground cayenne pepper

2 tablespoons pepper jelly

2 tablespoons sweet relish

2 tablespoons Major Grey's chutney (or more pepper jelly)

1. Preheat the oven to 375°F. Line a baking sheet with parchment paper.

2. In a medium bowl, stir together the black-eyed peas, oil, and Creole seasoning to coat. Pour onto the prepared baking sheet and spread in an even layer. Bake for 15 minutes, then reduce the oven temperature to 325°F, give the black-eyed peas a stir, and continue baking for 10 minutes more. Test one of the beans to see if it is dried out all the way through. If not, give another stir and continue baking until they are dried and crunchy, 5 minutes more. Cool completely.

3. While the black-eyed peas are cooking, put the diced sweet potato in a medium pot and cover with cold water. Bring to a boil over medium-high heat and cook until just tender, 7 to 10 minutes. Drain, transfer to a paper-towel-lined plate to cool completely, then place in a large bowl. Add the peppers, celery, tomatoes, cilantro, parsley, and scallions to the bowl.

4. When ready to serve, add the crispy black-eyed peas, puffed rice, peanuts, and sev to the bowl and stir to combine. Stir in the paprika, cayenne, pepper jelly, relish, and chutney. Taste and adjust the seasoning, if needed. Serve immediately as a great drinking snack, accompanied by anything from beer to Champagne!

MAKE AHEAD
The black-eyed peas can be roasted up to 1 week ahead and stored in an airtight container. The raw veggies can also be prepped 1 day in advance and kept in a bowl in the fridge, covered, overnight. But as soon as you mix them together, you have to commit to consuming immediately. So have your serving bowls ready!

Third Coast Shrimp Toast

I got such a kick when I visited a Chinese restaurant in New Orleans one time and found that their shrimp toast was bursting with Creole flavors. The way cultures and traditions can seamlessly merge through food is endlessly fascinating to me. Especially when they manage to both highlight their similarities *and* celebrate their differences!

MAKES 16 TOASTS

2 scallions, white and green parts, trimmed and sliced

1 small garlic clove, sliced

½ pound shrimp (any size), peeled and deveined, cut into small pieces

½ teaspoon kosher salt

1 tablespoon rendered bacon fat (optional but highly recommended—if you don't have any, you can substitute extra-virgin olive oil)

1 teaspoon fish sauce or Worcestershire sauce

1½ teaspoons chopped fresh ginger

1 tablespoon chopped parsley

1 tablespoon chopped cilantro, plus whole leaves for garnish

1½ teaspoons Creole or blackening seasoning (if yours doesn't contain salt, add ½ teaspoon salt), plus more for garnish

1 egg white

1 lime

5 slices brioche or white sandwich bread

2 tablespoons raw white sesame seeds

1 teaspoon celery seeds (optional)

Vegetable oil, for pan-frying

1. In a food processor, combine the scallions, garlic, shrimp, salt, bacon fat, fish sauce, ginger, parsley, cilantro, Creole seasoning, and egg white.

2. Use a Microplane or small grater to shave the zest of the lime into the processor, and cut the remaining zested lime into wedges for later. Process the ingredients together for 20 to 30 seconds, or just until smooth.

3. Cut the crusts off of the bread slices and place them on a flat surface. Divide the shrimp mixture onto the bread and spread evenly, all the way to the edges.

4. In a small bowl, combine the sesame seeds and celery seeds and sprinkle the mixture over each slice, making an even coating. Press the seeds down lightly so they stick, and shake the excess seeds off.

5. Cut each piece in half (so you have 2 rectangles), then cut each rectangle in half so you have 4 thin rectangles.

6. Preheat the oven to 375°F and lightly oil a baking sheet. Heat a wide skillet over medium heat and add just enough oil to barely coat the bottom of the pan. When the oil is hot but not smoking, place the rectangles shrimp-side down in the oil.

7. Fry until the sesame seeds are toasted and the surface is golden, 2 to 3 minutes. Flip the pieces and cook on the bread side for another 1 to 2 minutes, or until toasted (add a drizzle of oil if the pan is dry). Place the pieces on the prepared baking sheet, shrimp-side up. Repeat with the remaining pieces until they are all lined up on the sheet.

8. When you're ready to serve, pop the tray in the oven for 5 to 6 minutes, until the bread is crisp and the shrimp is warmed through.

9. Transfer the hot toasts to a serving plate and finish with a squeeze of fresh lime juice. Garnish with a sprinkle of Creole seasoning and cilantro leaves and place the remaining lime wedges around the platter.

TIME-SAVING TIP
You can skip the oven and finish cooking the toasts all the way in the pan if you plan on serving right away.

that special touch

Sauces

When you're undergoing training at Le Bernardin, the sauce station is the last place you work. That's because it takes a serious amount of finesse, using things like vegetable scraps and wilted herbs as well as aromatics with various degrees of potency, to produce consistently flavored and textured sauces that taste like you've captured ingredients at their peak freshness. No wonder there's such a high intimidation factor for at-home cooks. If you're already struggling to get something on the table as it is, who has time to stand over the stove simmering a sauce?

But the thing is, sauces really are game changers, and they require much less time than you might think. They can take a meal from merely good to totally restaurant-worthy. Plus, they can be made from almost anything you have sitting in your fridge or pantry. Just whisk some olive oil into your acid base, and you have an instant vinaigrette.

All the following sauces can be made ahead, and several can be kept in the fridge for a couple of weeks or more, so all you need to do is open a jar if you want to "Sunday Best" your supper. For instance, if you're searing a chicken breast, you can simply pour a bit of sauce from your fridge into your pan to deglaze it. It will both heat the sauce and provide a rich, loving blanket for your chicken, transforming something super plain, flavor-wise, into something incredibly complex and special. And it will impress the hell out of your dinner companions too!

It goes back to the idea of self-love—taking a few small steps to elevate your everyday.

Buttermilk Vinaigrette

Aretha Franklin used to come into Le Bernardin for her birthday every year. And she wouldn't order a single item that was actually on the menu. One of her standing requests was a shredded carrot salad with raisins and ranch dressing! Needless to say, we didn't have bottles of Hidden Valley squirreled away in Le Bernardin's kitchen. So since I was working the sauce station, the task of making ranch from scratch invariably fell to me.

Now, although I'd been dipping my pizza crusts in ranch for most of my life, I'd never actually made it before. So I tried to feel my way through it, touching down all the creamy, tangy, herbaceous qualities associated with ranch dressing while still creating a product worthy of a Michelin-starred restaurant (to say nothing of Ms. Aretha Franklin). This recipe is what I came up with. It's even more pronounced in flavor than HVR, but much lighter in body; it manages to further increase the versatility of an already all-purpose dressing (see Level Up for ideas).

MAKES 2½ CUPS

1 tablespoon Dijon mustard

½ cup buttermilk

½ medium garlic clove

2 tablespoons chopped shallot

Zest of ½ lemon

2 tablespoons fresh lemon juice

2 tablespoons apple cider vinegar

½ teaspoon whole black peppercorns

1 teaspoon kosher salt, plus more as needed

1 cup grapeseed oil or other neutral oil

1 cup good-quality extra-virgin olive oil

3 sprigs of parsley, stems and leaves, roughly chopped (about 2 tablespoons)

5 sprigs of dill, stems and leaves, roughly chopped (a scant ¼ cup)

1. Place the mustard, buttermilk, garlic, shallot, lemon zest, lemon juice, vinegar, peppercorns, and salt in a blender. Blend on low speed just so the ingredients get acquainted, about 45 seconds. They don't have to be completely puréed—that'll come later.

2. With the blender running, open the top. Increase the speed to medium and slowly drizzle in the two oils, turning the speed up a little more (to medium-high) as you go.

3. Stop the blender, *remove the jar from the base*, and taste for seasoning. (Do not dip your finger or a spoon in while the jar is on the base. Anything can happen—an electrical surge, a switch getting bumped. It's not worth the risk. Safety first!) If it needs more salt (highly likely), add a couple more pinches.

4. Add the parsley and dill, put the lid back on, and return the jar to the base. Starting on low speed and slowly

increasing to high, purée for about 15 seconds to partially break down the parsley and dill.

5. Serve immediately or refrigerate, covered, for up to 5 days. The flavors meld really nicely after a few hours in the fridge.

LEVEL UP

Use this vinaigrette as a marinade for chicken, since the buttermilk will tenderize the meat. Pour it over a piece of fish and bake in the oven with a bit of salt and pepper. Drizzle it over a pile of greens topped with grilled shrimp. Swap it in for mayo in a lightened-up egg, tuna, or pasta salad, or use as a dressing for Hominy Tabbouleh (page 145), Collard Green Salad (page 172), or Cornbread Panzanella (page 214). It will add brightness to fried items such as Best-*Ever* Hush Puppies (page 74) and Humboldt Park Fried Chicken (page 118), and break up the richness of meats, braises, and stews, including Hanky-Pankies (page 56), Berbere-Spiced Mini Lamb Meatballs (page 77), and Boudin-Stuffed Calamari (page 208).

Cha-Cha

(TABLETOP PEPPER SAUCE)

In some families, cha-cha (or chowchow) refers to a green tomato condiment. But in the Terry-Washington-Cheatham family in Jackson, Mississippi, it was this pepper sauce that everyone would shake on every item on their plates. And then they'd do a little shimmy or "cha-cha," because it made the food so much better.

There was no real recipe that my family used. All you do is soak hot peppers in vinegar and sugar and let them infuse indefinitely, topping off the bottle with extra vinegar or water as you go. Cha-Cha can sit on your table and just stay there forever.

While this particular recipe yields 8 ounces, it's incredibly easy to scale up or down. Essentially, you can let the size of your bottle determine how much cha-cha you make. Just save any empty jar from the kitchen that looks nice, whether it's a bourbon bottle with a cork stopper or an old soy sauce bottle, which has a convenient slotted cap for shaking out one dash at a time. If you're not sure of the volume of your jar, fill it ¾ of the way with equal parts white wine vinegar and rice wine vinegar. So for an 8-ounce jar, this would be a total of 6 ounces of liquid: 3 ounces of white wine vinegar and 3 ounces of rice wine vinegar.

——— MAKES 1 (8-OUNCE) BOTTLE ———

3 ounces hot chile peppers (see Pick a Pepper)

2 garlic cloves, halved

1 tablespoon whole black peppercorns

3 ounces white wine vinegar (minimum 5% acetic acid)

3 ounces rice wine vinegar (minimum 5% acetic acid)

1 teaspoon sugar

SPECIAL EQUIPMENT
1 (8-ounce) glass bottle with cap or cork

1. Clean an 8-ounce glass bottle well with soap and hot water and let dry (hello, dishwasher!).

2. Place the peppers in a bowl and cover them with warm water. Swish the peppers around a few times, then drain them in a colander and rinse well under cold running water.

3. Wearing a pair of kitchen gloves to protect your hands from the chiles' oils, trim the tops off the peppers and cut a few peppers in half for show. Push the peppers through the neck of the bottle, along with the garlic and peppercorns.

4. In a small pot, combine the white wine vinegar, rice wine vinegar, and sugar and bring to a simmer over medium-high heat. Turn off the heat and, using a funnel if necessary, pour the mixture into the jar.

5. Let the liquid cool at room temperature, uncovered. Once it is cool, seal the bottle with a lid or cork and let macerate for 1 to 2 days at room temperature before using on EVERYTHING.

6. Whenever your liquid level gets low, top off with equal parts white wine and rice wine vinegar (it doesn't have to be heated) and let sit. There is enough acid to keep anything from growing in your bottle of goodness, and you can keep topping it off as needed for years.

7. The garlic will likely turn blue or green. This is a natural occurrence when garlic cells are exposed to acid. There's nothing wrong or dangerous about it, but you can take the garlic out after 1 to 2 weeks if you like.

8. When the peppers are spent (no longer giving off as much heat as you would like), eat them or use as garnish and add a few new ones to the bottle. I have a jar that I've been topping off for close to four years, and I occasionally add new peppers that I have left over from other recipes.

PICK A PEPPER

I like to use a combo of red and green peppers. Piri-piri (African bird's eye) chiles, cayenne peppers, and tabasco peppers are my favorites. But *any* hot pepper you have available will work great! I also like to add the Korean chili flakes known as gochugaru to mine, so you get those sparkly red flecks along with sliced fresh peppers.

LEVEL UP

Truly the gift that keeps on giving, Cha-Cha is an easy way to add a bit of funk, heat, and umami to anything from eggs to collard greens. Think of it like a finishing salt, since it contributes a piquant, vinegary flavor that'll wake everything up (even soups and stews). You can also whisk it into salad dressings. Just remember the vinaigrette ratio: 3 parts oil, 1 part vinegar, and a bit of cha-cha-cha! Use Cha-Cha to bring the heat to Green Tomato Shakshuka (page 51), Braised Turkey Necks (page 121), Pilsen Red Beans and Rice (page 141), or Controversial Gumbo (page 204).

Turnip-Top Pesto

Originating in the Italian city of Genoa, the name "pesto" directly translates to "to pound." So while this bright green sauce has become practically synonymous with basil and pine nuts, the truth is that the ingredients are a whole lot less important than the process.

Which is to say, never waste the greens when purchasing turnips! I love to swap the delicate tops for the expected basil in pesto, since they add a sharp and sweet quality that's wonderful in a pot of mussels or clams. You can also use sugary beet greens (which are somewhat easier to find outside of the South), fennel fronds for an interesting texture and anise-like flavor, or even grassy carrot tops!

— MAKES 2½ CUPS —

¼ cup raw sunflower seeds

2 cups (packed) torn turnip greens

1 cup (packed) fresh basil leaves

Juice of ½ lemon

2 garlic cloves, sliced

⅔ cup extra-virgin olive oil

½ cup grated Parmesan cheese

Kosher salt and freshly ground black pepper

1. Preheat the oven to 325°F. Line a small baking sheet with aluminum foil and scatter the sunflower seeds on the sheet. Toast until aromatic, 5 to 7 minutes. Remove from the heat and let cool to room temperature.

2. In a food processor, combine the toasted sunflower seeds, turnip greens, basil, lemon juice, and garlic and process for a few seconds. With the machine running, slowly drizzle the oil through the chute; continue to process until smooth. Add the Parmesan and pulse a few times to incorporate. Add salt and pepper to taste; pulse a few times to combine. Transfer to an airtight container with a lid and store in the refrigerator for 3 to 5 days or freeze indefinitely.

MASTER PESTO

The magical ratio for making pesto is 1 part nuts to 2 parts oil to 2 parts cheese to 8 parts herbs or greens. Plus lemon juice, garlic, salt, and pepper to taste. As long as you respect this balance, there are very few actual rules. Try using pistachios like they do in Sicily, or walnuts, which are a lot less expensive than pignolis. Or even pecans, for a taste of the American South! Instead of Parmesan, any hard grating cheese will do, from Asiago to Gruyère. And I've already demonstrated how you can play fast and loose with the basil, so if turnip tops aren't your thing, choose your own adventure when it comes to herbs or greens!

LEVEL UP

Toss the pesto with pasta, use it as a salad dressing, or drizzle it over roasted veggies (especially turnip bulbs, for a root-to-stem meal!). Portion it into ice cube trays and freeze, then drop in a cube when you're making soup. Slather liberally over your Grand Slam Breakfast Tarts (page 52), Brioche-Crusted Salmon (page 114), or Whole-Roasted Cauliflower (page 177).

Fermented Pepper Sauce

(CHA-CHA'S COUSIN)

I love identifying culinary kinships between cultures, and the art of preservation and fermentation is one of them. You've got sauerkraut in Central and Eastern Europe, kimchi in Korea, miso in Japan, and this pepper sauce from the American South! Back in the days before refrigeration, our cousins in the North could just bury stuff underground to preserve it. But it never got quite cold enough in the Southern states. So fermentation—the process of using yeast or bacteria to convert sugars and starches into shelf-stable alcohol or acids—was key. Like Cha-Cha, this sauce is a great way to add a kick of heat to your meals. But although the former is more of an infused vinegar, this smooth, blended, slightly thick purée contributes umami-rich, lacto-fermented funk!

MAKES 2½ CUPS

2 habanero peppers

1 pound Fresno chiles

4 garlic cloves, crushed

3 tablespoons sugar

3 tablespoons kosher salt

2 teaspoons whole black peppercorns

1 teaspoon coriander seeds

1 teaspoon yellow mustard seeds

1. Wearing a pair of kitchen gloves to protect your hands from the chiles' oils, trim the stems and tops off the habaneros and Fresnos, then cut the peppers in half. Pull out the ribs and seeds and tap out loose seeds that are stuck to the interior walls.

2. Place the peppers in a gallon-size glass jar (or other nonreactive container with a lid). Add the garlic, sugar, salt, peppercorns, coriander, and mustard seeds. Add 2 cups of warm water and swirl the mixture around until the salt and sugar dissolve. Add 4 more cups of warm water to the jar.

3. Place a zip-top bag partially filled with water on top of the ingredients, in order to keep them submerged. Set the lid on tightly and put the jar in the back of a closet or anywhere cool and dark.

4. Check on your jar once a day. After a few days it will start to get cloudy. This is good. You'll also want to open the lid at least once a day to vent the carbon dioxide that builds up.

Do this for at least 7 days and up to 2 weeks, depending on your preferred level of fermentation and the appearance of certain indicators: You should be able to hear the sound of pressure releasing/air escaping when you open the jar. You'll want to see little bubbles in the jar and a little cloudiness to know that fermentation is happening and you're developing all those beneficial probiotics (good bacteria). If you're not seeing a few bubbles after 5 to 7 days, keep it going another 3 to 4 days, checking each day and opening, or "burping," the jar.

5. After fermenting for 7 days (or more), strain the ingredients through a colander set over a medium bowl. Place the solids in a blender along with ½ cup of the brine and purée until smooth, adding up to ½ cup more brine as needed to reach your preferred consistency (some people like it thicker, some like it thinner).

6. Pour the sauce into a clean glass pint jar with a lid and store it in the refrigerator. The fermentation will slow but won't stop completely, and the flavor will continue to develop and mature. (Read: It will keep getting better!) The sauce will keep in the refrigerator for up to 4 months. Just make sure to open the lid once a week (or leave it slightly askew), for 5 minutes or so, so the carbon dioxide doesn't build up and cause the bottle to explode in your fridge!

LEVEL UP

Approach this sauce as you would sriracha. Spoon a dollop on top of a bowl of white rice with a fried egg and avocado for a complete meal. Slather it on ribs or mix it with store-bought barbecue sauce or other condiments to cut the sweetness and bring a depth of flavor. Start your day with a bang by adding sweet heat to breakfast items, such as Kick the Can Salmon Croquettes (page 38) or Cornbread Toad-in-the-Hole (page 45). Swap it in for the pepper jelly in Crunchy Hoppin' John Bhel Puri (page 80), spice up the custard of Kitchen-Sink Quiche (page 223), or add a dab to your Slow-Roasted Pork Shoulder (page 182).

Mustard-Green Chimichurri

Chimichurri—a kind of Argentinean pesto traditionally made from chopped parsley, red wine vinegar, and plenty of garlic—is another one of those workhorse condiments. It's particularly good friends with grilled meat, cutting through the fat by adding a bright herbal flavor and a touch of acidity. Those qualities are equally welcome when drizzled atop avocado toast, folded into eggs, or stirred into a pot of soup or beans.

Yet as much as I love it, I've always found chimichurri a little lacking in the spice department. And I don't just mean heat (although the Fresno chile I've included in this recipe is great for that). There's a certain vibrant pepperiness I've long thought it could benefit from, and experimentation led me to this winning combination, featuring naturally piquant mustard greens. They have a wasabi-esque back note that packs heat as well as flavor. You may just find that your steak plays second fiddle to your sauce!

MAKES 2 CUPS

½ bunch (about ½ pound) mustard greens

6 sprigs of cilantro

½ shallot, minced

1 medium garlic clove, minced (see Pro Tip)

⅔ cup extra-virgin olive oil

1 Fresno or any small, moderately spicy red chile, minced

Zest of 1 lime

⅓ cup red wine vinegar

1 teaspoon kosher salt

1 heavy pinch of freshly ground black pepper

1. Rinse and dry the mustard greens and cilantro. Remove the thick bottom stems from the mustard greens. Roughly chop the cilantro (stems and leaves) and the mustard greens together, then place them in a food processor with the minced shallot and garlic.

2. Pulse the ingredients a couple of times to combine, then add the oil, chile, and lime zest and process for 2 or 3 seconds.

3. Use a rubber spatula to scrape the mixture into a bowl. Whisk in the vinegar, salt, and black pepper.

4. Let the chimichurri sit for at least 10 minutes before using. Store in an airtight container in the fridge for 3 to 4 days.

LEVEL UP

Add a wow factor to even the simplest steamed fish, baked chicken breast, roast pork tenderloin, or grilled steak by spooning chimichurri on top. Or make a whole roast chicken and baste it with chimichurri when the skin gets crispy. This is also an awesome condiment for grain bowls and lends an herbaceous element to Overnight Grits with Fried Eggs (page 33), Stout-and-Soy-Roasted Chicken (page 117), and of course, Grilled Skirt Steak (page 124).

PRO TIP

Use a Microplane whenever minced garlic is called for. It saves time and keeps your hands from smelling for the rest of the day.

building bridges with sauces

When I began working in restaurants, I started seeing how ingredients and techniques from different cultures could be woven together. There are certain culinary touches that can live together on a menu and still make sense. Le Bernardin in particular was such a big eye opener, because as French as it is, the big mandate is that fish is the star of the plate. You maintain integrity by doing precious little to the protein itself, which allows you to play with everything else. Especially sauces.

I was fascinated by the use of chorizo emulsion on the pan-roasted cod and green tea consommé under the peekytoe crab. At culinary school there had been *rules*. Everything I learned was so classic, taught in the way it's always been taught and done in the way it's always been done. So it was freeing to see that even at the fine-dining level, cooking doesn't need to be so staid, and food doesn't need to exist in a vacuum. And even though it was a French restaurant, my coworkers from Japan and Peru and South Africa and Germany could see their food reflected in the menu of the great Le Bernardin.

The only thing I couldn't find on the menu at the time was Southern flavors. And I knew that was because soul food was still being pigeonholed as humble and ugly-delicious. Which is true, but if Korean food (which was long dismissed for the same reasons) could find its way into high-end cuisine, why not Southern cuisine? So during my time at the sauce station, which offers the most avenues for influence, I started to make a mental note of similarities. We ferment! Why couldn't one of our pepper sauces take the place of sriracha or gochujang? Our country gravy comes from the same family tree as béchamel! And remoulade is every bit as Southern as it is French. Oh, and jus? Southern cooks would never dream of letting flavor go to waste, from the browned bits left from a pan of roasted bones to the pot likker released from a mess of greens.

Those discoveries gave me creative permission to play. And I realized that sauces could do so much more than add another level of flavor. They could serve as a culinary love letter between cultures.

Charred Green Onion Relish

I fell in love with this condiment at Vanessa's Dumpling House on the Lower East Side, which my coworkers and I would make a pilgrimage to every Sunday on our day off. Off-the-charts awesome with everything from dumplings to noodles to Peking duck, my version is made with green onions (okay, that's actually just what Southerners call scallions) that have been charred for an extra smoky element and combined with lots of spicy ginger. I also add a healthy dollop of seed-dotted mustard, which makes this more of a relish and reminds me of the classic Southern condiment chowchow. Whatever you want to call it, it's a reliable staple in my fridge, because it instantly elevates just about anything.

--------- MAKES 1½ CUPS ---------

2 bunches scallions

4 tablespoons grapeseed oil (a light-bodied olive oil works too)

¼ teaspoon kosher salt, plus more as needed

3 tablespoons finely grated ginger (it's best to use a Microplane)

2 teaspoons sherry vinegar

2 tablespoons whole-grain mustard

¼ teaspoon sugar

1. Trim the root end off of each scallion and remove the flimsy outer layer. If your scallions are too long to lie flat in a skillet, cut them in half.

2. Toss the scallions with 1 tablespoon of the oil and a pinch of salt.

3. Heat a large skillet over high heat. Have a spatula or tongs ready to flip the scallions. When the pan is smoking hot, add some scallions in a single layer without crowding (depending on your pan size, it might be best to do this in two or three batches). After about 10 seconds, when the scallions are nicely blistered on the first side, flip the scallions and blister on the other side. Transfer to a plate to cool. Repeat until all the scallions are blistered.

4. In a medium bowl, stir together the remaining 3 tablespoons oil, ¼ teaspoon salt, and the ginger, vinegar, mustard, and sugar.

5. Working with a small handful at a time, group the scallions in straight, even lines and thinly slice them crosswise. They don't all have to be perfectly sliced, but you want the size to be relatively uniform. Add the scallions to the bowl and stir to combine thoroughly. Taste and adjust the seasoning, if needed.

6. Let the relish sit for at least 20 minutes before using. Store in an airtight container in the fridge for 5 to 7 days.

LEVEL UP

Use this as you would a mirepoix or sofrito, by sautéing a spoonful in a bit of oil in a hot pan before adding your protein or rice. You can also use it as a marinade for fish or chicken, rub it onto a seared steak, or fold it into stir-fries or noodle bowls. While it's obviously incredible in Asian-inspired dishes (such as Louisiana Yaka Mein, page 227), this relish adds the perfect final accent to just about any cuisine, be it Southern (Overnight Grits Arancini, page 217) or Italian (Boudin-Stuffed Calamari, page 208).

Red Miso BBQ Sauce

By toasting a dollop of the Japanese umami bomb known as miso—fermented soybean paste—before stirring it into a slathering sauce, you can add slow-cooked smokiness to oven-roasted meat without having to use an actual smoker or outdoor grill.

MAKES 4 CUPS

1 tablespoon vegetable oil

1 medium-size sweet onion, such as Vidalia, sliced

2 garlic cloves, sliced

¼ teaspoon kosher salt, plus more as needed

½ cup red miso paste

2 teaspoons smoked paprika

1 teaspoon ground coriander

1 teaspoon ground cumin

1 teaspoon freshly ground black pepper

½ teaspoon ground ginger

¼ cup bourbon or water

1 cup ketchup

¼ cup Thai sweet chili sauce

¼ cup apple cider vinegar

¼ cup (packed; 55g) dark brown sugar

1. Heat a medium saucepan over medium heat. Place the oil, onion, garlic, and ¼ teaspoon salt in the pan. Cook, stirring occasionally, until the aromatics are tender and just turning brown around the edges, about 4 minutes.

2. Add the miso, paprika, coriander, cumin, pepper, and ginger and stir to coat the onion and garlic. Reduce the heat a tiny bit to medium-low and cook, stirring frequently and scraping the bottom of the pan, until the miso has darkened and the spices are toasted and fragrant, about 5 minutes.

3. Pour the bourbon into the pan, stirring and scraping to dissolve the miso stuck to the bottom. (The mixture should look like a thick paste.) Add the ketchup, chili sauce, vinegar, and brown sugar and stir to combine well. Bring to a simmer, then reduce the heat to low and cook, stirring occasionally to make sure the sauce is not sticking and burning, until the sauce thickens and turns a deeper red, about 15 minutes. Taste and adjust the seasoning and sweetness, if needed. Remove from the heat and let cool to room temperature.

4. Purée the sauce in a blender or with a stick blender until smooth. Use immediately or store in an airtight container in the fridge for up to 5 days.

KNOW YOUR MISO

There are actually multiple types of miso paste, my secret weapon for sauces. And each kind has its strong suit. Use sweet and mild white miso for butter sauces (perfect for starches or fish); rich red miso for barbecue, braises, and bold cuts of meat; and versatile yellow miso for everything in between.

LEVEL UP

Swap this sauce in for tomato paste when braising short ribs, use it as a marinade or slathering sauce for poultry or pork, brush it over whole fish on the grill, or fold it into a pot of baked beans. Add slow-simmered smokiness to BBQ Quail (page 123), Pecan-Crusted Pork Rib Roast (page 187), or Slow-Roasted Pork Shoulder (page 182).

Smoky Red Gravy

My father didn't cook for us very often. But when he did, he was likely to make a dish of seared pork chops smothered with jarred tomato sauce, topped with croissant dough and baked (page 130). We loved it! This sauce is inspired both by his recipe—except I've actually put the pork *in* the gravy—as well as by the tomato-based sauce that Southerners often use to simmer up pig's feet.

MAKES 4 CUPS

1 celery stalk, roughly chopped

2 medium garlic cloves, crushed

1 large shallot or 1 small onion, roughly chopped

½ red bell pepper, seeded and roughly chopped

½ green bell pepper, seeded and roughly chopped

¼ cup vegetable oil (duck fat or pork fat are great substitutes here)

½ cup (70g) all-purpose flour

1 slice applewood-smoked bacon or pancetta

1 teaspoon kosher salt

½ teaspoon freshly ground black pepper

1 teaspoon dried Italian seasoning blend

2 teaspoons smoked paprika

1 cup dry red wine

2 cups tomato juice

1 (14.5-ounce) can high-quality diced tomatoes (I like San Marzano)

1. In a food processor, combine the celery, garlic, shallot, and bell peppers and pulse until finely chopped, 6 to 8 long pulses.

2. Heat the oil in a large skillet over medium heat. Whisk in the flour and cook, stirring regularly, until it forms a nice deep-brown roux. Not light brown. Not golden brown. A rich *brown* brown. This should take 10 to 15 minutes.

3. Add the bacon and the chopped veggies to the pan. Stir well to combine before adding the salt, pepper, Italian seasoning, and paprika. Continue cooking and stirring until the liquid from the veggies has evaporated and the mixture looks dry, about 8 minutes.

4. Whisk in the red wine to make a smooth paste (minus the texture from the veggies and bacon, of course). Bring to a simmer over medium heat and cook for 3 minutes, stirring occasionally. Whisk in the tomato juice, bring back to a simmer, then add the tomatoes with their juices and again bring to a simmer. Reduce the heat to low and cook at a low simmer, stirring occasionally, until the sauce is deep red and slightly thick, 20 to 30 minutes. (Note: If you have a splatter guard, this would be an excellent time to use it!) If it gets too thick, add a splash of water.

5. The sauce can be cooled and puréed (just make sure to remove the slice of bacon first) or used as is. It can also be stored for up to 5 days in an airtight container in the fridge.

LEVEL UP

This classic multipurpose gravy is great with pork dishes, of course, but equally well matched to veal, duck, and more. Sear chicken thighs and cook them in a skillet with this sauce, adding a little chicken stock. Ladle it over pasta or lasagna, or brown ground meat or chopped mushrooms and stir them into the gravy for a quick Bolognese sauce. Simmer it with veggies for a ratatouille or stew, or thin it out with stock and purée for a flavorful tomato soup. This gravy is a must for Mom's Stuffed Shells (page 197) as well as my dad's Smothered Pork Chops (page 130).

Beer-Apple Jus

What is a *jus*, you ask? It certainly sounds fancy. It's similar to gravy, since it's made with drippings. Except instead of being thickened with flour, it's reduced to a concentrated stock. So what makes jus different from stock? Besides being super concentrated, all of the ingredients the jus is composed of (bones, vegetables, fruit, what have you) get roasted first, as opposed to being added raw to simmering liquid. Thus, you get another layer of super-charged flavor, *and* a really cool name.

MAKES 4 CUPS

1 pound chicken bones (either raw or left over from a cooked chicken)

1 sweet onion, such as Vidalia, halved

1 medium carrot, scrubbed, cut crosswise into 3 pieces

1 celery stalk, cut crosswise into 3 pieces

3 tablespoons vegetable or grapeseed oil

4 cups unsalted chicken stock

1 dried bay leaf

1 teaspoon whole black peppercorns

1 teaspoon kosher salt, plus more as needed

3 medium garlic cloves, sliced

3 cups apple cider

1 (12-ounce) bottle of stout beer (such as Guinness or Old Rasputin)

1 sprig of sage

3 sprigs of thyme

1 teaspoon cornstarch (optional)

1. Preheat the oven to 375°F.

2. In a large bowl, toss the chicken bones, one of the onion halves, and the carrot and celery with 2 tablespoons of the oil. Spread out the mixture on a baking sheet in a single layer (this is one of the few times I advocate for not using foil; trust me on this). Roast until the bones are deep golden brown and the veggies are browned in places, 20 to 25 minutes. Use a spatula to scrape the bones, veggies, and any browned bits stuck to the baking sheet into a medium pot.

3. While the baking sheet is still hot, pour 1 cup water on the sheet and swirl it around, scraping the sheet to dissolve the rest of the caramelized juices and free the stuck-on bits. Pour the liquid into the pot with the bones and roasted veggies. Add the stock, bay leaf, peppercorns, and salt to the pot and bring to a boil over high heat. Reduce the heat to medium-low and simmer until the liquid is reduced by nearly half, 20 to 25 minutes. You want to end up with 2 to 2½ cups.

4. While the stock is simmering, slice the remaining onion half. Heat the remaining 1 tablespoon oil in a large pot over medium-low heat. When the oil is shimmering, add the sliced onion and garlic, along with a pinch of salt, stirring to coat, and sweat the aromatics for 5 to 7 minutes. A little browning around the edges is fine, but try to avoid too much color. Add the apple cider, raise the heat to high, and bring to a boil. Reduce the heat to medium-low and simmer until the cider has reduced to a thick syrup, 15 to 20 minutes. Whisk in the beer and bring back to a simmer. Cook until reduced by a little more than half, 5 to 7 minutes.

5. Strain the chicken stock through a colander into the pot with the beer-cider reduction. Add the sage and thyme and simmer until reduced by one-third, 10 to 12 minutes. Remove and discard the sage and thyme and season the sauce with salt to taste. If the sauce is too thin for your liking, dissolve the cornstarch in 2 tablespoons of warm water, whisk it into the pot, and simmer until the sauce reaches your desired thickness.

6. Use immediately or store in an airtight container in the fridge for up to 4 days.

MASTER THE JUS
Once again, this recipe can be taken as a jumping-off point to create a jus flavored with pretty much anything at all. I use chicken bones and carrots deglazed with apple cider and beer for a sauce that's basically the distilled essence of fall. But you can do fish, corn, and white wine for summer; beef, mushrooms, and Madeira for winter; and chicken, ramps, and tarragon for spring!

LEVEL UP
I like pairing this jus with lighter proteins, like chicken, pork, or duck, or making a veggie-centric main by using it to sauce roasted steaks of cauliflower or squash. This makes a beautiful, decadent accompaniment to cool-weather dishes such as Barley Grits (page 147), Whole-Roasted Cauliflower (page 177), Slow-Cooked Ham Hocks (page 134), or Roger's Park Meat and Potatoes (page 190).

Bacon-Miso Sauce

As I've mentioned, mango gazpacho (the inspiration for the Mango Tajín Gazpacho Shooters on page 73) was the first full recipe of mine to make Le Bernardin's menu. But this sauce was my first component.

If you haven't already guessed it, I have a bit of a miso obsession. It sprang from one of my greatest lessons at the restaurant: that food doesn't have borders. Just because a dish is French doesn't mean it can't be improved by ingredients from another country! In this sauce, I toast a bit of miso in the bottom of a pan—just like you might do with tomato paste—to create smoky undertones that are positively magical. The addition of bacon makes for a double punch of smoky umami.

--- MAKES 2½ CUPS ---

1 tablespoon grapeseed oil or other neutral cooking oil

4 slices applewood-smoked bacon, cut into ½-inch pieces

2 medium shallots, sliced

2 garlic cloves, sliced

Kosher salt and freshly ground white pepper (okay, black is fine)

¼ cup white miso paste

¼ cup white wine

2 teaspoons Hondashi granules

4 tablespoons unsalted butter

1. Heat a medium pot over medium-low heat for a couple of minutes. Put in the oil, then add the bacon and cook, stirring occasionally, for 5 to 6 minutes.

2. When the bacon has rendered most of its fat and browned, use a slotted spoon to scoop out most of the crispy bacon bits (more than half) and transfer them to a small plate lined with a paper towel. Reserve this bacon for another use.

3. Add the shallots and garlic to the pot with the remaining bacon and fat. Stir in a bit of salt and a heavy pinch of pepper and cook over medium-low heat until the shallots and garlic are just softened, 3 to 4 minutes.

4. Add the miso to the pan and stir it in well. It should start to make a paste with the fat. It will stick and make a thin coating on the bottom of the pan. Keep cooking, stirring and scraping frequently, until the miso begins to look toasted and a little browned in places, about 2 minutes.

5. Raise the heat to medium and pour in the wine to deglaze. Use a whisk to scrape up everything stuck to the pan and dissolve it into the liquid. Bring the liquid to a simmer over medium heat and let it cook until it has reduced by half, 2 to 3 minutes.

6. Add 2 cups of water and the Hondashi (or 3 cups of stock or miso soup) and whisk again to fully incorporate the ingredients. Raise the heat to high and bring the liquid to a boil. Boil for 1 minute, then reduce the heat to medium to simmer until reduced by about half, 8 to 10 minutes.

7. Strain the sauce through a fine-mesh strainer into a clean small pot and discard the solids (you can also use a slotted spoon to remove all of the solids from the sauce). Bring the sauce back to a simmer over medium heat and whisk in the butter, one tablespoon at a time. Let the sauce simmer for a few seconds after the last of the butter is whisked in.

8. The sauce can be served immediately or kept in an airtight container in the refrigerator for up to 7 days. Just bring it back to a boil before serving (if the fat separates, use a blender or hand blender to re-emulsify it). Use the reserved bacon as garnish for whatever you use the sauce with, such as Sweet Potato Gnocchi (page 152).

DIAL IT UP WITH DASHI

Made with kombu and bonito, dashi is like the Japanese version of a delicate chicken stock. But like any stock, it takes a certain amount of finesse. To save time, I use Hondashi granules (sold in Asian grocery stores), which produce instant dashi. If you can't find them, you're welcome to use 3 cups of vegetable stock in this recipe, or even leftover miso soup!

LEVEL UP

Since it brings tons of umami to the table, as well as an outsize amount of salty, layered flavor, you can stay totally basic with whatever you combine this with. Dilute it with broth for soup. Slather it on a simply seared chicken breast or pork chop. Toss it with spaghetti. Stir it into rice. Drizzle on top of roasted vegetables. And the sky is the limit when it comes to spuds. Fold it into mashed potatoes, or dollop atop baked sweet potatoes. And Bacon-Miso Sauce isn't exclusively friends with Sweet Potato Gnocchi (page 152). It's also best buds with Kick the Can Salmon Croquettes (page 38), Turnip Latkes (page 159), Whole-Roasted Cauliflower (page 177), and Pan-Fried Spaghetti Rösti (page 226).

how to "sunday best" sauces

MASTER THE VINAIGRETTE: A 3:1 ratio of oil to vinegar is the key to making vinaigrettes of all sorts. After that, what you add (or don't) is up to you. Try buttermilk for creaminess and garlic and herbs for flavor, or mustard as an emulsifier (see below) so that it doesn't break.

KNOW YOUR EMULSIFIERS: Natural emulsifiers are your ace in the hole when it comes to perfectly creamy vinaigrettes. To keep your oil and vinegar from separating, simply whisk them into a beaten egg yolk, a dollop of mayo or mustard, a drizzle of honey, a smidge of tomato paste, or (my favorite discovery) a bit of puréed mango.

EMBRACE AROMATICS: Whether caramelized, deeply roasted, or raw (run through the blender or puréed finely on a Microplane), aromatics like onion, garlic, ginger, chiles, and fresh herbs make *all* the difference when it comes to complex, flavor-forward sauces.

TAKE YOUR TIME: The reason the best sauces and stocks are cooked loooow and sloooow is that time is flavor's best friend. What happens is you're simmering out all the water released by your vegetables and meat, and leaving nothing but their pure, concentrated essence.

CREATE A CUBE COLLECTION: One of the most intimidating things about sauces is the perception that they need to be made last-minute (or cooked for a long time; see previous tip). And who really has that kind of time to add to their midweek dinner routine? The good thing is, lots of sauces, like pesto, chimichurri, jus, and more, can be made in batches, portioned into ice cube trays, and frozen. That way, they can be popped out and used to liven up a meal at a moment's notice!

THICKEN IN AN INSTANT: One of the best things about sauces is how they (ideally) cling to food. So if yours is looking a little thin, you can always stir in a slurry of equal parts cornstarch and water to thicken it up.

ENLIVEN YOUR LIQUIDS: You can *absolutely* use water as a base for your sauces, so don't let a lack of stock hold you back. You'll just have to love it up a bit with a few more aromatics (see third tip). That said, water and stock are just the tip of the iceberg when it comes to sauce building. You can use wine, beer, juice, tomato purée—I think you get the picture.

BETTER WITH BUTTER: A simple pat of butter added to a basic pan sauce will make it impossibly creamy, luxurious, and rich. And that's not the only way butter comes into play. Compound butters are sauces all their own. Just stir something crazy flavorful into softened butter (I looove using white miso, but herbs, pesto, garlic, ramps, truffle salt, chiles, and sun-dried tomatoes are also great). Place your compound butter on a large sheet of plastic wrap, use the wrap to guide it into a log, wrap it well and freeze it. Then you can cut off chunks whenever you need, for topping a seared steak; melting over vegetables; folding into rice, potatoes, or pasta; or creating a simmer sauce for chicken or fish.

REDUCE: Pan sauces—the simplest sauces of all—are made by pouring a bit of liquid into a pan that's been used to sear vegetables or meat. This is called *deglazing*; using liquid to release all those flavor-packed bits. Choose whatever you think will best complement your meal, such as red wine for beef, whiskey for pork, marsala for chicken, or stock for fish (yes, water works too). The next step is to reduce the sauce by one-half to two-thirds by raising the heat and cooking that liquid out.

REUSE: Despite what the food police say, you can safely reuse marinades. Boil for 5 minutes in order to kill any potentially harmful bacteria, then cool before storing in the fridge for a couple of days, or in the freezer indefinitely.

RECYCLE: Save all your scraps, like a squirrel storing nuts for the winter. Onion ends, carrot peels, cheese rinds, chicken bones, that bunch of celery that's starting to go limp in the fridge—keep these goodies in food storage bags in the freezer for putting toward your next spectacular sauce.

Country Gravy

(AKA THE SOUTHERN MOTHER SAUCE)

What you may know as béchamel is called country gravy in the South. It's a staple sauce that can be used as a base for just about anything. Mushrooms, bell pepper, minced onion, garlic, or dried herbs and spices can be added to the oil before the flour goes in. Bacon, sausage, ham, or any sort of meat can also be browned in the oil—just make sure to add 1 to 2 more tablespoons of flour to make up for the extra fat that the meat will render out. Chopped greens like spinach or kale as well as purées of veggies like butternut squash, carrots, or parsnips can be whisked in at the end.

—— MAKES 2 CUPS ——

¼ cup vegetable or grapeseed oil

⅓ cup (45g) all-purpose flour

½ teaspoon kosher salt, plus more as needed

½ teaspoon freshly ground black pepper

2 cups whole milk, plus more as needed

1. Heat the oil in a large skillet over medium heat. Whisk in the flour, salt, and pepper until smooth (it should look like wet sand). This is called a *roux*. Reduce the heat to medium-low and cook, stirring regularly, until the roux has become a light sandy brown, 7 to 10 minutes.

2. Whisk in the milk little by little, making sure there are no lumps. Bring to a simmer, whisking frequently, and cook until thickened, about 5 minutes. Adjust the seasoning as needed; thin with more milk if you wish, to achieve your desired consistency. Use immediately or store in an airtight container in the fridge for up to 5 days.

SIMPLE SWAP

You can use nondairy milk (the ones labeled as creamers or Califia's Barista Blend work best), or swap out the milk completely for stock.

LEVEL UP

Whenever you're searing any kind of meat in a pan, remove the browned piece of meat, deglaze the pan with a little wine or beer, and whisk in a few spoonfuls of this gravy to make a quick pan sauce. Or stir in a bit of mushroom stock to make a mushroom sauce. When roasting meat in the oven, heat as much gravy as you like in a small pot and whisk in the pan drippings. Or you can fold in a little cheese and, congrats! You've just made an elegant French Mornay sauce. Flaky Layered Biscuits (page 23) aren't the only match made in heaven for this velvety gravy. Try it with Chicken and Cornbread Dumplings (page 195), Elote Macque Choux (page 168), and Green Cabbage Gratin (page 178).

Poor Man's Remoulade

For most of my life, I'd associated remoulade with the South, and the accepted recipe as a pinkish, mayo-heavy, tartar-esque sauce with something tangy mixed in. And while I grew to appreciate the French version, which uses crème fraîche, fines herbes, cornichons, and red wine vinegar, I'm far more likely to whip up this so-called "poor man's" remoulade, spiked with pickle juice from pepperoncini or whatever sharp, nonsweet pickles you have on hand.

––––––––––––––––––– MAKES 2 CUPS –––––––––––––––––––

1½ cups mayonnaise (I love Kewpie, Blue Plate, or Duke's)

¼ cup Dijon mustard

1 garlic clove

1 tablespoon smoked paprika

2 tablespoons sweet relish

2 teaspoons Creole seasoning (I like Tony Chachere's)

2 teaspoons prepared horseradish (or freshly grated horseradish root, if available)

2 teaspoons pickle juice (red wine vinegar works too)

1 to 2 teaspoons Tabasco sauce

Kosher salt and freshly ground black pepper

1. In a medium bowl, combine the mayonnaise and mustard and grate in the garlic using a Microplane. Add the paprika, relish, Creole seasoning, horseradish, pickle juice, and Tabasco and whisk together. Season with salt and pepper to taste.

2. You can use the sauce right away, but the flavors improve if allowed to meld in the fridge for a few hours. The sauce can be stored in an airtight container for 5 to 7 days in the refrigerator.

SUNDAY BEST FINESSE

While I clearly have a soft spot for Southern remoulade, you're perfectly welcome to upgrade to French style. Simply add finely chopped herbs like parsley, chives, chervil, and tarragon, fold in diced capers or cornichons instead of the relish, and swap in some of the mayo for tangy crème fraîche.

LEVEL UP

Remoulade makes a glorious dipping sauce for anything fried, and is incredible with seafood, whether raw, poached, grilled, fried, or steamed. Jazz up salad dressings that otherwise call for standard mayo, drizzle it over vegetable skewers, or use it as a go-to sandwich spread. And bring on the appetizers! This is the ultimate dip for Best *Ever* Hush Puppies (page 74), Oven-Fried Okra Chips (page 67), and Candied Chicken Wings (page 63), as well as a great sauce for Brioche-Crusted Salmon (page 114).

remaking the dinner plate
Protein, Starch, and Veg

Once my sister and I were born, my mom stayed home to take care of us while my father worked overnight shifts at the Oscar Mayer plant. But no matter how late it was or how busy everyone was, we'd always eat dinner together as a family. Generally, the meal would consist of your standard meat + starch + vegetable, or some sort of stew or casserole. And always a salad, served in this big wooden bowl straight out of the seventies.

Yep, dinner was a rotating meal, and all my mom needed to do was plug dishes in or swap them out. She'd root through the pantry for dry goods like rice, pasta, or grits, and roast or steam whatever vegetable she happened to have on hand. She'd make the most out of any meat she could find that wasn't too expensive, be it chicken thighs, top round of beef, or pork shoulder; serve it up in some combination; and then switch up the combos from week to week.

And let's be honest: two of the three elements generally got short shrift. If my mom was expending energy preparing a roast, it was probably going to be accompanied by peas and a rice packet. So by all means, if you take the time to make Sweet Potato Gnocchi (page 152) or Grilled Green Tomato Salad (page 171), feel free to pick up a rotisserie chicken on the way home from work! Or treat yourself to the kind of slow-braised item you'd generally save for Sundays by making use of an electric cooker. Start your recipe off first thing in the morning and let it slowly simmer all day, so it's ready and waiting by the time you return for dinner.

The point is, whether you choose to lavish love on one part of your plate or go for broke by elevating all three, these updated takes on your classic protein + starch + veg are guaranteed to make every meal feel special.

Protein

——

Brioche-Crusted Salmon

This technique of crowning salmon with buttery brioche was borrowed from Laurent Gras, who was a leading chef in Chicago when he popularized it using sourdough. It's so much fun to play around with. As long as you slice the bread thinly enough, you don't need to use any binder, since the protein from the fish allows it to stick all by itself. I especially like using salmon, because it tends to release all of that white albumin. It's the perfect glue for toasty brioche bread, which also keeps it from pooling unappealingly on the plate.

4 skinless salmon fillets
(8 ounces each)

1½ teaspoons kosher salt

1 loaf brioche, unsliced

2 tablespoons vegetable oil

4 tablespoons (½ stick)
unsalted butter

1 garlic clove, crushed

2 or 3 sprigs of thyme

1. Preheat the oven to 350°F with a rack in the center position.

2. Season the salmon fillets with the salt and set aside.

3. Using a serrated knife, trim away the crust from the sides of the brioche loaf, then make four long lengthwise slices that are about ⅛ to ¼ inch thick. Lay a slice of brioche on a cutting board and place a salmon fillet lengthwise in the center; it should fall within the border of the crust. Use your knife to trim away the bread around the salmon. It's best to hold the knife flat against the edges of the salmon and press straight down (using the same motion as with a cookie cutter) to get an even cutout around the fish. Repeat with the remaining fillets and brioche slices, setting the finished fillets brioche-side down on a plate or tray.

4. Heat a large oven-safe skillet over medium heat. Put in the oil and butter; when the butter begins to bubble and foam, gently place the salmon, brioche-side down, in the pan. Work in batches if you can't fit all the fillets in the pan at once. Shake the pan a little to make sure the brioche is not sticking, then scatter the garlic and thyme sprigs around the fish. Cook, swirling the pan occasionally and basting the oil-butter mixture over the fish with a spoon until the bread is golden brown, about 1 minute.

5. Flip the fillets brioche-side up, transfer the pan to the center oven rack, and bake for 3 to 4 minutes, or until the salmon is cooked through but still has a touch of dark pink inside (about 145°F). Keep in mind, it will continue cooking a little even after you remove it from the oven!

6. Blot the fish with a paper towel and transfer to plates, brioche-side up. Serve immediately.

MAKE AHEAD
Complete the recipe through step 4, then transfer the fish, brioche-side up, to a parchment-lined baking sheet. Keep at room temperature for up to an hour, or refrigerate for up to 4 hours, uncovered. When you're ready to cook, place the fish in a 375°F oven and cook for 3 to 4 minutes on each side.

IDEAL MEAL
Serve with Elote Macque Choux (page 168).

Stout-and-Soy-Roasted Chicken

This is a version of the very first dish I learned how to cook on my own, when I was about twelve years old. When my mom left for work one morning, she realized she'd forgotten to marinate the chicken she'd pulled from the freezer to defrost the night before. Since she was going to be working especially late that evening, she called me before I left for school, full of instructions. She had me sprinkle salt on that chicken, pour a beer in a big plastic bag, stick the chicken in the bag along with some bay leaves and celery, and stand the bag in a bowl in the fridge to keep it upright.

When I got home from school, I was so proud of myself. I said, "I marinated this chicken, and now I'm going to cook it!" I had my dad turn on the oven for me, and I roasted that chicken, so it was ready by the time my mom returned from work. Of course, I've played with the rubs and marinades since then, but this is definitely the dish that started it all.

— SERVES 3 OR 4 —

1 (3- to 4-pound) whole chicken

1 cup soy sauce or tamari (wheat-free soy sauce)

1 (12-ounce) bottle stout beer (such as Guinness or Old Rasputin)

1 tablespoon fish sauce or Worcestershire sauce

½ teaspoon ground white pepper (black works too)

6 garlic cloves, crushed

2 large white onions, sliced into rounds

2 tablespoons unsalted butter, at room temperature

1. Using kitchen shears or a sturdy knife, cut out the backbone of the chicken and set it aside. Cut the chicken in half lengthwise, between the breasts.

2. Combine the soy sauce, beer, fish sauce, pepper, and ½ cup of water in a large bowl. Add the garlic, half of the sliced onions, the backbone, and the chicken halves, skin-side down. Marinate for at least 2 hours and up to 8 hours, stirring occasionally.

3. Preheat the oven to 450°F and position a rack in the upper third of the oven.

4. Arrange the unmarinated sliced onions on a baking sheet. Remove the chicken pieces from the marinade, pat them dry, and place them skin-side up in the center of the sheet, on top of the onions. Rub the butter over the chicken skin, getting it into all those hard-to-reach places!

5. Add ⅓ cup of water to the baking sheet and transfer it to the oven. Roast for 20 minutes, then baste the chicken with its juices and continue cooking until the skin is deep brown and crispy, 10 to 20 minutes more.

6. I suggest eating the super-crispy skin and tender morsels from the backbone immediately (I firmly believe in rewarding yourself for your hard work), then plating and serving the rest!

EASY UPGRADE

To make this a one-pan meal, toss sliced mushrooms, halved brussels sprouts, split carrots, or other smallish vegetables in a little oil and salt and add them to the sheet to roast along with the chicken.

IDEAL MEAL

Serve with Trinity Rice Pilaf (page 157) and Blistered Green Beans (page 166).

Humboldt Park Fried Chicken

When I was a kid, I used to get really *hangry*. Once I had my mind set on what I wanted to eat, I refused to deviate from it. One time, I was out all day with my mom for doctor's appointments and decided I needed fried chicken to make up for it. Southern fried chicken with that thick, craggy crust—nothing else would do.

Well, we happened to be in the largely Puerto Rican neighborhood of Humboldt Park, and my mom took me to one of the places she sold to through Kraft. It was a market with a counter in the back, and she ordered me a fried half chicken. When it came out, I started bawling. "This isn't fried chicken! Where's the craggy crust?" See, their style was to dust it lightly with adobo and flour.

My mom put the smack down, and I reluctantly tried it. And I couldn't believe how good it was. Of course, I couldn't backtrack in front of my mom right then, because I'd thrown such a fit. I guess I'm admitting it for the first time now! Sorry I was such a brat, Mom.

SERVES 4 TO 6

---

1 (3½-pound) chicken, cut into pieces (see Note)

3 garlic cloves, sliced

1½ teaspoons kosher salt

1 teaspoon whole black peppercorns

1 teaspoon dried oregano

2 tablespoons distilled white vinegar

2 tablespoons fresh orange juice (fresh lime juice works too)

1 tablespoon olive oil

Vegetable oil, for frying

1 cup (140g) all-purpose flour

1 cup (140g) cornstarch

1½ teaspoons adobo all-purpose seasoning

¼ teaspoon freshly ground black pepper

Lime wedges, for garnish

Torn cilantro, for garnish

1. Place the chicken pieces in a large bowl.

2. Combine the garlic, salt, peppercorns, oregano, vinegar, orange juice, and olive oil in a mini food processor, in a blender, or in a mortar if you want to go old-school. Process, blend, or mash the ingredients until you have a mostly smooth paste.

3. Pour the marinade over the chicken and toss, making sure to rub it evenly over each piece. Transfer the chicken to a nonreactive container, cover, and marinate for a few hours or up to overnight.

4. When you're ready to fry, fill a large deep cast-iron skillet with 2 inches of vegetable oil. Heat over high heat until the oil reaches 325°F; adjust the flame to maintain this temperature.

5. In a large baking dish, whisk the flour, cornstarch, adobo, and ground pepper to combine. Working in batches so as not to overcrowd the pan, shake any excess marinade off the chicken pieces before tossing them in the flour mixture, shake off excess, and carefully place them in the hot oil.

6. Fry, turning as needed, until the chicken is golden brown on all sides, 20 to 25 minutes. Use a slotted spoon or tongs to transfer the chicken to a wire rack or to a baking sheet lined with paper towels or newspaper.

7. When all the chicken pieces have been fried once, raise the oil temperature to 375°F. In batches, fry the pieces a second time (it's okay to crowd them this time) until they are a deeper brown on all sides and the internal

(recipe continues)

temperature reads 165°F, about 7 minutes. If you don't have a thermometer, make a small slit in one of the chicken thighs, down to the bone. If there's still redness around the bone, it needs more time to cook.

8. Drain the chicken on the wire rack or clean paper towels, then transfer to a serving plate.

9. Garnish with lime wedges and cilantro and eat ASAP!

PLAYING CHICKEN

When dividing a whole chicken yourself, I highly recommend cutting it into 12 pieces instead of the traditional 8. If you start by purchasing a cut-up chicken, you'll want to cut each thigh in half: Slice the meat until you get to the bone, place the heel of your blade directly on the bone, put a folded towel on top, and hit the top of the knife hard, downward to cut through. Then cut each breast crosswise in half. You'll get more surface area for marinating and more of those crispy edges this way.

IDEAL MEAL

Serve with Pilsen Red Beans and Rice (page 141) and Grilled Green Tomato Salad (page 171).

Braised Turkey Necks

Southern turkey necks are super country, served in a heavily seasoned Creole-style gravy. My mom had a version too, although she swapped in turkey legs and used canned golden mushroom soup. Creamed soup was kind of all the rage in the eighties, so I'm not mad at her for that. But it wasn't until I moved to New York City as an adult that I discovered a third inspiration for my favorite dish—Jamaican brown stew chicken. The sweet and spicy sauce is so gooey and unctuous, it clings to the turkey necks. You're gonna want to do what I do and suck all of the sauce and bits of tender meat from the bones.

SERVES 4 TO 6

4 pounds turkey necks (you can substitute chicken thighs or legs)

Kosher salt

2 tablespoons vegetable oil

1 medium onion, halved and thinly sliced

2 scallions, white and green parts, sliced

4 garlic cloves, chopped

½ teaspoon ground allspice

¼ teaspoon ground ginger

¼ teaspoon freshly ground black pepper

¼ teaspoon ground cayenne pepper or 1 Scotch bonnet pepper

2 teaspoons molasses

1 tablespoon soy sauce

1 beefsteak or large vine tomato, seeded and chopped

1 dried bay leaf

4 sprigs of thyme

4 cups unsalted chicken stock (you can substitute vegetable stock or water)

1. Preheat the oven to 375°F.

2. Rinse the turkey necks and pat them dry. If they are whole, cut into pieces 3 to 4 inches long. Generously season with salt.

3. Heat a large deep cast-iron skillet over medium-high heat, then add the oil. Heat for 30 seconds then add the turkey necks (in batches if necessary), and sear until well browned on both sides, 5 to 6 minutes per side. Remove to a plate.

4. Reduce the heat to medium-low and add the onion and a pinch of salt to the pan. Cook, stirring occasionally, until the onion is nicely browned, 4 to 5 minutes. Add the scallions, garlic, allspice, ginger, black pepper, and cayenne (if using a Scotch bonnet, wait until the chicken stock goes in to add it). Cook, stirring, for about 1 minute to toast the spices; make sure they don't burn.

5. Add the molasses, soy sauce, and tomato and cook for another minute. Add the bay leaf, thyme, and stock (along with the Scotch bonnet, if using) and return the seared necks and any accumulated juices to the skillet. Bring to a boil, partially cover the pan with a piece of aluminum foil, and place it in the oven. Braise the turkey necks for 1½ hours, or until the meat is fall-off-the-bone tender when tested with a fork.

6. Let the necks cool in the braising liquid at room temperature for 5 to 7 minutes before serving, spooning the braising liquid over top of each serving, like a sauce.

TAKE IT SLOW
Brown the turkey necks in a skillet, then finish off the rest of the recipe in a slow cooker for 2 to 2½ hours instead of a pot.

IDEAL MEAL
Serve with Barley Grits (page 147) and Red Cabbage and Beet Slaw (page 165).

Red Miso BBQ Quail

Quail is a fun dinner option, whether you're feeding two people or twenty. Everyone gets their own bird. And since quail are so small and lean, they cook quickly (you can roast one in seven minutes!) and respond well to strong seasonings like my Red Miso BBQ Sauce. Quail cooks quickly, so have your plates and side dishes ready before you begin grilling. When the birds are done, you'll want to sit and eat right away.

─────────────── SERVES 2 ───────────────

4 semi-boneless quail

1 teaspoon kosher salt

½ cup Red Miso BBQ Sauce (page 98), plus more for serving

2 tablespoons plus 1 teaspoon vegetable oil

1. Rinse the birds and pat them dry. Season them evenly with the salt, making sure to season inside the cavity as well as all over the skin. Let the birds sit on a paper-towel-lined plate for 15 minutes.

2. Brush or rub the barbecue sauce all over the outsides of the quail and refrigerate, uncovered, for at least 45 minutes and up to 4 hours. You want the sauce to form a thin, dry layer.

3. Prepare a grill for direct high heat.

4. Evenly coat the quail with the 2 tablespoons of oil. Drizzle an old kitchen towel with the remaining 1 teaspoon oil and use it to oil the grill grates.

5. Place the quail on the hottest part of the grill, breast-side down, cover the grill, and cook until the barbecue sauce is charred and caramelized, about 3 minutes. Flip the quail, moving them just off the grill's hottest spot, cover the grill, and cook for another 5 minutes, or until the birds are cooked through (internal temperature should be around 150°F) and the sauce is dry.

6. Transfer the quail to individual plates or a serving platter. Serve with extra barbecue sauce on the side.

PICK YOUR PROTEIN
You can swap the quail for chicken drumsticks and thighs. Just make sure you cook them until the interior temperature registers 165°F.

IDEAL MEAL
Serve with Sour Cream Cornbread (page 144) and Collard Green Kimchi (page 161).

Grilled Skirt Steak *with* Mustard-Green Chimichurri

Whenever my dad took us to the diner on Sundays, I always ordered steak and eggs. That's when I fell in love with skirt as a cut. It's not overly lean, which means it stays juicy no matter how hard you sear it and has enough fat to coat your mouth. That fattiness plays really well with Argentinean-style chimichurri, a type of acidic, bright pesto with lots of fresh herbs. Although, of course, I had to add in mustard greens for a bit of Southern flair!

SERVES 4

¼ cup plus 1 tablespoon extra-virgin olive oil

3 garlic cloves

1 teaspoon kosher salt

½ teaspoon freshly ground black pepper

½ teaspoon onion powder

1 (2½-pound) skirt steak

½ cup Mustard Green Chimichurri (page 94), for serving

1. Pour ¼ cup of oil into a small bowl and grate in the garlic using a Microplane. Add the salt, pepper, and onion powder and stir to thoroughly combine.

2. Place the skirt steak on a tray or in a large bowl and rub the oil mixture all over. Cover and refrigerate for at least 2 hours or up to overnight.

3. When you're ready to get cooking, remove the steak from the fridge and let it sit at room temperature for 5 to 10 minutes.

4. Prepare a grill for high heat or heat a large grill pan over high heat. Drizzle a paper towel with the remaining 1 tablespoon oil and use the towel to oil the grates. Lay the steak crosswise over the grates and cook until grill marks develop, 3 to 4 minutes, then flip and cook on the other side until you have nice dark grill marks, another 3 to 4 minutes. This should result in medium rare meat, so cook a minute or so longer if you prefer. Transfer the steak to a serving platter and let rest for 3 to 4 minutes before slicing on an angle across the grain into thinnish slices.

5. Serve immediately with the chimichurri.

IDEAL MEAL
Serve with Hominy Tabbouleh (page 145) and Bourbon-and-Brown-Sugar-Glazed Root Vegetables (page 175).

REMAKING THE DINNER PLATE: PROTEIN, STARCH, AND VEG

learning to cook like a grown-up

When we were in college, my sister and I never lived on campus and we never had meal plans. We essentially had to figure out how to be adults together, and that included learning to feed ourselves. My crash course started the summer before my freshman year.

My sister was a junior, living abroad in Japan for the summer. My parents declined to join me for orientation, so I had to find my way from Chicago to Florida by myself. I flew standby to Atlanta, took a Greyhound to Tallahassee, and finally found myself sitting alone on campus, so hungry, with no car and hardly any money, in 110-degree heat. I was literally about to start bawling when this big-bodied Ford Taurus with blackout tints rolled up on me and a woman with giant doorknocker earrings and a broad Brooklyn accent stuck her head out the window. "You have to be Jacqui's sister," she yelled at me. "Get in the car."

Now, I had heard stories about my sister's friend Amani, and she did not disappoint. She was pure Bed-Stuy, landed as if by alien spaceship in Florida. She was about twenty-two years old, hung out with Brooklyn rappers she grew up with, and was high-energy in the best possible way. She was also my guardian angel that summer. She took me back to her apartment, proceeded to cook me dinner, and began a series of life lessons.

"How do you plan a meal?" she asked me. I was damned if I knew. "Tell me something your mom used to cook," she prompted. I offered up a basic dinner. She's like, "Look at it this way. Protein, starch, veg." Which is exactly what my mom had said during her own attempted lessons, but I guess I wasn't paying attention. Amani told me that whenever I was planning dinner, I should be sure to pick a veggie or salad because I had to have something green. And that a starch could be something easy that you stir in a pot with water, or one of those Knorr rice packets with sauce and seasoning in it. That's the mantra she taught me when it came to learning how to feed myself. "If it's breakfast or lunch, you can skip one of the three," she added. "But when it comes to dinner, you've gotta have your protein, starch, and veg."

Cheerwine-Braised Oxtail

You don't need to break the bank to feed a crowd. Though they're not quite as inexpensive as they once were, thick cuts of oxtail go a long way. And they taste impossibly rich and indulgent when braised in red wine or a sweet Southern soda like Cheerwine, which contributes a delicious sticky sweetness. Can't find Cheerwine? Use Dr Pepper or Cherry Coke. Or try a combo of both, which means you'll get to drink half a can of each.

This is also a great make-ahead meal. If you braise your oxtails the day before serving, cool everything at room temperature, then refrigerate overnight. The fat will congeal and harden and it will be easy to lift off the top of the liquid.

--- SERVES 4 ---

2 teaspoons kosher salt, plus more as needed

1 teaspoon freshly ground black pepper

1 teaspoon gumbo filé powder (optional)

½ teaspoon ground coriander (optional)

5 pounds beef oxtails (try to get all large pieces, if possible)

2 tablespoons vegetable oil

2 medium onions, halved and sliced

6 garlic cloves, halved

2 carrots, cut into 2-inch pieces

4 celery stalks, cut into 2-inch pieces

2 tablespoons tomato paste

3 cups dry red wine

1 bottle or can (about 12 ounces) Cheerwine soda

2 cups unsalted chicken stock, plus more as needed

2 dried bay leaves

2 sprigs of thyme

2 small sprigs of rosemary

1 tablespoon cornstarch

1. In a large bowl, stir together the salt, pepper, and the filé powder and coriander (if using). Pat the oxtails dry with paper towels, then toss them with the seasonings. Refrigerate, covered, for at least 2 hours or up to overnight. About 30 minutes before cooking, take the oxtails out of the fridge to let them come to room temperature.

2. Heat a large Dutch oven or other heavy-bottomed pot over medium-high heat, then put in the oil. Working in batches to avoid crowding, sear the oxtails until well browned all over, about 3 minutes per side. Transfer to a plate.

3. Add the onions, garlic, carrots, and celery to the pot. Turn down the heat to medium and cook, stirring occasionally, until the vegetables have browned at the edges and begun to soften, about 5 minutes. Add the tomato paste and cook, stirring frequently with a heatproof rubber spatula or wooden spoon to prevent burning, for 2 minutes, or until the paste starts to stick to the bottom of the pot. Pour in 1 cup of the wine, scraping the bottom of the pan to dissolve all the tomato paste before adding the remaining 2 cups of the wine. Raise the heat to medium-high, bring to a boil, and cook, stirring occasionally, until the liquid is reduced by about half, 8 to 10 minutes. Add the Cheerwine and cook until reduced by one-third, about 6 minutes.

(recipe continues)

4. Return the oxtails to the pot, along with any accumulated juices, then add the stock, bay leaves, thyme, and rosemary. If necessary, add just enough extra stock or water to cover the oxtails. Season with a couple of pinches of salt, bring to a boil, then reduce the heat to medium-low to simmer. Cook the oxtails, partially covered, until the meat is super tender, about 3 hours, checking occasionally to make sure nothing is sticking or burning.

5. Transfer the oxtails to a plate or tray. Skim off the fat from the braising liquid and remove and discard the herbs.

6. In a small bowl, stir the cornstarch with just enough warm water to create a slurry (a thinnish paste). Drizzle the slurry into the simmering liquid and stir to combine. Simmer until the sauce thickens, about 5 minutes, then return the oxtails to the pot, basting to coat the meat. Serve the oxtails with ample sauce.

SLOW COOKER ALERT
Brown the oxtails in a skillet, then finish off the rest of the recipe in a slow cooker instead of a pot.

IDEAL MEAL
Serve with Barley Grits (page 147) and Brussels Sprouts with Brown Butter (page 174).

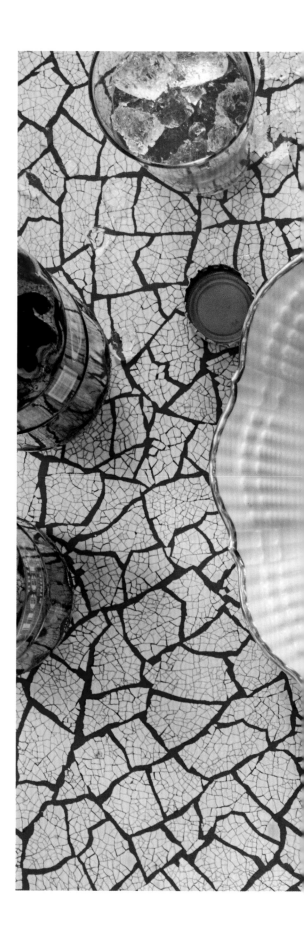

Smothered Pork Chops
with Smoky Red Gravy

I'd never really seen my dad cook when my parents were together (aside from late-night snacks that he would share with me, his nocturnal counterpart), but once they got divorced, he'd come over to take care of Jacqui and me if my mom was working late, and if she hadn't left something to reheat, he was tasked with making dinner. Since it was super easy, this saucy, savory, pastry-covered pork was his go-to dish. He'd layer it into one of those white casseroles with blue flowers on the side that everyone seemed to have in the eighties (and was inevitably missing a lid). It was awesome. I mean, who doesn't like digging into a crust of croissant dough? My Southern-born dad would call this "smothered and covered," but if you want to sound fancy, you can refer to it as pork chops *en croute*!

SERVES 4

4 bone-in pork chops (each about 1 pound and 1 inch thick)

1 tablespoon sweet paprika

2 teaspoons kosher salt, plus more as needed

1 teaspoon freshly ground white pepper (black works too)

1 tablespoon vegetable oil

1½ cups peeled pearl onions (either fresh or frozen)

2 garlic cloves, minced

1 cup dry white wine

1 (14.5-ounce) can diced San Marzano tomatoes or 1 (13.8-ounce) box Pomi chopped tomatoes

2 cups Smoky Red Gravy (page 99) or your favorite jarred tomato sauce

1 strip orange zest

2 or 3 sprigs of oregano, leaves picked

2 cups (about ¾ pound) small Yukon Gold potatoes, skin-on and halved

1 (½-pound) sheet puff pastry dough, thawed if frozen, or 1 (8-ounce) can croissant dough

1 large egg, beaten

1. Heat a large sauté pan over medium-high heat. Pat the pork chops dry with paper towels. In a small bowl, combine the paprika, salt, and pepper and evenly sprinkle over both sides of the pork chops. Put the oil in the pan and sear the pork chops until golden brown, 3 to 4 minutes per side. (If necessary, work in batches to avoid crowding the pan. Most pans are not big enough to hold all 4 chops at once!)

2. Transfer the seared chops to a 9 × 13-inch baking or casserole dish. Reduce the heat under the pan to medium-low and add the pearl onions; cook, stirring occasionally, until the onions get a little bit browned, about 5 minutes.

Stir in the garlic and cook for 30 seconds, until fragrant. Pour in the wine and stir with a wooden spoon to dissolve any fond (yummy brown bits). Bring to a simmer and cook until the wine has reduced by about half, 3 to 4 minutes.

3. Add the tomatoes, red gravy, orange zest, oregano, and potatoes; stir to thoroughly combine. Simmer for 5 minutes. Taste and add salt if needed. Remove the tomato mixture from the heat and let it cool for 10 minutes, then pour it over the pork chops in the baking dish. Cover and refrigerate for 30 to 45 minutes.

4. Preheat the oven to 400°F.

(recipe continues)

5. Lay the puff pastry sheet flat on a work surface. Use a rolling pin (or wine bottle) to roll the dough to about half of its original thickness, making sure it will completely cover your casserole dish.

6. Lay the puff pastry on top of the dish of chops, then pinch and crimp the edges to seal the dish. If the overhang is more than ½ inch, trim away the excess, then crimp. Brush the pastry evenly with egg and cut a couple of slits in the top to vent steam.

7. Bake until the sauce is bubbling and the dough is puffed and golden brown, 30 to 40 minutes. Serve each chop with some sauce and a section of puff pastry.

SUNDAY BEST FINESSE

Scoring the dough is totally optional, but it looks really nice. Use a knife to score the top of the dough in a diamond pattern—first make scores in one direction, about 1 inch apart, then score in the opposite direction, about 1 inch apart—being careful not to cut all the way through.

IDEAL MEAL

Serve with Collard Green Salad (page 172).

Herb-and-Mustard-Slathered Veal Chops

Consider veal the other, other white meat. Like chicken and pork, it's light, tender, and end-lessly versatile, and yes, it's also controversial. So by all means, use pork chops or bone-in chicken breasts if you feel some sort of way about it.

SERVES 4

4 veal rib chops (each about ¾ pound and 1 to 1½ inches thick)

2 teaspoons kosher salt

½ teaspoon freshly ground white pepper (black pepper works too)

1 cup plain bread crumbs

3 to 4 tablespoons Dijon or deli-style/rustic mustard

Canola or vegetable oil, for searing

4 garlic cloves, skin on, lightly crushed with the side of your knife

4 sprigs of thyme

2 sprigs of rosemary

½ cup grated Parmesan cheese

2 tablespoons chopped fresh parsley

1. Pat the veal chops dry and season liberally on both sides with the salt and pepper.

2. When you're ready to cook, sprinkle the bread crumbs into a shallow dish and set aside. One by one, slather each chop all over with the mustard (don't neglect the bone!) and place it into the bread crumbs. Turn and lightly press the bread crumbs to coat the chop evenly, shake off the excess, and transfer the chop to a baking sheet.

3. Line another baking sheet with parchment paper and lightly oil the paper. Heat a large sauté pan or cast-iron skillet over medium-high heat. Put a drizzle of oil in the pan, and when the oil is just smoking, place 1 or 2 chops in the pan (as many as you can fit without crowding).

4. Toss 2 cloves of the crushed garlic, 2 sprigs of thyme, and 1 sprig of rosemary into the pan and continue cooking, shaking the pan occasionally, until the first side of the chops is nicely browned, 4 to 5 minutes.

5. Flip and continue cooking until both sides are nicely browned. Be sure to flip or remove the garlic and herbs when they turn deep brown. Transfer the browned veal chops to the prepared baking sheet and repeat with the remaining chops, garlic, and herbs.

6. Preheat the oven to 425°F. In a small bowl, combine the Parmesan and parsley. Sprinkle 2 tablespoons of the Parmesan mixture on top of each chop.

7. Place the baking sheet in the oven and cook the veal for 9 to 10 minutes, or until the Parmesan is toasted and the chops are cooked to a nice medium (about 145 to 150°F). Let the chops rest for about 5 minutes and serve!

PRO TIP
Seasoning your meat and letting it sit in the fridge makes a noticeable difference in the amount of internal seasoning, especially with thick cuts. So if you have time, keep seasoned chops on a plate or tray in the refrigerator for 1 to 2 hours, then hold them at room temperature for 10 minutes before cooking.

IDEAL MEAL
Serve with Turnip Latkes (page 159) and Blistered Green Beans (page 166).

Slow-Cooked Ham Hocks

It was a game changer for me when I realized you could purchase fresh ham hocks, not just the smoked and cured ones used to cook down greens. When you stew them slowly, you end up with an inexpensive, porky play on osso bucco that can be served with any starch or veg you please. They also make for great leftovers that can be reimagined in all manner of ways. There are also tons of great ways to simplify this recipe. For one, you can prepare it in a slow cooker instead of a pot. And if you don't have the Beer-Apple Jus, you can mix one bottle or can of beer with 2 tablespoons of honey instead.

This stock is amazing for cooking cabbage, beans, and greens; turning into sauces; or using as a base for soups. Don't let all that goodness go to waste, I beg you.

SERVES 4

4 fresh (not smoked) ham hocks (about 1½ pounds each)

1 large onion, peeled and quartered

3 garlic cloves, crushed

1 carrot, cut into 1-inch pieces

1 large turnip, quartered

1 tablespoon kosher salt

1 teaspoon whole black peppercorns

1 teaspoon caraway seeds

2 or 3 whole allspice berries

2 or 3 juniper berries

1 dried bay leaf

3 sprigs of thyme

1 cup Beer-Apple Jus (page 100)

1. Place the ham hocks in a large pot with the onion, garlic, carrot, turnip, salt, pepper, caraway, allspice, juniper, bay leaf, and thyme. Fill the pot with water to cover the hocks by 2 to 3 inches. Bring to a boil over high heat, skimming off any foam that accumulates on the surface as it heats up.

2. Reduce the heat to around medium, cover the pot, and simmer until the hocks are tender, 2 to 2½ hours. You may need to add a little water occasionally, as you want to keep the hocks submerged the entire time. Check the meat for doneness with a small knife, making sure to stab into the exposed meat, not the skin. It should be super tender and almost falling off the bone. With a large slotted spoon, transfer the hocks to a baking dish, taking care not to tear the skin.

3. Strain the cooking liquid into a large bowl. Reserve ¼ cup of the liquid for the recipe and save the rest for future use.

4. Preheat the oven to 375°F.

5. Use a sharp knife to score the skin of the hocks in a crisscross pattern. Your slits should be about ½ inch deep.

6. Stir together the reserved cooking liquid and the Beer-Apple Jus and pour it over the hocks. Transfer the baking dish to the oven and cook for 20 minutes. Flip the hocks and continue to cook, basting occasionally, until the skin is a deep honey brown and crispy at the edges, another 30 to 40 minutes. Let rest for a few minutes and serve!

SUNDAY BEST FINESSE

If you want to get the skin super crunchy, instead of roasting the ham hocks with the jus, fry them in a pan. After scoring, heat 1 to 2 cups of canola or vegetable oil in a pan and add the ham hocks, basting frequently with the hot oil and turning as necessary until the skin is blistered and crunchy all around. Serve with the jus on the side.

IDEAL MEAL

Serve with Mashed Parsnips (page 156) and Green Cabbage Gratin (page 178) or Split Pea Salad (page 150) and Red Cabbage and Beet Slaw (page 165).

Roasted Catfish
with Herby Yogurt

Even after my parents' divorce, my dad still came for dinner every Sunday. But since they were no longer married, my mom officially excused herself from having to prepare the kind of Southern dishes he was used to. One of her earliest expressions of independence was to experiment with catfish—instead of serving it fried or blackened, she roasted it.

It was so shocking (and smelled so good) that despite my seventeen-year-old hangover (which I had been passing off as the flu all day), I had to take a taste. It was a revelation. I could actually appreciate the flavor and texture of the fish without it being crusted in something. That's the day I learned that I loved catfish for exactly what it was.

SERVES 4

2 teaspoons kosher salt

½ teaspoon dry mustard

½ teaspoon celery seeds or celery seed powder

½ teaspoon freshly ground black pepper

4 catfish fillets (8 ounces each)

½ cup Greek yogurt (choose your preferred fat content)

2 tablespoons Dijon mustard

Zest of 1 lemon, plus lemon wedges for serving

2 tablespoons finely chopped fresh parsley

2 tablespoons finely chopped fresh dill, plus a handful of sprigs for garnish

1. In a large shallow bowl, combine the salt, dry mustard, celery seeds, and pepper. Evenly season the catfish fillets on both sides with the mixture and set on a paper-towel-lined plate. Refrigerate, covered, for 30 minutes.

2. Preheat the oven to 425°F. Line a baking sheet with parchment paper.

3. Blot any moisture from the fillets with paper towels and transfer the catfish to the prepared baking sheet. In a small bowl, stir together the yogurt, Dijon mustard, lemon zest, parsley, and dill and spread the mixture evenly over each fillet.

4. Bake the fillets until just barely opaque throughout, about 8 minutes (internal temperature should be around 145°F).

5. Plate the fish, squeeze a little lemon juice over the top, and garnish with dill sprigs.

IDEAL MEAL
Serve with Hominy Tabbouleh (page 145) and Charred Okra (page 167).

Starch

———

Sky-High Popovers

Popovers are a very technique-based dish, using a batter similar to that of crepes but yielding a fluffy rise like you expect from a well-executed soufflé. No wonder they're making a resurgence at high-end restaurants! You certainly knew Sunday dinner was going to be extra special if you spotted them on my family's table. They were a treat we really looked forward to at every holiday gathering.

MAKES 6 FULL-SIZE OR 12 MUFFIN-SIZE POPOVERS

4 large eggs

1½ cups whole milk

1 teaspoon kosher salt

1 teaspoon sugar

1½ cups (210g) all-purpose flour

2 tablespoons unsalted butter, melted, plus 2 to 3 tablespoons for the pan

1. Combine the eggs, milk, salt, sugar, flour, and melted butter in a blender. Purée on medium speed until just combined and smooth, about 30 seconds. Transfer to a covered container, and let the batter rest in the fridge for at least 30 minutes and up to overnight (just let it come back to room temperature before baking, about 10 minutes).

2. Preheat the oven to 425°F with one rack positioned in the lower third of the oven and one positioned in the center.

3. Place about ½ tablespoon of butter in each well of a popover pan or muffin tin. Set the pan on the low rack in the oven and let it get wicked hot (5 to 7 minutes). Pull the pan from the oven and grab a pastry brush. Moving quickly, brush the butter to coat the wells. Using a ladle, immediately pour the batter into the wells, filling them about three-quarters full.

4. Set the pan on the middle rack in the oven and bake for 15 minutes. Reduce the oven temperature to 350°F and continue baking until the popovers are puffed and a beautiful, deep golden brown, about 15 minutes more. Try to avoid the urge to open your oven before they're done.

5. Use oven mitts or a folded towel to bring the pan to the dinner table, then grab and toss the hot popovers to your loved ones while they are fresh (and before they deflate).

SUNDAY BEST FINESSE
Instead of using butter for greasing the pans, try duck fat!

Pilsen Red Beans and Rice

In Mississippi, where my dad grew up, there's a huge Mexican American population. And Chicago, where I grew up, boasts the third-biggest Mexican community in the United States—much of it concentrated in the Pilsen neighborhood, where my mom took us for treats like elotes and paletas. So I've always seen how Southern and Mexican traditions can blend together seamlessly, especially when it comes to red beans and rice, a staple in both cultures. This version starts with the Southern trinity of onion, bell pepper, and celery, which functions as a flavor builder just like Latin American sofrito (which adds tomatoes and cilantro to the equation). I also love folding in morsels of smoky dried chorizo and earthy spices like coriander and cumin. If you don't have time to soak them, bring the beans to a boil in a pot of water. Boil for 5 minutes, cover, turn the heat off, let sit for an hour, and then drain and proceed with the recipe.

SERVES 8 TO 10 AS A SIDE, OR 4 TO 6 AS A MAIN COURSE

1 pound dried red kidney beans

2 scallions, white and green parts, thinly sliced

3 garlic cloves, sliced

1 large Spanish onion, chopped into large pieces

1 large green bell pepper, seeded and chopped into large pieces

3 celery stalks, sliced

1 teaspoon dried thyme

4 sprigs of parsley, roughly chopped, plus more for garnish

¼ cup plus 1 tablespoon extra-virgin olive oil

2 medium vine tomatoes, cored and finely chopped

1 tablespoon kosher salt, plus more for seasoning

2 teaspoons smoked paprika

1 teaspoon ground coriander

½ teaspoon ground cumin

Freshly ground black pepper

1 dried bay leaf (or 2 fresh)

½ pound dried chorizo, thinly sliced

Trinity Rice Pilaf (page 157) or cooked white rice, for serving (about ½ cup per person)

Chopped fresh cilantro, for garnish

1. Put the beans in a colander and check for any pebbles or debris. Rinse the beans with cold water, then transfer them to a large container or pot and add enough water to cover them by 2 inches. Soak the beans overnight, covered, then drain.

2. Place half of the scallions along with the garlic, onion, bell pepper, celery, thyme, and roughly chopped parsley in a food processor. Pulse 5 to 6 times to chop a bit and integrate. You don't want the mixture too fine or liquidy, so use your judgment after each 1-second pulse. By the way, congratulations! You just made a sofrito using a Southern-style trinity. Let's call it Trinity Sofrito!

3. Heat a large pot over medium heat. Put in the ¼ cup of oil, then all but ½ cup of the trinity sofrito (save the remainder for other uses). Cook, stirring occasionally, until the liquid has evaporated slightly and the bell pepper is a brighter green, about 5 minutes. Stir in the tomatoes, salt, paprika, coriander, cumin, and black pepper to taste. Cook for another 3 minutes.

4. Add the soaked beans, bay leaf, and 6 cups of water. Partially cover the pot and bring to a boil over high heat. Reduce the heat to medium-low to simmer, and cook for 2 hours.

(recipe continues)

5. Heat the remaining 1 tablespoon oil in a medium sauté pan over medium-high heat. Add the chorizo and cook until nicely browned, 2 to 3 minutes per side. Transfer the chorizo and all of its rendered fat to the pot with the beans and continue cooking, partially covered, until the beans are very tender, another 45 minutes to 1 hour.

6. Use a fork to mash about one-quarter of the beans against the side of the pot. This is traditional and serves to thicken the beans and make them more stewy. Season to taste with more salt and pepper, give the pot a good stir, and let sit for a few minutes before serving.

7. Serve over Trinity Rice Pilaf or white rice and garnish with parsley and cilantro and the remaining scallions!

LEFTOVER ALERT
Set aside ½ cup of the Trinity Sofrito for making Trinity Rice Pilaf (page 157).

TIMING TIP
Right after you add the chorizo is a good time to start your rice so that it will be done at the same time as the beans (takes about 40 minutes).

Sour Cream Cornbread

There were two cornbread camps in our family: one that made it from scratch, and one that used Jiffy. And each talked shit about the other side. The people who made it from scratch said the Jiffy was too crumbly and cakey, while the Jiffy people complained that the from-scratch cornbread was too dry and gritty.

Well, when I was working at Red Rooster, I discovered the best of both worlds. The restaurant's homemade cast-iron cornbread had sour cream in the batter, which balanced the sandy texture of cornmeal with the dense moisture of pound cake. Since my version has a higher fat content than most cornbread, it grills up really well—try using it as a base for avocado toast.

MAKES ONE 12-INCH ROUND LOAF

4 tablespoons (½ stick) unsalted butter

1½ cups fresh sweet corn kernels (frozen is okay in a pinch)

3 large eggs

16 ounces (2 cups) sour cream

1½ cups buttermilk

1 cup plus 2 tablespoons (135g) cake flour (can substitute all-purpose)

1½ cups (210g) fine cornmeal

⅔ cup (200g) sugar

4 teaspoons baking powder

½ tablespoon Aleppo pepper flakes or other dried red pepper flakes (optional)

2 teaspoons kosher salt

1. Preheat the oven to 375°F.

2. Heat a small saucepan over medium heat. Place the butter, the corn, and 1 tablespoon of water in the pan and cook, stirring occasionally, until the corn is just cooked (or defrosted and warmed through), 5 to 7 minutes. Remove from the heat and let cool to room temperature.

3. In a large bowl, whisk the eggs, sour cream, and buttermilk until thoroughly combined. In another large bowl, whisk together the cake flour, cornmeal, sugar, baking powder, red pepper flakes (if using), and salt. Use a rubber spatula or wooden spoon to gently fold the egg mixture into the flour mixture until just combined. Fold the corn into the batter and let rest for 15 minutes.

4. Heat a 12-inch cast-iron skillet over medium heat. Pour the batter into the skillet (make sure to use the spatula to get all that goodness out), then immediately transfer the skillet to the oven.

5. Bake the cornbread until the top has crowned and the middle is cooked, 20 to 25 minutes. Test by inserting a wooden skewer into the middle of the cornbread. If it comes out clean, you're good; if not, continue cooking for up to 10 minutes more.

6. Transfer the pan to a wire rack and let it cool to room temperature. Slice and serve directly from the skillet, or transfer slices to a serving plate. Enjoy!

EQUIPMENT SWAP
You can use cake or loaf pans instead of cast iron. They don't need to be heated, just oil them well and line the bottoms with parchment paper. Begin checking them at around 20 minutes for doneness.

Hominy Tabbouleh

Hominy is such a huge part of African American culture. After all, it's what we use to make grits. But it's got so much more potential than that. Produced from dried nixtamalized corn, the fluffy kernels are great at absorbing flavor. So what better substitute for bulgur wheat in Middle Eastern–style tabbouleh, which essentially serves as a sponge for soaking up olive oil, lemon juice, and herbs?

SERVES 4 TO 6

3 cups canned hominy, rinsed in cold water

2 teaspoons kosher salt

½ cup good-quality extra-virgin olive oil (it really makes a difference here)

1 bunch of parsley, leaves and stems roughly chopped (about ¾ cups)

3 large collard green leaves, stemmed and roughly chopped

1 cup fresh mint leaves, chopped

½ cup chopped fresh cilantro leaves and stems

2 scallions, halved lengthwise and thinly sliced

1 pint cherry tomatoes, quartered

1 garlic clove, minced

Zest and juice of 2 lemons

½ teaspoon freshly ground black pepper

1. Place the hominy in a food processor. If your processor is a small guy (like the one I use most frequently), only fill it by about one-third. Trust me, it's best to work in batches. Pulse the hominy 6 or 7 times, until it is finely chopped, with a consistency resembling coarse bulgur wheat; transfer to a large bowl. (Don't wash the food processor.) Stir 1 teaspoon of the salt and ¼ cup of the olive oil into the hominy until well combined.

2. Place the parsley and collard greens in the processor (again, working in batches to avoid overpacking the machine) and process for 5 to 10 seconds (no pulsing this time), until the leaves are chopped small but not too fine. If some large pieces remain, add them to the next batch. Transfer to the bowl with the hominy, but don't mix.

3. Add the herbs to the hominy, along with the scallions, tomatoes, garlic, lemon zest, lemon juice, pepper, and the remaining 1 teaspoon salt and ¼ cup olive oil. Gently fold together to thoroughly combine. Taste and adjust the seasoning, if needed.

4. The tabbouleh can hold for up to 1 day in the refrigerator, but it is best served within a few hours of mixing, when the flavors are melded but still bright.

Barley Grits
with Roasted Grapes and Almonds

Starting around 2017, I began making cholent every Friday with my kosher friends. Cholent is a type of overnight stew made from broken barley. It made me think of Southern grits, which are broken hominy. That was a lightbulb moment. It showed me that any grain could be made into grits, and barley is a great option, because it's earthy and nutty and has a higher nutritional content than corn.

--- SERVES 4 TO 6 ---

2 cups pearled barley

1 cup unsweetened almond milk, plus more as needed

2 teaspoons kosher salt

2 tablespoons extra-virgin olive oil

3 sprigs of thyme, leaves picked

2 cups whole seedless red grapes, plus 4 sliced grapes for garnish

¼ cup balsamic vinegar (or any slightly sweet, dark vinegar, such as pomegranate, cherry, etc.)

¼ teaspoon freshly ground black pepper

¼ cup skin-on sliced almonds, lightly toasted

1. Preheat the oven to 350°F.

2. In a food processor, pulse the barley in 3-second intervals until the grains are broken into pieces. Place the barley in a fine-mesh sieve and sift off the barley dust.

3. Combine the almond milk and 3 cups of water in a medium pot and bring to a simmer over medium heat. Stir in 1 teaspoon of the salt and the barley grits, reduce the heat to low, and cook, stirring occasionally, until the grits are tender, about 20 minutes. Thin with more almond milk or water, if needed, to achieve your desired consistency. Taste and adjust the seasoning, if needed.

4. While the grits are cooking, heat the oil in an oven-safe nonstick skillet over medium-high heat. Add the thyme and whole grapes and cook until the grapes are browned and blistered, about 2 minutes. Remove from the heat and add the vinegar, pepper, and remaining 1 teaspoon of salt. Stir to combine.

5. Place the skillet in the oven and roast until the grapes are wrinkled and softened, 7 to 10 minutes. Remove from the oven, stir in half of the sliced almonds, and let cool to room temperature.

6. Portion the warm grits among serving bowls and top with the roasted grapes and almonds and any accumulated juices. Garnish with the sliced grapes and remaining almonds. Yum!

FYI
The sifting is totally optional. Just know that the dust will add more starch and thicken the grits, so you may need to add a little more liquid if you don't remove it.

how to "sunday best" your protein, starch, and veg

PLAY WITH PROTEINS: Take a chance on an unfamiliar cut. For instance, if you like lamb, try shoulder steaks instead of chops. They're cheaper, and you can braise or sear them.

SUPPLEMENT WITH SAUCES AND SPICES: Even the most simply prepared protein, vegetable, or starch can soar if you sprinkle it with a compelling spice such as berbere or fenugreek powder or slather on an awesome sauce. One from chapter 2, preferably! But even a basic coat of miso paste or a baste of butter and soy will do.

GO SLOW: Slow-roasting keeps meat moist. Give this method a try on proteins that don't have skin or bones, such as chicken breasts or thighs, that would otherwise allow them to naturally maintain tenderness.

USE BOOZE: When you roast a chicken or steak in the oven, add wine or beer to the bottom of the pan instead of just letting the juices accumulate and evaporate. It will help create an especially flavorful liquid that you can use at the end to make sauce.

CRUST IT UP: To form a really great crust, sear proteins in a cast-iron pan before you put them in the oven.

LIVE LARGE: If you cook bigger proteins than you technically need—such as pork shoulders, beef roasts, or whole birds—you'll have the makings for multiple midweek meals.

LIVEN UP YOUR LIQUIDS: Use a seasoned liquid like stock instead of plain water to cook your starches. They really need to pick up flavor while they're still cooking, instead of at the end. That said, if you only have water, supplement it with aromatics like a chunk of onion or a clove of garlic.

RETHINK RISOTTO: When cooking hearty grains like barley or farro, stir them frequently to pull out the starches and give them a creamier, risotto-like texture.

CULTIVATE CRUNCH: Leftover grains can be fried or baked in the oven for a crunchy component to use later.

MAKE GOURMET GRAINS: Season your grains or starches with a balance of fat and acid, like olive oil and lemon juice.

PUMP UP YOUR PASTA: Don't drain your pasta water away. Save 1 to 2 cups to toss with the sauce, since the starchy liquid will thicken it slightly and help it cling to the pasta.

SEASON EVENLY: When preparing veggies to roast, toss them in a bowl with oil and seasoning (instead of adding oil and salt to the tray) so that you don't get greasy, dry, or salty spots.

RAISE THE HEAT: Don't be afraid of cooking vegetables at a higher heat than you're used to. A screaming-hot pan or 425°F oven will give them delectable caramelized edges.

PERFECT THE BLANCH: Any green nonroot vegetable can be added to well-seasoned, rapidly boiling water, cooked for a few seconds until brightly colored and tender, then transferred to an ice bath. Prepared this way, greens can be kept in the fridge or frozen as a quick, ready-to-use addition to stir-fries, starches, or roasts.

ADD DIMENSION TO SALADS: The best salads have a combination of textures and flavors. Do a raw and cooked combo of any veg you have on hand, like raw and blanched green beans or raw and roasted radishes.

MAKE VEGGIES THE STAR: When vegetables are the main meal, cook them whole instead of cutting them into pieces, and treat them like a protein. Marinate them. Roast them. Sear them. Sauce them. Give all the love you can to your whole-roasted carrots, head of cauliflower or broccoli, or cluster of maitake mushrooms. You'll still get that sensation of cutting through something hefty with a fork and knife, which contributes a lot to the mental aspect of feeling sated.

Split Pea Salad *with* Warm Bacon-Sherry Vinaigrette

The Exorcist kind of ruined split peas for a lot of people. But in my husband's family and in mine, there's nothing more beloved than a bowl of split pea soup simmered with a ham bone. So I thought I'd take everything great about the flavors of split pea soup and reimagine them as a salad, thereby eliminating the color and texture associations that tend to turn people off.

SERVES 6 TO 8

1 pound green or yellow split peas (you can also use any color of lentils), sorted through to remove any stones

1¼ teaspoons kosher salt, plus more as needed

2 small shallots

2 garlic cloves, minced

4 sprigs of thyme

4 slices thick-cut applewood-smoked bacon

⅓ cup extra-virgin olive oil, plus more for drizzling

1 teaspoon freshly ground black pepper

2 tablespoons Dijon mustard

¼ cup sherry vinegar

3 tablespoons sliced fresh chives

3 cups torn (1- to 2-inch pieces) red lettuce leaves (yes, red; green won't look pretty)

4 small radishes, thinly sliced

1. Place the split peas and 1 teaspoon of the salt in a medium pot and fill with enough water to cover the peas by 1 inch. Cut 1 shallot in half lengthwise and add it to the pot along with half of the garlic and all of the thyme sprigs.

2. Cover the pot and bring to a boil over high heat, then reduce the heat to medium-low and simmer until the peas are tender but not mushy or falling apart, about 15 minutes. Drain in a colander, pick out and discard the thyme and shallot, and place the split peas in a medium bowl. Set aside to cool to room temperature.

3. Meanwhile, slice the remaining shallot crosswise into paper-thin rounds. Place the slices in a small bowl with cold water to cover and an ice cube. Soak until ready to use.

4. Slice the bacon in half lengthwise and slice the strips ¼-inch thick. Heat a medium sauté pan over medium-low heat. Drizzle with oil and add the bacon and pepper. Cook, stirring occasionally, until the bacon is browned and crisp and the fat has rendered, about 7 minutes. Reduce the heat to low, add the remaining half of the garlic, and cook for

30 seconds, until fragrant. Whisk the mustard in followed by the vinegar and the ⅓ cup of the oil. The vinaigrette won't be fully emulsified, but don't worry—it's still a vinaigrette and it will still make the salad delicious.

5. Use a rubber spatula to scrape *all* of the warm vinaigrette into the bowl of split peas, then add the remaining ¼ teaspoon salt and the chives. Gently fold everything together. Taste and adjust the seasoning, if needed.

6. Drain the shallot slices and transfer them to paper towels. Blot dry, then fold into the split peas.

7. Place the lettuce and radishes in a large bowl and toss with a drizzle of oil and a pinch of salt. Gently fold in the split peas and serve.

DOUBLE-DUTY DRESSING

There's nothing this vinaigrette doesn't elevate, from grains of any sort, to spinach leaves and bitter greens like endive and chicory, to simply grilled chicken or pork.

Sweet Potato Gnocchi *with* Bacon-Miso Sauce

As I've mentioned, Bacon-Miso Sauce was the first menu element I personally developed for Le Bernardin. We often served it with Japanese sweet potatoes, since I loved the sweetness and tenderness of potato paired with the salty and umami-filled sauce. Basically, it's amazing with potatoes of any sort, of any color, and from any country. So if you don't feel like making gnocchi, go on and roast up some sweet potato wedges to serve with this luscious sauce instead. Think of it as a fancy answer to french fries and ketchup!

SERVES 2 AS AN ENTRÉE OR 4 AS AN APPETIZER

⅔ cup whole milk ricotta cheese

2 pounds sweet potatoes (about 3 medium sweet potatoes)

1 large egg

½ cup grated Parmesan cheese

2 teaspoons kosher salt

3 cups (420g) all-purpose flour, plus up to 1 cup (120g) more as needed

2 tablespoons olive oil

1 cup Bacon-Miso Sauce (page 102)

3 tablespoons crumbled cooked bacon, for garnish

2 teaspoons sliced chives, for garnish

1. Place the ricotta in a towel-lined colander set in the sink or over a bowl, and let sit for about 2 hours to remove excess liquid (if you don't have time to drain, no worries, you may just need a little more flour).

2. Rinse the sweet potatoes, prick all over with a fork, and place in a microwave-safe container, uncovered. Microwave on high until completely tender when poked with a fork, at least 7 minutes. Let cool for 10 minutes.

3. Cut the sweet potatoes in half and scrape the flesh into a food processor (discard the skins, or sprinkle them with salt and snack away). Purée the flesh until smooth, with no strings remaining, about 10 seconds, then scrape it into a large bowl.

4. Add the egg, ricotta, Parmesan, and salt, and mix well with a wooden spoon. Fold in the flour 1 cup at a time until a soft dough forms. The dough should be soft but not sticky, so add up to 1 cup flour in ¼-cup increments if needed.

5. Dust a baking sheet with flour. Turn the dough out onto a lightly floured work surface and divide it into 8 pieces. Take one piece at a time, pressing and rolling it with your palms into a long rope about ½ inch thick. Cut the rope into pieces about ½ inch long and place the cut gnocchi on the prepared baking sheet while you roll and cut the remaining dough.

6. Bring a large pot of salted water to a boil over high heat. While the water comes to a boil, heat a large nonstick sauté pan over medium heat, and have a large slotted spoon or handheld strainer basket ready to lift the gnocchi out of the water. When the water is boiling, carefully add the gnocchi to the pot and gently stir to make sure they are not sticking together. Add the oil to the sauté pan and swirl to coat.

7. When the gnocchi begin to float to the surface, in about 4 minutes, they are almost ready. Let them continue cooking for 10 seconds, then lift them out of the pot, shaking off the excess water. Carefully lower the boiled gnocchi into the sauté pan (the oil will splatter a little, so tilt the pan away from you as you add the gnocchi).

8. Shake and swirl the pan occasionally, and carefully toss the gnocchi to make sure they all make contact with the pan. Sauté for 4 to 5 minutes with the occasional toss, until all of the gnocchi have spots of caramelization.

9. Pour the Bacon-Miso Sauce into the pan, toss to coat, and add a spoonful of cloudy pasta-cooking water.

10. Divide the gnocchi and sauce among serving bowls, garnish with crispy bacon and chives, and serve immediately.

SUNDAY BEST FINESSE

As an additional (but completely optional) step, roll each cut gnocco along the back of a fork to make indented lines, then return it to the flour-dusted sheet until ready to cook. Rolling the gnocchi on the fork will help the sauce adhere better but is a little time consuming if you're working solo. The gnocchi can also be frozen at this point. To freeze, place in the freezer in a single layer on a sheet tray (or in multiple layers in an airtight container, with parchment placed between the layers). When frozen, transfer the gnocchi to a freezer-safe bag or airtight container, and freeze indefinitely.

Mashed Parsnips

I love potatoes, don't get me wrong. But did you know that in the United States, parsnips were more popular than potatoes up until the 1800s? I say it's time for a comeback. I like to slow-roast them so that they get all caramelized and brown on the outside. And they fry up really well. But I especially love them mashed or puréed in place of potatoes, because they have a little less starch, a little earthy sweetness, and a little more vitamins. So I still get all the comfort of mashed potatoes but feel like I'm being healthier. Whether that's true or not.

— SERVES 4 TO 6 —

8 large parsnips, peeled and cut into ½-inch lengths

2½ to 3 cups whole milk (half-and-half, nondairy creamer, oat milk, or almond milk also work great)

2 garlic cloves, trimmed

4 sprigs of thyme

1 teaspoon kosher salt, plus more for seasoning

2 to 3 tablespoons unsalted butter

1. Add the parsnips to a pot along with 2½ cups of milk, the garlic, thyme sprigs, salt, and 2 tablespoons of butter. Bring to a simmer over medium-high heat and cook until the parsnips are very tender, 15 to 20 minutes. Pick out and discard the thyme.

2. Use a slotted spoon to transfer the parsnips to a food processor. Process for a few seconds at a time until smooth. With the motor running, stream in as much of the cooking liquid as necessary to achieve your desired consistency, processing until just combined. (Some people prefer a thick mash, while others like it richer and smoother. Who am I to tell you what's right?) Add more milk, butter, or salt if needed and process for a few seconds to incorporate the adjusted seasonings. Plate and serve.

MAKE AHEAD

The mash can be cooled at room temperature, refrigerated, then microwaved or reheated in a pot with a little splash of milk and/or a bit of butter.

Trinity Rice Pilaf

In 2017, I did a three-month stint as a teacher at the Institute of Culinary Education. And one of the basic techniques we taught our students was how to make rice pilaf. I couldn't help adding one of my Southern twists, though, using a classic trinity base (onion, bell pepper, and celery) to infuse lots of extra flavor. I especially like using it for my Boudin Stuffing (page 208).

SERVES 4 TO 6

3 cups unsalted chicken or vegetable stock

1 dried bay leaf

1 tablespoon bacon fat, chicken fat, or extra-virgin olive oil

2 cups long-grain rice

½ cup finely diced sweet onion, such as Vidalia

¼ cup finely diced celery

¼ cup finely diced green bell pepper

1 large garlic clove, minced

1 teaspoon kosher salt

½ teaspoon smoked paprika

Heavy pinch of freshly ground black pepper

½ cup sliced scallion greens and/or chopped fresh parsley

1. Pour the stock into a small pot with the bay leaf and bring to a bare simmer over medium heat.

2. Place a medium pot with a wide bottom (insert peach emoji) over medium heat. Add the fat and when it's hot, add the rice. Cook, stirring frequently, until the grains are well coated and beginning to get toasty brown and nutty smelling, 4 to 5 minutes. Stir in the onion, celery, bell pepper, and garlic. Cook for about 2 minutes, then stir in the salt, paprika, and pepper.

3. Carefully pour in the hot stock, give one good stir, and cover the pot tightly with a lid. Reduce the heat to low and cook for 15 minutes. Turn off the heat and let stand for 10 minutes (don't lift the lid!).

4. Uncover the pot and sprinkle in the scallion greens and/or parsley. Fluff the rice with a fork and transfer to a serving plate if serving right away. If not, scoop and fluff the rice onto a wide, flat tray and cover with a damp kitchen towel for up to half an hour.

SOFRITO FROM SCRATCH

If you don't already have extras of Trinity Sofrito (page 141) handy, finely dice half an onion, 1 clove of garlic, a half stalk of celery, and one-quarter of a green bell pepper, and combine in a bowl with a pinch of dried thyme, and a couple of sprigs of parsley.

LEFTOVER ALERT

Leftover pilaf makes excellent fried rice! Any rice you don't serve, lay out on a plate and refrigerate overnight, then transfer to an airtight container until ready to use.

Turnip Latkes

Part of my family is Jewish, and one of my dearest friends, Israel, keeps kosher, so I've done a deep dive on the cuisine of the Jewish diaspora. Just like that of the African diaspora, the cuisine of this singular culture branched off in so many directions, crossing into so many different cultures and countries. The cookbooks of Helen Nash were the first kosher books I discovered in which traditional dishes were brought into the modern day by changing up ingredients and techniques. They showed me that no matter how sacred family traditions are, there's always room to grow and change.

SERVES 4 TO 6

- 3 medium turnips (about 2 pounds), peeled
- 2 teaspoons kosher salt
- 1 small onion
- ½ teaspoon granulated garlic
- ½ teaspoon ground black pepper
- 1 large egg, beaten
- Scant ¼ cup potato starch
- Vegetable oil, for frying
- Sliced scallions or chives, for garnish
- Sour cream and applesauce, for serving

1. Grate the turnips on the large holes of a box grater (watch your knuckles!) and transfer to a large pot. Add enough water to just cover the grated turnips, along with 1 teaspoon of the salt, and bring to a boil over high heat.

2. While the water is coming to a boil, grate the onion on the large holes of the box grater and transfer to a clean kitchen towel. Gather the edges of the towel and squeeze out a bit of the excess liquid, then shake the onion into a medium bowl. Save the towel for the turnips.

3. As soon as the water begins to boil, drain the turnips in a colander and rinse with cold water for 1 minute. Transfer the turnips to the kitchen towel, gather the edges, and wring out the excess moisture.

4. Add the turnips, the remaining 1 teaspoon salt, and the granulated garlic, pepper, and egg to the bowl with the grated onion. Use a fork to gently stir the ingredients together, then sprinkle in the potato starch and mix again.

5. Heat a large, wide skillet over medium heat and pour in enough oil to thinly coat the pan. When the oil begins to shimmer, spoon 2-tablespoon-size mounds of the latke mixture into the skillet, about 2 inches apart. Use a spatula to flatten the latkes to a ¼-inch thickness. Cook until browned and crispy, about 5 minutes per side. Transfer the latkes to a paper-towel-lined plate to drain, and season with a small pinch of salt. Repeat with the remaining mixture, adding oil to the pan as needed.

6. Transfer the latkes to a serving plate and sprinkle with sliced scallions. Serve hot, with sour cream and applesauce on the side.

CASE IN POINT
I'm a big fan of swapping in sweet and crunchy turnips (one of the dominant root vegetables in the South) for standard starchy potatoes when making latkes. The end result is deliciously light and crisp with a wonderfully tender center.

Veg

Collard Green Kimchi

I used to exclusively purchase kimchi at the store until a couple of Korean coworkers piqued my curiosity by telling me of how their families used to make it in huge batches, let it ferment, and have a stockpile that would last them for months. Southerners certainly aren't strangers to fermenting and pickling, so I thought I'd give it a go.

I went traditional at first with napa cabbage, before testing my way through all of our go-to greens. Turnip got too soft, and mustard was aggressively spicy—although I appreciated the peppery bite it had, which was similar to daikon. Collards, however, stood head and shoulders above the rest. They were nice and hearty and had a grassy but neutral flavor that really picked up the brine.

----- MAKES 3 QUARTS -----

2 pounds collard greens

¼ cup kosher or sea salt

¼ cup gochugaru (Korean red chile flakes)

3 tablespoons fish sauce or 2 tablespoons salted shrimp paste, or 1½ tablespoons of each

1 teaspoon sugar

1 tablespoon finely grated garlic

2 teaspoons finely grated fresh ginger

1 small daikon radish, peeled and cut into matchsticks (about 1½ cups; see Note)

1 large carrot, peeled and cut into matchsticks (about ½ cup; see Note)

4 scallions, halved lengthwise and cut into 1-inch pieces

1. Bring 4 cups of water to a boil in a large pot. While it heats, trim the stems that extend past the ends of the collard leaves, cut the stems in half lengthwise, and set aside in a large heat-safe bowl. Cut the collard leaves crosswise into 2- to 3-inch-wide strips and place them in the bowl with the stems.

2. Sprinkle the salt over the greens and gently massage it into the leaves until they begin to soften.

3. When the water comes to a boil, turn off the heat and let stand for 3 minutes, then pour the water over the collards. Wait 5 minutes, then add 2 to 3 cups of ice to the bowl. Let

the collards stand for about 30 minutes, gently massaging them occasionally.

4. Drain the collards in a colander and rinse under cold running water; rinse out the bowl too. Return the collards to the bowl, fill with cold water to cover, and let stand for 10 minutes. Drain the collards again and run cold water over them for 5 minutes, tossing occasionally to ensure the water gets between the leaves.

5. Combine the gochugaru, fish sauce, sugar, garlic, and ginger in a small bowl. Add 2 tablespoons of water and stir to make a paste.

(recipe continues)

6. Squeeze any excess water from the collards and return them to the bowl. Add the daikon, carrot, scallions, and gochugaru paste and use your hands (wearing kitchen gloves, if you don't feel like getting messy) to work the paste into the veggies. Try to peel apart the collard leaves as much as possible so that the paste can get all up in there.

7. Transfer the collard mixture to a 3-quart glass jar (or multiple smaller jars) with an airtight lid, leaving about 2 inches of headspace at the top. Pour ¼ cup of water into the large bowl and swirl it around to pick up any seasonings left behind, then pour it into the jar.

8. Screw the lid onto the jar and set it in a cool, dark place. Check the kimchi every day. After 2 or 3 days, you should start to see some bubbles forming near the bottom. Loosen the lid to allow gas to escape for about 5 minutes before re-tightening the lid. After about 5 days (fewer if your bubbles are very active), transfer the kimchi to the refrigerator to continue maturing. Loosen the lid periodically to vent gas.

9. The kimchi can be eaten at any point, but it is best after a few days in the fridge (and stays good for about a month). The fun part is tasting a little each day and seeing how it's coming along! It should develop more and more rich, melded, umami flavor the longer it sits. Next time you make it, you can adjust the seasonings to your taste.

SPEED SLICING

I recommend using a mandoline with the julienne attachment as the easiest route to matchstick cuts!

Red Cabbage and Beet Slaw

The Southern classic red velvet cake originally got its color from raw beets. But if you were going to eat a beet on my dad's side of my family, it had to be *cooked*. I had never really experienced them raw until I started eating out at Polish spots in Chicago. That's when I discovered that as long as they're shredded small, beets make an incredible slaw or salad.

SERVES 4

¼ cup extra-virgin olive oil

1 teaspoon poppy seeds

½ teaspoon celery seeds

½ small head of red cabbage (about ¾ pound)

1 large beet, peeled

1 large shallot or ½ small red onion, halved and thinly sliced

Kosher salt and freshly ground black pepper

2 tablespoons Dijon mustard

¼ cup sherry vinegar

Greek yogurt or sour cream, for serving (optional)

Dill, parsley, and/or tarragon, torn, for serving

1. Heat a small sauté pan over medium heat. Put in the oil, swirl to coat the pan, and then add the poppy seeds and celery seeds. Cook, stirring frequently, until the seeds are fragrant, about 4 minutes. Transfer to a large bowl.

2. Cut the half a head of cabbage in half, remove the core, then slice into ¼-inch-thick ribbons. Transfer to another large bowl. Grate the beet in a food processor with the shredding disk (which will save your hands from turning red) or on the large holes of a box grater. Add to the cabbage. Add the shallot and season with a couple of pinches of salt and pepper.

3. Add the mustard and vinegar to the bowl with the seeds and whisk to combine. Add the vegetables and toss with your hands or a couple of forks until thoroughly combined. Taste and adjust the seasoning as needed.

4. Transfer the salad to a serving bowl or individual bowls, top with a spoonful of Greek yogurt, if using, and sprinkle with herbs.

PRO TIP

If the acidity from the mustard and vinegar is too strong for you, add a pinch of sugar to balance it out (although the sweetness from the beets should do the trick!).

Blistered Green Beans
with Crushed Peanuts and Soy

My mom has always looked for ways to make green beans new and interesting, such as tossing them in a cast-iron skillet or throwing them on the grill. The blistered effect makes them so much more layered in flavor than your basic steamed bean. I like adding a splash of soy and some toasty crushed peanuts, because the end result reminds me of a charred cabbage dish that I enjoyed while visiting Vietnam.

SERVES 4

1 tablespoon vegetable oil, plus more if needed

½ pound green beans, trimmed (you can also use half green beans, half wax beans)

Pinch of kosher salt

¼ teaspoon cracked black pepper

¼ cup unsalted peanuts

2 tablespoons soy sauce (if you can get your hands on sweet soy sauce, use that, but no pressure!)

1 teaspoon fish sauce (optional; I like Red Boat)

¼ teaspoon dried red pepper flakes (totally optional)

1. Heat a large cast-iron griddle or skillet over high heat, then add the oil. When the pan is smoking hot, add the beans in a single layer, working in batches if necessary, and season with the salt and pepper.

2. Cook, tossing frequently so that all the beans make contact with the pan, until the beans are deeply blistered in spots and just tender, 5 to 7 minutes. (If working in batches, remove the beans to a plate while you blister the remaining beans. When done, return all the beans to the pan.) Turn off the heat.

3. Put the peanuts in a small skillet over medium-low heat and toast until fragrant, 3 to 4 minutes. Spread the peanuts on a cutting board. Using a rolling pin or the bottom of a sturdy glass, crush the peanuts into pieces. Don't press too hard: we don't want dust, just smaller pieces. Stir the crushed peanuts into the beans, reserving a few pinches for garnish. Stir in the soy sauce and fish sauce, if using, then transfer the beans to a serving dish.

4. Sprinkle with the reserved crushed peanuts and the red pepper flakes, if using, and serve hot.

Charred Okra
with Roasted Tomatoes

Okra is one of my favorite vegetables. It was introduced to America by West Africans during the slave trade and quickly became an integral part of the cuisine throughout the South and up to Philadelphia. It became an important sustenance crop for enslaved Africans, giving heft to stews made with meager rations, and the seeds were often roasted and simmered with coffee and chicory to make them stretch. I'm in a constant battle against people who don't like okra because I tend to believe that if there's an ingredient you don't like, you probably just haven't had it prepared the way that you'd like it. The issue with okra tends to come down to goo (it's in the marshmallow family, after all). But if you cut it in half lengthwise, you can caramelize all of the slimy stuff, sidestepping any textural issues and allowing okra's incredible flavor to shine.

SERVES 4

2 pounds okra pods, halved lengthwise

1 pint small cherry tomatoes, halved

⅓ cup vegetable oil

1½ teaspoons kosher salt, plus more for seasoning

½ teaspoon freshly ground black pepper

½ teaspoon smoked paprika

½ teaspoon ground turmeric

½ teaspoon grated fresh ginger

Pinch of ground allspice

Pinch of ground cloves

1. Preheat the oven to 425°F with a rack positioned in the upper third of the oven. Line a baking sheet with aluminum foil. Set a medium oven-safe skillet over medium-high heat.

2. Place the okra and tomatoes into separate medium bowls. Divide the oil, salt, and pepper between the bowls and toss well to coat. Add the paprika, turmeric, ginger, allspice, and cloves to the tomatoes only and toss to combine.

3. Arrange the okra on the prepared baking sheet in a single layer. Roast on the top rack of the oven until blistered in places and slightly shrunken, 10 to 12 minutes. Transfer to a serving plate while hot.

4. Meanwhile, pour the tomatoes into the hot skillet and cook, undisturbed, until blistered and charred, 1 to 2 minutes. Give the pan a little toss, then transfer to the top rack of the oven until the tomatoes are wilted a bit and the liquid has thickened, 7 to 8 minutes. Remove from the oven, stir in a splash of water, and spoon the tomatoes over the okra. Serve immediately.

Elote Macque Choux

I'd never heard of macque choux— sort of like a cross between succotash and fried corn— until dining with my husband and his mom at a restaurant in their hometown of New Orleans. I couldn't believe I hadn't known about it before, but his mother was like, "Girl, that's because your family is from Mississippi." It really drove home to me how regional Southern food is! That said, someone from New Orleans would probably roll over and die if you tried to serve them macque choux made with cilantro, poblano, and lime, and no roux. But that hasn't stopped me from pulling in some of my favorite elements from the Mexican corn dish elote. Mexico is the birthplace of corn, which is a fundamental part of the cuisine. Elote vendor carts were omnipresent on the corners of Chicago when I was growing up. I'm talking steamed corn cobs skewered on sticks, slathered with mayo, sprinkled with Tajín or some sort of chile mixture, rolled in cotija cheese, and finished with a squeeze of lime. Sweet, creamy, crunchy, and spicy, it's pretty much the perfect food.

SERVES 4 TO 6

5 ears sweet corn, cleaned of husk and silk and rinsed

2 tablespoons unsalted butter

3 sprigs of thyme

1 medium yellow onion, diced small

2 celery stalks, chopped small

2 cloves garlic, minced

1 teaspoon kosher salt, plus more to taste

Freshly ground black pepper

1 poblano pepper, seeded and diced small

1 red bell pepper, seeded and diced small

1 teaspoon smoked paprika

Grated zest and juice of 1 lime, plus wedges for serving

3 tablespoons crème fraîche

¼ cup chopped cilantro leaves and stems

1. To cut the kernels from the corn cobs, stand a cob upright in the center of a baking dish or Bundt pan. While holding the top of the cob steady, use a paring knife to cut down the side of the cob from the top to the base. The corn kernels will stay in the baking dish instead of scattering all over your counter and floor.

2. Heat a large skillet over medium heat. Put the butter, thyme, onion, celery, and garlic in the skillet. Season with ½ teaspoon of the salt and a generous pinch of black pepper, and cook, stirring occasionally, until the onion and celery are tender, about 6 minutes.

3. Stir in the poblano and bell peppers, paprika, and corn kernels. Add another ½ teaspoon of the salt and cook for 2 to 3 minutes, until the corn and peppers are just warmed through.

4. Turn off the heat, pull out the thyme stems and stir in the lime zest, lime juice, and crème fraîche. Stir in half of the chopped cilantro; taste and adjust the seasoning, if needed. Transfer the macque choux to serving bowls and garnish with the remaining cilantro and lime wedges.

WASTE NOT, WANT NOT
Save the cobs in the freezer and boil with water later to make corn stock for chowders and summer soups!

REMAKING THE DINNER PLATE: PROTEIN, STARCH, AND VEG

Grilled Green Tomato Salad *with* Buttermilk Vinaigrette and Pepitas

History suggests that cooking green tomatoes was passed on to the Black people of the South by Indigenous Americans from Mexico, of which there was a large population in Mississippi. Green tomatoes share similarities with tomatillos, which are also native to Mexico and commonly used to make sauces and stews. This dish is a great way of demonstrating that not all Southern food needs to be fried. I dry tomato slices between paper towels before grilling, drizzle them with buttermilk dressing, and sprinkle on toasted pepitas—an ode to Mexico—for crunch.

--- SERVES 4 TO 6 ---

Vegetable oil, for greasing

4 large green tomatoes, cored and sliced crosswise into ½-inch-thick rounds

¼ cup extra-virgin olive oil

2 teaspoons kosher salt

1 teaspoon freshly ground black pepper

½ cup Buttermilk Vinaigrette (page 86)

2 tablespoons torn fresh basil leaves

2 tablespoons fresh dill fronds

3 tablespoons toasted pepitas (hulled pumpkin seeds)

1. Prepare a grill for high heat or heat a large grill pan over high heat. Dip a paper towel in a little vegetable oil and rub it on the grates. Let the oil burn off for 2 minutes.

2. Lay the tomatoes on a baking sheet, brush both sides with the olive oil, and season both sides with the salt and pepper. Working in batches if necessary, use tongs to lay the tomato slices on the grill. Cook until charred and tender, 2 to 3 minutes per side.

3. To serve, spoon a little of the buttermilk vinaigrette onto a serving platter, then arrange the grilled tomatoes on top as they come off the grill. Drizzle with the remaining vinaigrette and scatter the basil, dill, and pepitas over the top.

Collard Green Salad
with Sesame Vinaigrette

Forget kale—raw collard greens kick ass! They have a higher nutritional value, if you don't cook the life out of them, and they pick up flavor really well. They're not even that bitter, especially if you slice them thin, massage them with a bit of oil and acid, and dress them with an amazing vinaigrette.

――――――――――――――――――――――― SERVES 2 TO 4 ―――――――――――――――――――――――

2 tablespoons sesame seeds (white, black, or mixed)

1 pound collard greens

1 small shallot, halved lengthwise and thinly sliced

¼ teaspoon kosher salt

2 tablespoons rice vinegar

2 tablespoons soy sauce

½ teaspoon ground white pepper (black is fine too)

½ teaspoon sugar

¼ teaspoon dry mustard

1 tablespoon white miso paste

2 tablespoons toasted sesame oil

1. Heat a small sauté pan over medium-low heat. Put the sesame seeds in the dry pan and toast, tossing occasionally, until fragrant, 2 to 3 minutes. Set aside in a small bowl to cool.

2. Cut the collard greens in half lengthwise and remove the thick center ribs. Stack 4 or 5 of the halved leaves at a time and slice crosswise into ribbons about ¼ inch thick. (The ribbons don't have to be perfectly uniform.) Place the ribbons in a large bowl and add the shallot and salt, tossing to distribute.

3. In a small bowl, combine the rice vinegar, soy sauce, pepper, sugar, dry mustard, miso, and 2 teaspoons of water. Using a fork or the back of a spoon, mash the miso paste, stirring to dissolve it. Whisk in the sesame oil, then pour the dressing over the collards and toss well—like, really get in there. Go on and use your hands to massage it in.

4. Sprinkle the toasted sesame seeds over the greens and let sit for at least 10 minutes before serving. The salad can also be made a few hours ahead and chilled until ready to serve!

5. Before serving, toss again and transfer to a pretty bowl.

greens by any other name

When my dad married my mom, the women in his family were like, "Look. We don't care that you married a white girl, but we *do* care that she doesn't know how to cook Southern food." So Lula (my dad's grandmother, who raised him), Big Sister (my dad's aunt, who I pretty much consider my grandmother), and my great-great-aunt Nona drove from Mississippi to Chicago with seeds and cast-iron skillets to teach my mother how to cook.

They spent close to three months there, planting a garden, growing collard greens and mustard greens and tomatoes and turnips. One of the first things they asked was if she knew how to make anything Southern. She said, "I don't know, tell me what's Southern, and I'll tell you if I know how to make it." Her fried chicken wasn't their style, so she had to relearn that. Then they asked her if she knew how to make greens and she said yes, of course. They went, "Okay, get some greens started for dinner and we'll get started on some other stuff." Great. So she makes a big salad and says, all proud, "The greens are ready!" And they looked at her like she was crazy.

Another of my mom's favorite memories from that time was of sitting around with them on the back porch, stringing beans and shelling peas. It was summer in Chicago, and it was quiet, everyone in rocking chairs, just shelling away. Someone says, "Woo, sho is hot." A couple of seconds pass and someone else repeats, "Woo, chile, sho is hot," in agreement. And my mother didn't know if she was supposed to fake a Southern accent and chime in or just let it pass. But eventually she chirps her own "Sure is hot!" And they answer, "Sho is."

Brussels Sprouts
with Brown Butter and Hazelnuts

I'd say I've passed my physical peak for stripperdom. But if I *were* ever to become an exotic dancer, my stripper name would be Beurre Noisette (Brown Butter).

Brown butter is especially great with brussels sprouts, which, unsurprisingly, I hated as a kid. I didn't change my mind until my twenties, when I put them under the broiler by mistake. They got all blistered and blackened and the leaves were really crunchy and they were so damn good. The brown butter balances out their bitterness and makes them a little sweet, while the hazelnuts give you a bit more texture.

──────────────── SERVES 2 ────────────────

1½ pounds brussels sprouts

2 tablespoons vegetable oil

1 teaspoon kosher salt, plus more for seasoning

¼ teaspoon freshly ground black pepper

4 tablespoons (½ stick) unsalted butter

⅓ cup roughly chopped hazelnuts

Juice of ½ lemon

1. Preheat the oven to 450°F.

2. Trim the root ends of the brussels sprouts, removing any discolored outer leaves, and cut the sprouts in half. Place them in a large bowl and toss with the oil, salt, and pepper before placing them on a foil-lined baking sheet in a single layer, cut-side down. Don't wash the bowl, just wipe it out with a paper towel to reuse later.

3. Roast the sprouts until the outer leaves are blistered and crispy and the cut sides are browned, 7 to 8 minutes.

4. Meanwhile, put the butter in a small sauté pan over medium heat. Cook for 3 to 4 minutes. As the butter melts, swirl the pan occasionally to keep the milk solids from sticking to the bottom. The butter will start to bubble a little as the water cooks out, leaving just the fat and milk solids behind. When the bubbling starts to subside, swirl the pan again. You'll see a bit of foam on top and the liquid butter will become a deeper, golden yellow. The milk solids in the butter will go through a couple of color changes before it hits the chocolatey color we're looking for, so keep a close eye on it—it can go from deliciously browned to coffee-bean-burned in a few seconds.

5. As soon as the milk solids achieve the desired chocolate hue, add the chopped hazelnuts, stirring to coat. Remove the pan to a cool burner and squeeze the lemon juice over the top. (Be careful: It will sizzle and splatter a little—we are adding liquid to hot fat, after all—but it will only last a few seconds.) Stir again and set aside.

6. Transfer the roasted sprouts back to the bowl and use a rubber spatula to scrape all of the browned butter and hazelnuts over the top. Toss to coat. Taste and season with a pinch of salt, if needed. Serve hot and crispy.

MAKE AHEAD
Although best served fresh, these can be reheated on a tray in the oven at 375°F for 2 to 3 minutes, if needed.

Bourbon-and-Brown-Sugar-Glazed Root Vegetables

Bourbon and brown sugar is one of my favorite combinations of all time. Using it as a glaze for roasted root vegetables enhances their inherent sweetness without going over the top. Especially since the bourbon cuts right through it all, adding a hint of smokiness that balances everything out in a really fun way.

SERVES 4

2 pounds mixed root vegetables (carrots, parsnips, turnips, small potatoes, sweet potatoes, rutabagas, beets, etc.)

1 medium red onion, halved

3 tablespoons vegetable oil

2 teaspoons kosher salt, plus more for seasoning

4 garlic cloves, halved

3 sprigs of rosemary

2 teaspoons chopped fresh thyme

¼ cup (packed; 55g) dark brown sugar

1½ teaspoons freshly ground black pepper

2 tablespoons bourbon

1 tablespoon chopped fresh parsley and/or chives (optional)

1. Preheat the oven to 450°F. Line a baking sheet with parchment paper.

2. Peel any of the root veggies that have thick skins (rutabagas, beets); leave any thin-skinned ones intact (carrots, parsnips, potatoes). As long as it is scrubbed well, the skin cooks and looks beautiful on roasted veg. Cut the root vegetables into 1-inch pieces and the red onion into ½-inch pieces; transfer to a large bowl.

3. Add the oil, salt, garlic, rosemary, and thyme to the bowl and toss to combine. Spread the vegetables in an even layer on the prepared baking sheet. Roast until the vegetables are browned and just barely tender when pierced with a knife, 10 to 12 minutes. Return them to the large bowl; reduce the oven temperature to 375°F.

4. Put the brown sugar, ground pepper, and bourbon in a small saucepan over medium heat. Bring to a simmer, stirring occasionally, and cook until the brown sugar is melted and bubbling, about 3 minutes. Pour the warm brown sugar glaze over the roasted veggies and toss to thoroughly combine.

5. Pour the veggies back onto the baking sheet and roast until the glaze is bubbling and caramelized but not burned, 5 to 7 minutes.

6. Season with a heavy pinch of salt and let cool for a couple of minutes before transferring to a serving dish. Garnish with the parsley and/or chives, if using.

Spicy and Crispy
Whole-Roasted Cauliflower

Whole-roasted cauliflower and Buffalo cauliflower have both exploded in popularity in recent years, and this dish is the best of both worlds. The coating of Greek yogurt creates a wonderful thick crust on the outside, and when you slice it into wedges, you see the dramatic contrast of creamy white cauliflower on the inside.

— SERVES 4 TO 6 —

1 large head cauliflower (a little less than 2 pounds)

2 tablespoons plus 1 teaspoon kosher salt

2 dried bay leaves

¼ cup (35g) cornstarch

1½ cups raw sunflower seeds

2 teaspoons smoked paprika

1 teaspoon garlic powder or granulated garlic

1 teaspoon onion powder

½ cup Greek yogurt (or nondairy yogurt)

Olive oil cooking spray

2 tablespoons unsalted butter, melted

¼ cup hot sauce (preferably Tabasco)

1 tablespoon honey

1. Trim the leaves and stem from the cauliflower and place in a pot just large enough to hold it. Fill the pot with enough water to just cover and add the 2 tablespoons of salt and the bay leaves. Cover and bring to a rapid boil over high heat. Turn off the heat and let sit for 8 minutes before draining the cauliflower. Rinse under cold water for a few seconds, then transfer to a paper-towel-lined plate and refrigerate for about 15 minutes, until cool.

2. Preheat the oven to 400°F. Line a baking sheet with parchment paper.

3. In a food processor, combine the cornstarch, sunflower seeds, paprika, garlic powder, onion powder, and the remaining 1 teaspoon salt. Process until the seeds are finely chopped and the mixture looks like coarse meal. Transfer to a wide bowl.

4. With a spatula or brush, spread the yogurt all over the cauliflower. Using a couple of forks or your gloved hands, carefully lift the cauliflower and place it, upside down, in the sunflower seed mixture. Get your fingers around the center stem and rotate the head to coat the cauliflower completely

in the mixture. Scoop up mixture as needed to coat all the way up the sides.

5. Place the cauliflower on the prepared baking sheet and lightly spray it all over with olive oil. Roast, rotating the baking sheet halfway through, until the coating is golden and crispy, about 20 minutes.

6. Stir the melted butter, hot sauce, and honey in a small bowl until combined. Brush the mixture all over the cauliflower, then return it to the oven and continue cooking until the sauce has caramelized, 10 to 15 minutes more.

7. Let the cauliflower cool for about 5 minutes before slicing it into wedges and serving.

MAKE AHEAD
The cauliflower can be prepared through step 2 up to 3 days ahead and kept loosely covered in the fridge.

MAKE IT A MEAL
So much more than a side, this can totally be treated as an entrée, paired with everything from Hominy Tabbouleh (page 145) to Split Pea Salad (page 150) to Barley Grits (page 147).

Green Cabbage Gratin

You can gratin just about any vegetable and make it even more delicious. So as much as I love cabbage on its own, simply charred or shredded in a salad, this is a way to turn a humble, inexpensive vegetable into something outrageously rich and decadent. Got leftovers? Shred them up and stir into pasta, alongside every last remnant of cheesy bread crumbs and sauce.

SERVES 4 TO 6

1 large head savoy cabbage (about 2 pounds)

2 tablespoons vegetable oil, plus more for greasing

¾ teaspoon kosher salt

¾ teaspoon freshly ground black pepper

⅓ cup dry white wine

2 large garlic cloves, minced or grated on a Microplane

4 sprigs of thyme

1 teaspoon Worcestershire sauce

2 cups heavy cream

½ lemon

½ cup grated Parmesan cheese

½ cup grated Gruyère cheese

½ cup bread crumbs

1. Preheat the oven to 400°F.

2. Remove the outer leaves and cut the cabbage into 8 wedges through the core (you want the leaves to stay together). Drizzle the wedges with the oil, rub to coat evenly, and sprinkle both sides with ½ teaspoon each of the salt and pepper. Arrange the wedges in a pinwheel shape, facing the same direction, in a large, shallow baking dish or 12-inch oven-safe skillet that has been lightly greased with oil (it's okay if the wedges overlap a little, as they will shrink as they cook). Roast until the cores are tender and the leaves are slightly charred, about 10 minutes. Let cool.

3. Meanwhile, pour the wine into a medium bowl and stir in the garlic, thyme, Worcestershire, and cream. Season with the remaining ¼ teaspoon each of salt and pepper and stir to combine. Grate the zest of the ½ lemon into a separate small bowl (keep the zested lemon for later). Stir the Parmesan, Gruyère, and bread crumbs in with the zest; set aside.

4. Reduce the oven temperature to 375°F. Pour the cream mixture over the cabbage, cover with a lid or foil, and return to the oven. Bake for 20 minutes.

5. Remove the foil, squeeze the juice of the zested ½ lemon over the pan, and sprinkle the bread crumb mixture over the cabbage wedges. Return to the oven and bake until the cream is reduced and the crust is beautifully browned, another 15 to 20 minutes. Let cool slightly before digging in.

pure sunday vibes
Family-Style Feasts

The way I see it, the Sunday Best vibe doesn't have to be relegated only to Sundays. My aunt Dottie lived in a really rough neighborhood in Jackson, Mississippi. She had become a den mother of sorts for anyone in town who was down on their luck. She wasn't rich, but what she did have were pots and pans full of food lining her stove each and every day. She'd sit at home while people filed in and out of her house. "Hey, Miss Dottie, how you doing?" And she'd be like, "How are *you* doing?" and offer them a plate. I remember being at her house and watching at least twelve people come in during the five or so hours I was there. There was always more than enough food for everyone. That's when I started to see that there are all kinds of ways you can take care of people just through the simple act of feeding them.

This chapter is devoted to the dishes more commonly associated with celebratory Sunday meals—prepared in large quantities, made with both inexpensive ingredients that require a little more love to shine and top-of-the-line ingredients that can cook all day. With that said, there's no reason you need to save them for parties, holidays, and crowds. Why not roast a whole pork shoulder, even if you have two to four mouths to feed instead of ten to twelve? My mom's and dad's respective families on both sides of Chicago cooked massive amounts of food on the weekends. This meant there was always plenty left if you visited them during the week, or freezer inventory for unexpected lean times. That's why almost all of the following recipes make incredible leftovers that can be enjoyed as is or reimagined and reinvented (see Transformations: Leftovers Reimagined) all week long!

Slow-Roasted Pork Shoulder

(PERNIL)

Since it's an inexpensive cut that feeds so many people, we often prepared pork shoulder for family meal at Le Bernardin. When it was my responsibility to cook it, I would make pernil, which I regularly enjoyed as a kid with my friend Suheily's family in the largely Puerto Rican neighborhood of Humboldt Park.

The beauty of pernil is that the tender meat is capped by a layer of skin that gets cooked until it's seriously crispy. Chopped into pieces and set on top for serving, it's referred to as *cuerito*. Everyone clamors for a taste, and your pork will absolutely be judged by how crunchy you get that skin.

——————————— SERVES 6, WITH LEFTOVERS FOR SANDWICHES ———————————

2 heads of garlic, cloves separated and peeled

1 large shallot, chopped

1 tablespoon black peppercorns

2 tablespoons coriander seeds

2 tablespoons dried oregano

1 tablespoon annatto (achiote) powder or paste (if you can't find it at your local store, simply leave out)

½ cup chopped fresh cilantro stems and leaves, plus more for garnish

¼ cup kosher salt

Zest and juice of 1 orange

2 tablespoons red wine vinegar

3 tablespoons olive oil

1 (5- to 6-pound) bone-in pork shoulder (aka Boston butt—hehe), *with* skin

Lime wedges, for garnish

1. In a food processor, combine the garlic, shallot, peppercorns, coriander, oregano, annatto, cilantro, salt, orange zest, orange juice, vinegar, and oil. Process to a smooth-ish paste.

2. Blot the pork dry and use a small, sharp knife to cut through the fat cap and skin and peel it back; don't separate it completely—leave a hinge at one end and open it like a book. Make 8 or so slits, 1½ to 2 inches deep, into the meat. (Leave the skin alone.) Rub as much of the seasoning paste into the slits as you can, then rub the rest over the outside of the meat.

3. Flip the fat and skin back over the top, wrap the shoulder in plastic or place it in a really big zip-top bag, and refrigerate it for at least 8 hours and up to 3 days.

4. Pull the roast from the fridge about an hour before cooking to get the chill off.

5. Preheat the oven to 325°F with a rack in the center position.

6. Place the pork in a roasting pan and pour 3 cups of water around it. Cover with foil and roast on the middle rack for 2 hours. Remove the foil and continue roasting for 2 hours more. Check the tenderness of the meat: If it is not falling-apart tender, cook for another 30 to 45 minutes. Crank the oven to 450°F and roast until the skin gets really crispy, 15 to 20 minutes more.

7. Remove from the oven and let the pernil rest, loosely tented with foil, for 30 minutes. Remove the crunchy-fatty skin (cuerito) to a cutting board and use a chef's knife to cut it into large pieces. With two forks, pull the meat apart into large chunks, place on a serving platter, and place the cuerito on top.

8. Garnish with lime wedges and cilantro.

DO-AHEAD ALERT
Marinate the pork 1 to 3 days ahead of time. Trust me, it makes a huge difference.

Black Garlic Roasted Leg of Lamb

Leg of lamb was definitely a special-occasion meal in my house. Since it's a terrific family-style cut, though, leftovers can be sliced into sandwiches or tucked into soups or stir-fries the whole week through. My mom used to cut slits in the meat and stuff garlic cloves in them before roasting, which is why I decided to showcase black garlic in my version. Aged, supple black garlic adds a concentrated, caramelized sweetness that's almost like balsamic vinegar, and makes an excellent foil for deeply earthy roasted lamb.

SERVES 6 TO 8

1 large onion

1 bone-in leg of lamb (about 6 pounds)

4 large garlic cloves

¼ cup (tightly packed) black garlic cloves or paste

1½ teaspoons freshly ground black pepper, plus more for seasoning

3 tablespoons anchovy paste or chopped oil-packed anchovy fillets

1 tablespoon chopped fresh thyme

1 heaping tablespoon chopped fresh rosemary, plus 4 whole sprigs

6 sprigs of oregano

2 tablespoons Dijon mustard

¼ cup extra-virgin olive oil, plus more for drizzling

1 lemon, zested and halved

Kosher salt

2 cups dry white wine

2 pounds small red potatoes

1. Heat the oven to 450°F with a rack in the center position.

2. Slice the onion crosswise into 1-inch-thick rounds (it's okay if the rings separate). Evenly line a roasting pan with the onion slices.

3. Blot the lamb dry and place it fat-side up on top of the onions. (Leave the netting in place if your leg has it.) Using a paring knife, make a series of small, deep cuts straight down 2 inches into the center of the lamb in a straight line, every 2½ inches or so. You should have about 12 deep incisions.

4. In a mini food processor or with a mortar and pestle, combine the garlic, black garlic, pepper, anchovy paste, thyme, and chopped rosemary. Process or crush until you have a chunky paste and the ingredients are well combined. Transfer half of the paste to a small bowl.

5. You're going to have to get hands-on for this part. Scoop the remaining paste in the food processor onto the lamb and use your fingers to smush it into each incision. The idea is to really get it in there, as much as you can, down to the bone. Scatter the rosemary sprigs and oregano sprigs around the bottom of the pan.

6. Whisk the mustard, olive oil, lemon zest, and the juice of one half of the lemon into the paste in the bowl until combined. Smear the mixture all over the outside of the lamb, then season with a couple of heavy pinches of salt. Feel free to throw the lemon halves into the roasting pan as well—they lend a nice aroma to the roasting lamb.

(recipe continues)

7. Pour the wine and 1 cup of water into the bottom of the roasting pan. In a large bowl, toss the potatoes with a drizzle of oil and some salt and pepper and scatter them around the lamb.

8. Roast on the middle rack for 12 minutes. Reduce the oven temperature to 350°F and continue cooking until the lamb registers 145°F on an instant-read thermometer inserted into the thickest part, near the bone, about 1½ hours more. Baste the lamb with pan juices every 20 minutes or so, adding a little water as needed to keep the onions and pan from scorching.

9. Remove the pan from the oven, tent it loosely with foil, and let rest for 20 minutes before slicing and serving.

Pecan-Crusted Pork Rib Roast

Think of this as the pork version of prime rib. It's really impressive looking, with a big wow factor, but since it's considerably less expensive than similar cuts such as veal crown roast or rack of lamb, you don't need to save it for special occasions. I like to coat mine with a Southern catfish-inspired pecan crust, which besides looking awesome helps seal in the juices. What a great way to make something "fancy" for a whole lot less money.

SERVES 6 OR 7

1 (4- to 5-pound) pork rib roast, from the loin end, chine bone removed

8 large garlic cloves, crushed

8 sprigs fresh thyme, plus 2 tablespoons picked leaves

⅓ cup kosher salt, plus 1 tablespoon

⅓ cup dark brown sugar

2 tablespoons vegetable oil, plus more for drizzling

1½ cups raw pecans, broken

½ cup panko breadcrumbs or gluten-free breadcrumbs

2 teaspoons granulated garlic

2 teaspoon onion powder

1 teaspoon freshly ground black pepper

1 egg white

2 tablespoons Dijon mustard

2 medium onions, quartered

1. First, brine the rib roast overnight. Place the roast in a large zip-top bag with 4 cloves of the garlic and 4 sprigs of the thyme. Combine the ⅓ cup salt, brown sugar, and 4 cups of room temperature water in a mixing bowl and whisk until fully dissolved. Pour the solution into the bag.

2. As you close the seal on the bag, tilt the bag and squeeze out the air so the liquid is dispersed around the meat. Place the bag in a baking dish and refrigerate overnight. In the morning, lean the roast back so the brine can work its way into the bone-side and keep refrigerated until ready to cook.

3. Transfer the roast to a plate. Reserve the garlic and thyme. Blot the roast dry with a paper towel and season all over with the remaining 1 tablespoon of salt (bone side too).

4. Heat a large skillet over medium-high heat. Add the oil and when it is just beginning to smoke, place the roast meat-side down in the pan along with the reserved garlic and thyme. Sear the meat for 5 to 7 minutes or until deeply browned on one side. Rotate the roast so it is standing, and continue to sear the bottom for 5 to 7 minutes. Keep an eye on the garlic cloves, flip them as needed, and discard them if they begin to burn. Use the oil in the pan to baste the top of the roast around the bones. Remove to a large plate to cool.

5. Place the pecans, breadcrumbs, 2 tablespoons of thyme leaves, granulated garlic, onion powder, and black pepper in a small food processor and pulse 5 times or until the pecans are chopped finely. Pour into a shallow dish.

6. Combine the egg white and mustard in a small bowl and beat with a fork until thoroughly combined. Brush the egg white mixture over the seared meat on all sides, including the bottom. Pick the roast up by the bones and place directly onto the pecan mixture. Roll the roast forward and spread the pecan mixture on all sides of the roast so it has an even crust all around, including between the bones. Press the pecan mixture onto the meat to compact the crust.

7. Preheat the oven to 375°F and lightly oil a baking sheet. Place the roast in the center of the baking sheet. Place the quartered onions around the roast with the remaining 4 garlic cloves and 4 sprigs of thyme. Drizzle the onions and garlic with a little oil and place the tray on the center rack in the oven.

8. Cook the roast for 1½ hours to 1 hour 45 minutes, or until a thermometer reaches 150°F when inserted into the thickest part. Remove from the oven and let rest for 15 minutes before slicing.

sundays on the north and south sides

When it came to our Sunday celebration schedule growing up, my sister and I would generally spend the afternoon with my dad's family on the South Side of Chicago, either at his father's house or one of his sister's houses, joined by his mother. My mother didn't come with us very often. There'd be people drinking and smoking and talking shit and playing cards, while my sister and cousins and I played in another room. It was all pretty ad hoc. Sometimes my dad's family would get together and sometimes they wouldn't. But there was always food. It was pretty casual and potluck style. Aunt Cookie made the best collard greens, so she'd bring them over. My grandmother Ceola would cook the meat, maybe pot roast or fried chicken or catfish, and my aunt Giselle would provide other sides like cornbread, green beans, potato salad, or candied yams. Everything would just sit in pots on the stove, and people would pile up their own plates.

My mom often elected to stay home to do laundry. Until the evening, that is, when without fail, we'd take a forty-five-minute drive to the North Side of Chicago to *her* parents' house. Sunday dinner was a serious tradition over there, and a lot more formal by comparison, but it was still very communal. Sixteen adults plus their kids

would gather at the dining room table and pass around platters of turkey or ham or lamb—plus a big iceberg salad, of course—all served family style. Popovers or dinner rolls were the last thing to come out of the oven. And whoever went to fetch them would just stand at the kitchen door and throw them into the room, while all us kids would jump out of our seats to catch one, piping hot!

Mississippi Pot Roast

Italians were recruited to work in the South after slavery was outlawed; ships would depart from Southern Italy three times a month for New Orleans, bringing immigrants over to work. Just as Italian immigrants had a big influence on New Orleans cuisine (the lower French Quarter was once known as Little Palermo), they've equally inspired food in southern Mississippi, including this roast. It's cooked down with trinity mirepoix as well as tomatoes, red wine, and plenty of herbs, such as oregano, basil, and thyme. But the real signature addition is piquant pepperoncini, which add a welcome hit of acid to an otherwise deeply savory dish.

—————————————————————— SERVES 6 ——————————————————————

1 boneless beef chuck roast (about 4 pounds)

1 tablespoon kosher salt, plus more for seasoning

2 teaspoons freshly ground black pepper

2 tablespoons vegetable oil

2 tablespoons olive oil

4 large garlic cloves, halved

3 medium yellow onions, chopped

1 medium carrot, quartered lengthwise and cut into ½-inch slices

2 celery stalks, sliced

1 small green bell pepper, seeded and chopped

2 tablespoons tomato paste

1 cup dry red wine

5 plum tomatoes, seeded and chopped (or 1½ cups drained canned plum tomatoes)

5 sprigs of thyme

1 teaspoon dried oregano

1 teaspoon dried basil

1 dried bay leaf

2 cups unsalted beef stock

6 to 8 whole pepperoncini, according to taste

2 tablespoons Wondra or all-purpose flour

1 tablespoon roughly chopped fresh parsley, for garnish

1. Heat a large Dutch oven or other heavy-bottomed pot over medium-high heat. Sprinkle the beef all over with the salt and pepper.

2. Put the vegetable oil in the Dutch oven and sear the meat on all sides until well browned, 7 to 8 minutes per side. Remove the meat to a plate.

3. Reduce the heat to medium. Use a paper towel, held with tongs, to carefully sop up the remaining oil in the pot, then add the olive oil. Add the garlic, onions, carrot, celery, and bell pepper and season with a couple of pinches of salt. Cook, stirring occasionally, until lightly browned, 6 to 8 minutes. Stir in the tomato paste, followed by the red wine, tomatoes, thyme, oregano, basil, and bay leaf. Stir everything together, scraping the bottom of the pot to release any browned bits, and bring to a boil.

4. Return the seared roast to the pot, pour in the stock, and add the pepperoncini. Add a pinch of salt and give the pan a little shake to help everything get settled. Bring back to a boil. Cover tightly with a lid, then reduce the heat to low and cook, turning the roast occasionally, until the meat is super tender, about 3 hours.

5. The pot roast can be served immediately, but it is even better and easier to cut the next day after sitting overnight in the sauce. To serve, carefully remove the meat to a large cutting board. Bring the sauce to a low boil over medium heat. Dissolve the flour in 3 tablespoons of room-temperature water and stir the slurry into the sauce. Simmer, stirring occasionally, until thickened, 5 to 7 minutes. Taste and adjust the seasoning.

6. Using a sharp knife, slice the meat into ½-inch slices and place them on a serving platter. Spoon the gravy over the top and garnish with the parsley.

Roger's Park
Meat and Potatoes

My mom grew up in a German-Irish family in Chicago's Roger's Park, which was a largely Irish neighborhood. And you could really see those influences when she made shepherd's pie. Seasoned with German ingredients like horseradish and caraway seed, it was one of her go-to dishes, because she could prepare a large batch, split it into two casserole dishes, freeze one, and bake the other one off for dinner.

— SERVES 4 TO 6 —

4 large russet potatoes (about 2 pounds), scrubbed

¼ cup crème fraîche or sour cream

2 tablespoons prepared horseradish

3 tablespoons unsalted butter, at room temperature

3 teaspoons kosher salt, plus more for seasoning

1 teaspoon ground white or black pepper, plus more for seasoning

1 egg yolk

3 tablespoons vegetable oil

1 pound ground beef

½ pound ground lamb (or ground pork or more beef)

2 medium onions, finely chopped

2 large garlic cloves, minced

2 medium carrots, diced small

1 teaspoon fresh thyme

½ teaspoon ground allspice

½ teaspoon caraway seeds (optional)

2 tablespoons Dijon mustard

2 tablespoons all-purpose flour

½ cup lager beer or beer of your choice

¾ cup unsalted chicken or beef stock (or water)

1 tablespoon Worcestershire sauce

1 cup frozen peas

1. Place the potatoes in a large pot with water to cover. Bring to a boil over high heat, then reduce the heat to medium and cook at a low boil just until tender (before the skin bursts open), about 30 minutes, adding water if needed to keep the potatoes covered.

2. Meanwhile, in a small food processor, combine the crème fraîche, horseradish (along with a splash of its liquid), butter, 1 teaspoon of the salt, ½ teaspoon of the pepper, and the egg yolk. Process until all the ingredients are incorporated.

3. Preheat the oven to 375°F.

4. Heat a large skillet or pot over medium-high heat; add the oil. Add the ground beef and lamb and sear, stirring occasionally and breaking up the meat with a spoon, until cooked through, about 8 minutes. There should be a fair amount of liquid in the pan.

5. Season the meat with the remaining 2 teaspoons salt and ½ teaspoon pepper and stir in the onions, garlic, and carrots. Cook, stirring, until the onions are translucent, about 7 minutes. Stir in the thyme, allspice, caraway, and mustard and cook for another 2 minutes. Sprinkle the flour over the ingredients, mix it in thoroughly, and continue cooking for 2 minutes, stirring frequently. The mixture should begin to look dry and the bottom of the pan should have a thin film of flour.

6. Pour in the beer, stock, and Worcestershire sauce, scraping the bottom of the pan with a wooden spoon or a spatula to dissolve any browned bits. Bring the liquid to a simmer and cook for 5 minutes, stirring occasionally. Taste and adjust the seasoning, if needed. Remove from the heat and let cool for a few minutes, then stir in the frozen peas and transfer to an 11 × 7-inch baking dish.

7. By now, the potatoes should be cooked—if a small knife slides easily into a potato with no resistance, they're ready. Drain the potatoes.

8. Get a kitchen towel, paring knife, potato ricer or masher, and large bowl ready. Hold a hot potato in one hand with the kitchen towel and use the knife to peel the skin off. Rice the potato into the bowl and repeat with the remaining potatoes. With a wooden spoon, stir the reserved horseradish mixture into the potatoes (or mash together with the potato masher). Use a spatula to carefully spread the potato mixture in an even layer over the meat.

9. Place the pan in the oven and cook until the potatoes are browned at the edges and peaks, 20 to 25 minutes. Let rest for 10 to 15 minutes before serving.

MIX UP YOUR MEAT
As long as it's ground, you can use whatever protein you'd like, and in any combination. I like beef and lamb, but you can do pork (if you'd really like to go German), veal, chicken, or turkey!

SUNDAY BEST FINESSE
Transfer the potato mixture to a piping bag with a star tip or to a zip-top bag with one corner snipped off and pipe little rosettes or kisses over the meat.

Slow-Roasted Harissa Short Ribs

Short ribs are often prepared using moist cooking methods, like braising. But I like a drier roast, as it allows the fat and collagen to break down and baste the meat in its own juices. The Tunisian pepper paste called harissa adds another dimension of flavor by permeating the meat and lending a sweet heat, while the addition of lemon (or preserved lemon) contributes a welcome brightness.

SERVES 4 TO 6

6 bone-in beef short ribs, about 1-pound each

1 tablespoon plus 2 teaspoons kosher salt, plus more for seasoning

1 teaspoon ground coriander

½ teaspoon ground cumin

2 bunches of carrots (about 2 pounds total), tops removed, halved crosswise on an angle

1 large red onion, halved and sliced ¼ inch thick

1 lemon, quartered, or 1 tablespoon finely chopped preserved lemon

2 tablespoons harissa paste

1 tablespoon tomato paste

2 tablespoons honey

3 tablespoons olive oil

1 medium garlic clove, finely grated

Pickled red onion, for garnish

Leaves from fresh herbs such as cilantro, dill, mint, and parsley, for garnish

1. Place the short ribs on a baking sheet. In a small bowl, combine 1 tablespoon of the salt, the coriander, and the cumin; sprinkle the mixture evenly all over the short ribs. Cover with plastic wrap and refrigerate for 8 to 12 hours.

2. Preheat the oven to 350°F.

3. Scatter the carrots, onion, and lemon in a roasting pan and season with a pinch of salt. Place the short ribs, meat-side up, on top of the veggies in a single layer. Add 2 cups of water to the pan (feel free to use wine or beer instead if you have some lying around) and cover tightly with foil. Place in the oven and cook for 2 hours.

4. In a small bowl, stir the remaining 2 teaspoons salt with the harissa, tomato paste, honey, oil, and garlic to combine. Carefully open the foil on the pan and slather the harissa mixture over the short ribs, using a spoon to spread it over the top of the meat. Cover the pan again and continue cooking until the meat is very tender, about 45 minutes more.

5. Raise the oven temperature to 375°F, remove the foil, and cook until the short ribs are browned on top, another 15 to 20 minutes.

6. Remove the pan from the oven and let it cool a bit, then arrange the veggies on a serving platter and top with the short ribs. Garnish with pickled red onion and any combination of fresh herbs.

Chicken and Cornbread Dumplings

Starting around the 1500s in the South, Indigenous Americans formed strong alliances with newly displaced Africans. In a sort of "the enemy of my enemy is my friend" situation, they shared important skills such as how to cultivate and use local crops, including nixtamalizing corn and various methods for preparing it. From this alliance we got grits, hominy, cornbread, hush puppies, hoecakes, and other corn-based foods. Native Americans even taught Africans how to form a sort of cornmeal batter and drop it into hot water or broth to create a stew. And thus, chicken and dumplings was born. It's easy to appreciate the dish for its comforting, rustic, homey qualities, but even more compelling is how many cultures have had a hand in creating it.

───────────── SERVES 5 OR 6 ─────────────

STEW

3 medium carrots

4 celery stalks

2 medium Spanish onions

1 large leek

2 tablespoons vegetable oil

3 pounds skin-on, bone-in chicken thighs

2½ teaspoons kosher salt, plus more for seasoning

2 teaspoons freshly ground black pepper

1 dried bay leaf

3 sprigs of thyme

2 tablespoons unsalted butter (can substitute vegetable oil, dairy-free butter substitute, or schmaltz), plus ½ tablespoon cold unsalted butter

¼ cup (40g) plus 3 tablespoons all-purpose flour

¼ cup dry white wine

½ cup heavy cream or whole milk (completely optional, depends on your mood and diet)

DUMPLINGS

¼ cup (45g) cornmeal

½ teaspoon sugar

¾ teaspoon baking powder

3 tablespoons chopped fresh dill

1 large egg, beaten

1 tablespoon chopped fresh parsley

1. MAKE THE STEW: Grab two bowls for veggie prep. Peel the carrots and trim ¼ inch from the tops and bottoms. Place the peelings and ends in one bowl. Quarter the carrots lengthwise and slice them thin; place into the second bowl. Trim 1 inch from the tops and bottoms of the celery stalks and place the ends in the bowl with the carrot scraps. Cut the stalks in half lengthwise, then slice thin; place in the bowl with the sliced carrots.

2. Slice the onions in half through the root ends, and remove and discard the skins. Chop the onions fine, leaving ½ inch at the root ends. Add the root ends to the veggie scraps; add the chopped onions to the sliced veggies.

3. Trim the root end and the top 2 inches from the leek. Remove the remaining green and light green parts, rinse them well under cold water, and add them to the scraps. Quarter the white part lengthwise, then slice thin and rinse well; add to the sliced veggie bowl.

4. Heat a large pot over medium-high heat, then add the oil. Season the chicken thighs on both sides with 1 teaspoon of the salt and 1 teaspoon of the pepper. Working in batches, add the thighs to the pot, skin-side down, and sear until golden brown all over, 5 to 7 minutes per side. Remove to a plate.

(recipe continues)

5. Add the veggie scraps to the pot and cook, stirring and scraping any stuck bits from the bottom, until softened, 3 to 4 minutes. Add the bay leaf and thyme, then return the chicken thighs and any accumulated juices to the pot. Pour in 8 cups of water and bring to a boil. Reduce the heat to medium-low and simmer, skimming any foam that rises to the top, until the chicken is cooked through and the liquid has reduced slightly, 30 to 40 minutes.

6. Using a pair of tongs, transfer the chicken to a plate. Strain the stock into a large bowl; discard the veggie scraps. Carefully skim the chicken fat from the surface and reserve it in a separate small bowl.

7. Set the pot back over medium heat and put in the skimmed chicken fat and the sliced veggies. Season with 1 teaspoon of the salt and the remaining 1 teaspoon pepper. Cook, stirring regularly, until the veggies begin to soften and brown at the edges, 5 to 7 minutes.

8. Stir in the 2 tablespoons of butter until melted, then dust with 3 tablespoons of the flour and stir to combine. Cook for 3 minutes, stirring occasionally. Whisk in the wine, stirring to create a thick paste. Gradually whisk in the reserved stock, making sure to dissolve the roux as you go so there are no lumps. Bring to a simmer and cook, uncovered, for 15 minutes.

9. Meanwhile, remove and discard the skin, bones, and cartilage from the chicken thighs. Pull the meat into large shreds. Add the meat to the pot and stir, making sure the sauce isn't sticking to the bottom. If you are using cream or milk, stir it in now.

10. MAKE THE DUMPLINGS: In a large bowl, whisk together the cornmeal, the remaining ¼ cup flour and ½ teaspoon salt, and the sugar and baking powder. Add the cold butter and rub it between your fingers until it is distributed throughout the dry ingredients. Add ½ tablespoon of the dill and the egg and stir to create a thick, spoonable batter. If the mixture seems too dry, add 1 to 2 tablespoons of stock or water.

11. Raise the heat under the stock to medium-high and bring the pot to a boil. Using two spoons or a cookie scoop, drop tablespoon-size mounds of the dumpling batter into the liquid. The dumplings don't have to be perfectly smooth and round, so don't waste time trying to make them pretty; just make sure the size is consistent so they cook evenly. When all of the dumpling batter is scooped, cover the pot, reduce the heat to medium-low, and simmer, undisturbed, for 15 minutes.

12. Open the lid and give the pot a gentle stir to get the dumplings completely bathed in the sauce. Taste the sauce and adjust the seasoning as you like. Lift out a dumpling, break it open, and check the center to make sure it is cooked through. The dumpling should look light and fluffy throughout. If needed, cover the pot and continue cooking for up to 7 minutes.

13. Just before serving, sprinkle the remaining 2½ tablespoons dill and the parsley over the stew, then ladle into bowls.

Mom's Stuffed Shells
with Smoky Red Gravy

You know you grew up in the eighties when stuffed shells were part of your regular dinner rotation. The fact that my mom managed an Italian restaurant in our neighborhood for three years only accelerated her shells obsession. She would make big batches of tomato gravy to keep in the freezer, then bust them out whenever she was able to bring home pasta from work.

Stuffed shells aside, I have very fond memories of my mom's time at Pasta Via. My friend Lisa and I liked to visit the strip mall where the restaurant was because there was a Blockbuster Video right next door. We'd pop over to the restaurant while she was closing up shop, lock the doors, listen to Tracy Chapman records on repeat, or dance to Michael Jackson's *Bad* in the window of the restaurant. Not to thoroughly date myself, or anything.

SERVES 4 TO 5

½ teaspoon kosher salt, plus more for the pasta water and seasoning

2 tablespoons extra-virgin olive oil

2 large garlic cloves, finely grated

1 pound fresh spinach

11 ounces jumbo pasta shells (about 30 of them)

3 cups Smoky Red Gravy (page 99) or 1 (24-ounce) jar of your favorite tomato sauce

16 ounces whole-milk ricotta cheese (about 2 cups)

2 cups shredded mozzarella cheese

2 cups finely grated Parmesan cheese

2 egg yolks

½ teaspoon freshly ground black pepper

1. Preheat the oven to 375°F. Bring a large pot of salted water to a boil over high heat.

2. Heat a sauté pan over medium-low heat. Put the oil and garlic in the pan. When the garlic just begins to sizzle, stir and cook for about 1 minute; don't let it brown.

3. Add the spinach to the pan, season with a pinch of salt, add a splash of water, and cook, stirring frequently, until just wilted, about 2 minutes. Remove from the heat and let cool.

4. Add the pasta shells to the boiling water and give them a little stir. Cook, stirring occasionally, until just barely al dente, 6 to 7 minutes.

5. In a large bowl, stir ½ cup of the starchy pasta-cooking water into the tomato sauce to incorporate. Drain the pasta in a colander and rinse under cold water; leave the colander in the sink.

6. In another large bowl, combine the ricotta, 1 cup of the mozzarella, 1 cup of the Parmesan, the egg yolks, the pepper, and the salt.

7. Gather the wilted spinach in a clean kitchen towel and squeeze to remove the excess water. Chop the spinach finely and add it to the bowl with the cheeses; mix well.

(recipe continues)

8. Spread half of the tomato sauce mixture over the bottom of a 9 × 13-inch glass baking dish. Fill each pasta shell with about 2 tablespoons of the ricotta mixture and line them up in the baking dish. If the shells have stuck together and become hard to separate, rinse them with a little cold water in the colander. Set aside any shells that are torn or broken and save them for another use. You should have 26 to 28 stuffed shells in the baking dish.

9. Spoon the remaining sauce over the shells, sprinkle with the remaining 1 cup mozzarella and 1 cup Parmesan, and cover the pan with foil. Bake until the sauce is bubbling, 15 to 20 minutes. Remove the foil and continue baking until the cheese is melted, bubbly, and browned in places, another 15 to 20 minutes. Enjoy!

MAKE AHEAD

This can be prepared up through step 9 and refrigerated for 1 to 2 days (or frozen for up to 3 months), then brought to room temperature for an hour before baking.

199 PURE SUNDAY VIBES: FAMILY-STYLE FEASTS

how to "sunday best" your family-style feasts

SATE 'EM WITH SNACKS: Keep visitors from breathing down your neck, asking if dinner is ready yet. Make sure there are plenty of nibbles on hand (by making good use of the Snacks chapter, for instance), and you'll have more wiggle room when it comes to getting the main meal on the table.

EXPEDITE SHARING: Make it easy for guests to help themselves: slice your roasts, cut up whole birds, and pre-portion anything that would otherwise be a pain in the butt to serve.

GO FOR BROKE WITH GARNISHES: Add final flourishes that look great *and* pump up the volume when it comes to flavor. Think fresh or fried soft herbs (because even the stems are edible), or halved lemons, seared cut-side down in a cast-iron skillet. You can also put out little bowls containing pickled onions, sliced chiles, condiments, or what have you, so guests can customize and round out the flavors of any given dish.

HANG TOUGH: Tenderloins and such can take a big bite out of your budget. Not only are tough cuts like shoulder a whole lot cheaper, they also take deliciously well to low-and-slow roasting or braising, which is a totally hands-off way to develop loads of extra flavor.

BE AMONG THE UPPER CRUST: It's hard to top the wow factor of salt-crusted whole fish. And preparing it is easier than you might think. Stuff the cavity of a 3- to 4-pound fish with lemon and herbs, then rub it all over with a thin film of vegetable oil. Make a paste with a ratio of 1 beaten egg white to 1 cup of kosher salt, and place a layer on the bottom of a baking pan. Lay the fish on top, and encase it with the rest of the salt paste. Bake at 400°F for 20 to 30 minutes.

GO FISH: Speaking of fish, fried catfish is a usual suspect at Southern-style spreads. So why not exceed expectations by serving sliced fillets of meaty, lobster-like monkfish instead?

SAY IT AIN'T SODA: Sticky Cheerwine or other sweet sodas make a great glaze for slow-braised meat.

THROW DIY DINNERS: Plan meals for which you take care of prep, but guests deal with their own assembly (think tacos, hot pots, or that throwback favorite, fondue). Not only is it fun for everyone, but it will also take lots of responsibility off your shoulders!

ENCOURAGE INVOLVEMENT: In the same vein, there's no need to load yourself down with responsibility. For the most part, partygoers *want* to get involved. So if they ask if they can bring something, don't be afraid to say yes. The less you have to think about snacks, sides, and beverages, the more attention you can lavish on main courses and desserts.

DITCH LAST-MINUTE DISHES: You don't want to deal with *à la minute* cooking when entertaining guests. Make dishes that actually taste better the longer they sit, such as stews, braises, roasts, and casseroles. That way, you can knock out almost everything a day or two before, and simply reheat the day of. Double bonus—you know you'll get great leftovers.

Grandma Lydia's Shrimp Creole

This was the first dish my husband, Stephen, cooked for me, back when he was just some guy I was dating. It's what let me know that I might have actually found a real self-sufficient man, not just one looking to mooch off the fact that his girlfriend was a chef! He learned this dish from his grandmother, who was always cooking with him at her side at their home in New Orleans. All he asked was that I find him the head-on shrimp, because he was still relatively new to New York City. I was mightily impressed. A guy who was inclined to make dishes like this, instead of throwing something in the microwave or ordering takeout? That's what I call a keeper.

SERVES 3 OR 4

2 pounds head-on jumbo (16/20) shrimp

1 teaspoon kosher salt, plus more for seasoning

2 teaspoons Creole seasoning (I like Tony Chachere's)

½ cup plus 2 tablespoons light olive oil

1 large onion, chopped

1 large green bell pepper, seeded and chopped

½ teaspoon ground black pepper

½ cup (70g) all-purpose flour

3 celery stalks, chopped

3 large garlic cloves, minced

1 teaspoon dried Italian seasoning blend

2 cups good-quality canned tomato sauce (not marinara!)

1 dried bay leaf

1 pound smoked andouille sausage (or other smoked spicy sausage), sliced ¼ inch thick

Tabasco sauce, Cha-Cha (page 88), or Fermented Pepper Sauce (page 92), for serving

2 tablespoons chopped fresh parsley, for garnish

Trinity Rice Pilaf (page 157) or cooked white rice, for serving (½ cup per person)

1. Line a tray with paper towels. Pinch the heads from the shrimp and place the heads in a large bowl (make sure you're not just pulling off the shells from the heads—you want all that flavorful goo inside). Remove the shells and tails from the shrimp bodies and discard or save for stock. Devein the shrimp; place the bodies in the bowl with the heads.

2. Toss the heads and bodies with a couple of pinches of salt and 1 teaspoon of the Creole seasoning, spread in a single layer on the prepared tray, and place in the refrigerator.

3. Heat a large deep skillet or Dutch oven over medium heat. Put in the ½ cup of oil, half of the onion, and half of the bell pepper. Add the salt and the black pepper and cook until softened, about 3 minutes.

4. Sprinkle the flour into the oil and stir to soak up the fat; it should look like wet sand with chunks of vegetables. Reduce the heat to medium-low and cook, stirring every couple of minutes, until the roux is dark brown, like almond butter, about 15 minutes.

5. Stir in the rest of the onion and bell pepper and the remaining 1 teaspoon Creole seasoning. Add the celery, garlic, Italian seasoning, tomato sauce, and bay leaf and bring to a simmer.

6. Heat the remaining 2 tablespoons oil in a medium sauté pan over medium-high heat. Add the sausage in a single layer and cook until well browned, 5 to 7 minutes per side. Transfer the sausage to the simmering pot, stirring to incorporate. Pour off all but 2 tablespoons of fat from

the sauté pan. Heat the remaining fat over medium-high heat and, when it's beginning to smoke, carefully place the shrimp heads in a single layer in the pan. Cook until bright red and blistered, 1 to 2 minutes. Flip and sear on the other side, another 1 to 2 minutes. Remove the pan from the heat.

7. Add 1½ cups of water to the sauté pan and return to the burner over medium heat. Simmer for 4 minutes, then pour everything—the seared heads and liquid—into the simmering sauce and stir to incorporate. Simmer for 10 minutes, then

add the shrimp bodies. Continue simmering for 3 minutes, then turn off the heat; the shrimp will finish cooking in the residual heat.

8. Add a few hits of Tabasco (or let people season their own portions), sprinkle with parsley, and serve over rice to soak up all that sauce.

Controversial Gumbo

My mom used to make gumbo every year around Christmastime, from a recipe she'd learned from a friend's Cajun dad. She used a pot that was so big, I could stand inside it until I was about eight years old and have it reach up to my shoulders! Once the gumbo was done cooking, it took two grown people to drag it out back into the snow, where it would stay clear through the remainder of the holidays. Since there wasn't time to make extra meals when preparing a big feast for Christmas or New Year's, we would just go into the backyard and ladle out bits at a time for reheating to enjoy for breakfast, lunch, or any time in between.

My mom was awfully proud of that gumbo. So much so that she was eager to show it off for Stephen and his New Orleans family when they came to spend their first Christmas with us. He told her that it was very good—but that it wasn't gumbo. At least as far as he was concerned. You see, in New Orleans, gumbo is thickened with either okra *or* filé powder, not both. And it's made with either seafood *or* chicken and andouille, not both. But that's not the case in communities like Baton Rouge, which is where my mom's recipe hailed from. Well, this Chicago clash of Creole and Cajun traditions sparked quite the controversy. I'm glad to report that Stephen and I got married anyway, but we did learn an important lesson: as many people as there are in Louisiana, there's that many ways to make gumbo.

SERVES 4 TO 6

1 cup duck fat (canola oil or another high-smoke-point fat will work too)

1¼ cups (175g) all-purpose flour

1 large bunch of celery, chopped (save the leaves for another use or for garnish)

4 large onions, chopped

5 green bell peppers, seeded and chopped

4 large garlic cloves, chopped

Kosher salt and freshly ground black pepper

2 quarts unsalted chicken stock

2 tablespoons vegetable oil

6 bone-in, skin-on chicken thighs

1 pound andouille sausage, sliced ⅛ inch thick

2 pounds king crab knuckle pieces (you can use legs instead), thawed if frozen

2 dried bay leaves

2 tablespoons Creole seasoning (I like Tony Chachere's)

3 tablespoons gumbo filé powder

¼ cup Worcestershire sauce

2 tablespoons Tabasco sauce, Cha-Cha (page 88), or Fermented Pepper Sauce (page 92), plus more for serving

Cooked white rice or Trinity Pilaf (page 157) for serving

3 scallions, white and green parts, thinly sliced, for serving

1. In the largest stockpot you can get a hold of, melt the duck fat over medium heat. Sprinkle in the flour, whisking to combine, and cook, stirring frequently, until the roux is *dark* brown but not black/burned. This will take a while, likely anywhere from 15 to 25 minutes. Be patient and don't be scared—you have to push the color to the point just before it burns.

2. Once it gets there, immediately add the celery, onions, bell peppers, and garlic and stir to thoroughly combine. Season with a few pinches of salt and a pinch of pepper. Cook for 10 minutes, stirring frequently. Gradually pour in the stock, stirring to dissolve the roux. Add 3 quarts of water and bring to a boil.

3. Meanwhile, heat 1½ tablespoons of the vegetable oil in a large skillet over medium heat. Season the chicken thighs lightly with salt and pepper and place them skin-side down in the skillet. Cook until the skin is a rich golden brown, about 6 minutes. Flip and sear the bone side until nicely browned, about 4 minutes. Transfer the thighs to the stockpot.

4. Add the remaining ½ tablespoon oil and the sausage (in batches, if necessary) to the skillet and sear until the sausage develops some nice color, about 2 minutes per side. Add to the stockpot. Deglaze the skillet with 1 cup of water, scraping up the bits stuck to the pan, and add to the stockpot.

5. Add the crab to the pot, along with a couple of pinches of salt, the bay leaves, and the Creole seasoning, and bring to a good boil over high heat. Reduce the heat to medium-low and simmer vigorously, stirring occasionally, until the chicken starts to fall off the bone, around 45 minutes to 1 hour.

6. Stir 1½ tablespoons of the filé powder, the Worcestershire sauce, and the Tabasco into the pot. Using a spider or tongs, remove the chicken thighs and crab to a platter. When they're cool enough to handle, remove the bones and cartilage from the chicken and pick the meat from the crab shells; return the chicken and crabmeat to the pot.

7. Continue simmering until the desired consistency is achieved, 20 to 25 minutes. We're looking for the liquid to be reduced by about one-third and the gravy to be thick enough to coat a spoon. If it still seems too runny, add up to 1½ tablespoons more of the filé powder in ½-tablespoon increments, until the desired consistency is reached.

8. Taste and adjust the seasoning, if desired, and serve with white rice, sliced scallions, and more Tabasco on the side.

DO-AHEAD DINNER
Although you can enjoy your gumbo right away, it's even better the next day. Let cool slightly at room temperature before storing in the refrigerator.

Boudin-Stuffed Calamari

I learned about boudin, a type of sausage made with livers and pork and bound with rice, when visiting New Orleans. My husband, his mom, and I were dining at the Gumbo Palace (see the story about Controversial Gumbo on page 204, ha ha), and I spotted it on the menu. Stephen's mom insisted I wouldn't like it—but I'm never one to pass up an opportunity to try something new. Unsurprisingly, to me anyway, I loved it.

When I started fiddling around with my newly discovered dish, I started by using it as a stuffing for pig trotters, a very labor-intensive protein that involves a lot of deboning, rolling, and time. So I decided to scale it down by swapping in calamari, inspired by Italian stuffed calamari dishes. This dish takes just minutes to sear, since the stuffing is essentially cooked and all you need to do is warm it through.

--- SERVES 3 OR 4 ---

12 to 14 squid bodies, cleaned, plus a few tentacles for frying, if using (about 1¾ pounds and thawed, if frozen

BOUDIN STUFFING

3 ounces chicken livers, chopped

1 large shallot, chopped

1 large garlic clove, sliced

1 celery stalk, chopped (save the leaves for garnish)

½ green bell pepper, seeded and chopped

1½ teaspoons extra-virgin olive oil

4 ounces ground pork (at least 30% fat)

½ teaspoon ground black pepper

½ teaspoon dry mustard

½ teaspoon Creole seasoning (I like Tony Chachere's)

¼ teaspoon kosher salt

¼ cup white wine

½ cup cooked white rice

¼ cup chopped fresh parsley

1 tablespoon Tabasco sauce or Fermented Pepper Sauce (page 92)

SQUID

½ cup (60g) Wondra or (70g) all-purpose flour (for tentacles)

½ cup (90g) fine cornmeal or masa harina (for tentacles)

½ teaspoon kosher salt, plus more for seasoning

3 tablespoons vegetable oil, plus more for deep-frying (for tentacles)

DIPPING SAUCE

¼ cup whole-grain mustard

¼ cup crème fraîche

2 teaspoons lemon juice

½ teaspoon Aleppo pepper flakes or hot paprika

1 tablespoon sliced fresh chives

Kosher salt

GARNISHES

Celery leaves, frisée, and/ or coarsely chopped fresh parsley

SPECIAL EQUIPMENT

Toothpicks

1. Line a tray with paper towels. Rinse the squid and spread out on the tray. Refrigerate.

2. MAKE THE BOUDIN STUFFING: Place the chicken livers in a food processor and pulse 5 or 6 times to purée. Scrape into a small bowl. Add the shallot, garlic, celery, and bell pepper to the food processor and pulse a few times, until finely chopped. Leave in the processor bowl until needed.

3. Heat the olive oil in a large skillet over medium heat. Add the ground pork and cook, breaking it up into small crumbles with a wooden spoon, until lightly browned and cooked through, about 4 minutes. Stir in the liver purée and cook just until the deep red color fades, about 1 minute.

4. Stir in the veggies from the food processor and turn the heat to medium-high. Season with the black pepper, dry mustard, Creole seasoning, and salt. Cook until the liquid released from the vegetables evaporates a bit, about 7 minutes. Pour in the wine and reduce until it just glazes the stuffing mixture and pan, about 4 minutes. Remove from the heat.

5. Stir the rice, parsley, and Tabasco into the filling and let cool to room temperature, about 10 minutes.

6. Using a teaspoon, fill each squid body three-quarters full with stuffing. Secure the top with a toothpick. Return the stuffed squid to the paper-towel-lined tray and place a layer of paper towels on top to absorb any excess liquid and help them sear better. Return the tray to the refrigerator.

7. COOK THE SQUID: In a small bowl, combine the flour, cornmeal, and salt; set aside. In a small pot, pour enough vegetable oil to deep-fry the tentacles and heat over medium heat until it immediately sizzles when a drop of water is added.

8. Toss the tentacles (and any of the sliced broken bodies) in the flour mixture, shake off the excess, and carefully drop the pieces into the hot oil. Fry until golden brown on all sides, about 4 to 5 minutes. Using a slotted spoon, remove the tentacles to a paper-towel-lined plate. Season with a pinch of salt.

9. Sprinkle the stuffed squid lightly with salt on both sides. Heat a large skillet over medium-high heat and add the 3 tablespoons of vegetable oil. Add the stuffed squid in a single layer, working in batches if necessary. Cook until browned, about 5 minutes, then flip them over. Reduce the heat to medium-low and partially cover the pan with a lid. (The filling is already cooked, so we're just making sure it gets heated through.) Continue to cook for about 5 minutes, until the squid is lightly seared and heated through, then transfer to a plate and remove the toothpicks.

10. MAKE THE DIPPING SAUCE: In a small bowl, combine the mustard, crème fraîche, lemon juice, Aleppo pepper, and chives. Season with a bit of salt.

11. To serve, smear a spoonful of the dipping sauce onto a serving plate and arrange the stuffed calamari on top. Place the fried tentacles on and around the calamari, garnish with celery leaves, frisée, and/or parsley, and serve with the remaining sauce on the side!

MAKE AHEAD
Both the stuffing and the sauce can be prepared up to 3 days ahead and refrigerated.

SUNDAY BEST SHORTCUT
I love frying up tentacles as a garnish for this dish but won't be mad if you leave them out.

tasty transformations
Leftovers Reimagined

The ultimate parent cooking trick is being able to work magic with leftovers. Since my mom knew we'd start complaining if we ate the same reheated meal over and over (unless it was specially ordered during one of her ingeniously invented "restaurant nights"; see page 219), she came up with all sorts of clever ways to completely transform a previous night's dinner. For instance, she managed to scrumptiously sneak already-cooked vegetables into stir-fry, shredded pot roast into lasagna, and roasted chicken into pot pie.

Not having the money to burn on expensive meat also increased her skills with another kind of "leftover," otherwise known as off-cuts. Since prime rib and tenderloins were generally saved for special occasions, she'd purchase cheaper, tougher proteins like oxtails or lamb shanks instead and braise

them down all day until they were flavorful, filling, and every bit as tender as a piece of pricey steak.

She picked up on more and more thrifty hacks once she started working at restaurants (as did I), where there's not a single fish head, chicken bone, or worn-out carrot that goes to waste. Since margins are slim, necessity becomes the mother of invention. Which is not at all dissimilar from running a budget-minded household!

This chapter is full of tips and recipes that will encourage you to work with what ya got—and flaunt it, proudly—by creating dishes that actively repurpose *Sunday Best* leftovers (hello, Overnight Grits Arancini, page 217!) or that can be easily pulled together from what you already have in your fridge (like Kitchen-Sink Quiche, page 223).

Cornbread (or Biscuit) Panzanella

From French toast to croutons to the Italian salad known as panzanella, it's cool how many cultures have found ways to revive old bread. It's the staff of life, after all, and requires a fair amount of time and attention to make. So why let even the smallest crumb go to waste?

Although panzanella is often made with crustier loaves like sourdough or ciabatta, I like using cornbread because it adds a little sweetness and stays a bit softer (no one wants shards of bread from an undersoaked panzanella shredding the roof of their mouth). It also reminds me of summertime in Mississippi, where the perfect seasonal meal was often little more than a hunk of cornbread and a sun-warmed tomato plucked from my great-aunt's garden.

——————————————————————————————— SERVES 4 TO 6 ———————————————————————————————

½ cup extra-virgin olive oil

3 cups cubed (1-inch) cornbread or biscuits (see Love Up Your Leftovers)

1½ pounds mixed heirloom tomatoes (the more colorful the better)

1½ teaspoons kosher salt

1 teaspoon freshly ground black pepper

¼ teaspoon sugar

2 garlic cloves, smashed and chopped

3 tablespoons red wine vinegar

1 small shallot or ¼ red onion, peeled and sliced into paper-thin rounds

1 tablespoon Dijon mustard

3 Persian cucumbers or ½ large cucumber

6 ounces fresh mozzarella or feta cheese, cut into bite-size pieces

½ cup torn fresh basil leaves

3 or 4 sprigs of parsley, roughly chopped

1. Preheat the oven to 325°F.

2. Grease a baking sheet with 2 tablespoons of the oil and arrange the cornbread on top in a single layer. Drizzle the cornbread with another 2 tablespoons of the oil and bake until toasted on top and browned on the bottom, 25 to 30 minutes. Let cool.

3. Core the tomatoes and cut into bite-size pieces, about 1 inch or less. Place them in a large bowl and add 1 teaspoon of the salt, the pepper, the sugar, half of the garlic, and 1 tablespoon of the vinegar. Toss to thoroughly combine.

4. Place the shallot in a small bowl with 2 ice cubes. Cover with cold water and let sit for at least 10 minutes and up to an hour (this crisps up the onion and mellows the flavor).

5. In a small bowl or a container with a tight-fitting lid, combine the remaining 4 tablespoons oil, ½ teaspoon of

salt, the remaining 2 tablespoons vinegar, the garlic, and the mustard. Whisk or shake well until you have a smooth emulsion.

6. If using Persian (or other small) cucumbers, cut them into rounds, about ¼ inch thick. If using a large cucumber, peel it, slice it in half lengthwise, scrape out the seeds with a spoon, then cut the halves into ¼-inch crescents.

7. Add the cucumbers, cheese, basil, parsley, and cornbread to the bowl with the tomatoes. Shake or whisk the vinaigrette one more time, then pour over the top. Using a large spoon, gently toss everything together. Taste and add a pinch of salt, if needed. Let sit for 5 to 10 minutes before enjoying!

LOVE UP YOUR LEFTOVERS

You can use Sour Cream Cornbread (page 144), Flaky Layered Biscuits (page 23), or cubes of any stale-ish, crusty-ish bread.

Overnight Grits Arancini

If you've ever stored cooked grits in the fridge, you know they turn into a solid brick that requires a lot of coaxing in a pot with milk, stock, or butter in order to loosen up. This is exactly how risotto behaves—made from Arborio rice, and popularly formed into the fried balls of love known as arancini. The lesson here is, whatever you do with risotto, you can totally do with any starchy grain, such as an excess batch of Southern-style grits.

MAKES 18 TO 20 ARANCINI

---

2 cups Overnight Grits (page 33) or other cooked grain (see Love Up Your Leftovers)

1½ cups Mushroom Ragout (page 33) or other mix-ins (see Love Up Your Leftovers)

⅓ cup grated Parmesan cheese

4 large eggs

1 cup (140g) all-purpose flour

1 cup fine bread crumbs

Kosher salt

Vegetable oil, for frying

1. Place the grits in a large microwave-safe bowl with the mushroom ragout. Microwave until just softened around the edges, about 2 minutes, and stir until smooth.

2. If steaming hot, allow the grits to cool until just warm before folding in the Parmesan and 1 beaten egg. Spread the mixture into the bottom of a shallow baking dish, cover with plastic wrap, and chill in the refrigerator until cold and firm, 1 to 2 hours.

3. In a medium bowl, beat the remaining 3 eggs. Place the flour in a second medium bowl and the bread crumbs, along with the heavy pinch of salt, in a third medium bowl.

4. Line a baking sheet with parchment paper. Scoop 2-tablespoon portions of the grits and roll into balls (dampen your hands as needed to keep them from getting sticky). Roll each ball in the flour, then transfer to the bowl with the egg and roll with two forks to coat completely. Use the forks to transfer the arancini to the bowl of bread crumbs and roll to coat again (congrats, you just executed the breading procedure "dry-wet-dry," which is the gold-standard technique for breading anything!). Place the breaded arancini on the prepared baking sheet.

5. Heat a large cast-iron skillet over medium heat; add enough vegetable oil to reach ½ inch deep. When the oil is hot but not smoking, gently place the arancini in the pan, working in batches, and cook, turning as they brown, until crunchy and GBD (that's golden brown and delicious) all over, about 8 minutes, adjusting the heat as necessary so they don't overbrown.

6. Transfer the arancini to a paper-towel-lined tray to drain. Season with salt while hot and serve as soon as they're cool enough to handle.

LOVE UP YOUR LEFTOVERS

You can use Overnight Grits (page 33), or any form of rice or starchy grain that becomes creamy and sticky when left to cool overnight. Mix-ins are entirely optional and can include Mushroom Ragout (page 33), ground meat, peas, or any cooked, finely chopped meat or veg of your choice.

MAKE AHEAD

These can be prepared through the rolling and breading step and refrigerated on a plate or baking sheet until you're ready to fry. You can also flash-freeze them in a single layer on a baking sheet, packaged into airtight bags or containers, and frozen for up to 2 weeks. Just thaw overnight in the fridge before frying.

end-of-week reservations at chez cheatham

My mom would occasionally declare Thursdays or Fridays "restaurant night." Our "dining room" was a raised counter with track lighting above it, set between the kitchen and living room. We'd sit at the counter, turn off all the lights except for the track lighting, and my mom would recite the menu. "Tonight, we have smothered pork chops, chicken marsala, and spaghetti!" or whatever the week's leftovers happened to be. We'd place our orders, and she'd microwave them or stick them in the oven. It was the best.

Clearly, my mom was just being resourceful, having neither the time nor the money to make a three-course dinner from scratch every night. But that's not how we saw it as kids. She turned eating leftovers into a fun game, and crafting interesting meals from whatever we could find in the fridge into a creative endeavor.

My mom's ingenuity has certainly served me well as an adult (there has been many a night when, coming back from a late restaurant shift, I've had to make quick magic from the sad contents of my fridge). It's definitely benefited me as a chef too, opening my mind to how infinitely transformable ingredients are and how easy it is to breathe life and love into just about anything you cook.

Cast-Iron Deep-Dish Pizza

Who doesn't love pizza? Chicago's famous deep-dish style, where the toppings are actually baked between the cheesy, molten layers, is the perfect catch-all for using up any type of leftover you have in your fridge.

As for dough, you can certainly buy a ball of it from most grocery stores or pizzerias. But making it from scratch is pretty rewarding, especially since it can be kept refrigerated for up to 5 days, or frozen for a month. Just thaw it overnight in the refrigerator, or let the cold dough sit at room temperature for 1 hour before using.

SERVES 4 TO 6

1 tablespoon sugar

2¼ teaspoons (1 packet) active dry yeast

1¼ cups warmish water (just above room temperature, but not hot)

¼ cup extra-virgin olive oil or melted butter, plus 2 tablespoons for coating the pan

2 cups (280g) all-purpose flour, plus more for dusting

½ cup (70g) fine cornmeal, plus 1 tablespoon for coating the pan

1½ teaspoons kosher salt

2 cups shredded mozzarella cheese (fresh mozz is ideal)

2 cups leftover veggies or meat (see Love Up Your Leftovers)

¾ cup good-quality tomato sauce (such as Smoky Red Gravy, page 99)

⅓ cup grated Parmesan cheese

1. In a small bowl, stir together the sugar, yeast, warm water, and the ¼ cup of oil. Let sit until foamy, about 10 minutes.

2. In a large bowl (if working by hand) or in a stand mixer with a dough hook attachment, combine the flour, the ½ cup of cornmeal, and the salt. Mix with a wooden spoon, or combine on low speed if using a mixer, then add the yeast mixture. Gently knead with your hands or combine in the mixer until you have a smooth dough that pulls away from the sides of the bowl, 4 to 5 minutes. Cover with a damp kitchen towel (one that's not super linty) and let rest for 30 minutes.

3. Turn the dough out onto a lightly floured work surface and knead again for 3 to 4 minutes. Cover with the damp

towel and let rise for 2 to 3 hours at room temperature until doubled in size, or overnight in the refrigerator (oil the dough lightly, place it in a bowl, and cover with plastic wrap). You can also freeze the dough at this point, wrapped tightly in plastic wrap or in airtight freezer bags.

4. Preheat the oven to 425°F with a rack positioned in the lower third of the oven.

5. Rub a 10-inch cast-iron skillet with the remaining 2 tablespoons oil (make sure to get into the sides and corners). Sprinkle the remaining 1 tablespoon cornmeal over the bottom, shaking it around to lightly coat. Set the pan aside.

(recipe continues)

6. Turn the dough out onto a lightly floured work surface and press and stretch it into a 12-inch round. Roll the dough around a rolling pin, then unroll it over the prepared skillet, giving it enough slack to sink into the pan. Lift the overhanging edges to let the dough settle into the bottom and edges of the pan without stretching it too much. Trim any overhang (fried dough anyone?).

7. Sprinkle 1 cup of the mozzarella over the dough, top with the leftovers, then layer with the remaining 1 cup mozzarella. Add the tomato sauce, spreading it into an even layer, and sprinkle with the Parmesan.

8. Place the skillet on the lower rack and bake until the crust is browned and the filling is bubbly, 30 to 40 minutes. Cool on a wire rack for 15 to 20 minutes before slicing.

LOVE UP YOUR LEFTOVERS
You can use leftover dough from Pecan Five-Spice Sticky Buns (page 25), Smoky Red Gravy (page 99), and bits of pretty much any leftover meat or veg. Try Berbere-Spiced Mini Lamb Meatballs (page 77)!

Crustless Kitchen-Sink Quiche

Quiche makes me think of Sunday School at St. Thomas in Hyde Park. The teachers were a mix of nuns and parent volunteers, and the parents would invariably bring food to share—which almost always included quiche. It made a lot of sense because quiche could be served warm, cold, or at room temperature, and included a starch, veg, and meat. What else did a bunch of kids need?

I continue to love the flexibility of quiche, which allows me to use up practically anything I have in my fridge. For the cheese, you can choose whatever kind goes well with your chosen filling, or totally leave it out. Most of the time, I don't even bother with crust if I don't have one in my freezer or the time to make it, and these days I'm more likely to go no-crust and save myself the calories (and make it easier for friends avoiding carbs or gluten). If you do want to add a crust, store-bought pie crust works great; just omit the cooking spray and bake the crust for 7 minutes at 350°F before filling.

SERVES 6 TO 8

Nonstick cooking spray or vegetable oil

5 large eggs

1 cup heavy cream

½ to 1 teaspoon kosher salt

½ teaspoon freshly ground black pepper

1 tablespoon unsalted butter

2 scallions, thinly sliced

1½ cups chopped leftovers of your choice (seriously, almost anything goes; see Love Up Your Leftovers)

½ cup grated cheese of your choice (optional)

1. Preheat the oven to 350°F.

2. Spray a 9-inch deep-dish pie pan liberally with oil and place it on a baking sheet.

3. In a large bowl, crack the eggs and whisk until well combined and a little foamy, about 3 minutes. Whisk in the cream, ½ teaspoon salt, and the pepper. Set aside.

4. Melt the butter in a large sauté pan over medium heat and add the scallions. Season with a little salt and cook until the scallions are just wilted, 1 to 2 minutes. Stir in whatever leftovers you're using and cook until heated through, 1 to 2 minutes. Remove the pan from the heat and let cool slightly before scraping everything into the bowl of eggs. Stir the filling into the eggs to combine, along with the cheese (if using).

5. If your leftovers are well seasoned, do not add the remaining salt. If they're not, they will suck the life (read: salt) out of the ½ teaspoon already in the eggs. Add as much of the remaining ½ teaspoon salt as you think you'll need. Trust your instincts!

6. Pour the mixture into the prepared pie pan. Place the baking sheet with the pan in the oven and bake for 20 minutes. Reduce the oven temperature to 325°F and continue to bake until the center of the quiche is set and the top is lightly browned, 25 to 30 minutes. Let cool to room temperature, slice, and serve.

LOVE UP YOUR LEFTOVERS

You can use the crab-andouille mix from Cornbread Toad-in-the-Hole (page 45), Candied Bacon (page 37), bits of Candied Chicken Wings (page 63), or any cooked veg that's started to wither and shrivel in your fridge. The possibilities are endless!

Pan-Fried Spaghetti Rösti

Reheating pasta can be a tricky undertaking, as it doesn't take much to get mushy. So it's a better bet to reimagine its texture completely by crisping it up in a pan. Anyone remember the Ramen Burger? Pan-frying is a great way to turn last night's dinner into a craveable brunch or easy lunch, by topping crunchy-edged, creamy-centered slices of rösti with a fried egg or pairing them with a simple green salad.

SERVES 2 OR 3

2 to 3 cups cooked sliced vegetables (see Love Up Your Leftovers)

⅓ cup grated Parmesan cheese, plus more for serving

4 cups cooked spaghetti

3 large eggs, beaten

Pinch of freshly grated nutmeg

Kosher salt and freshly ground black pepper

Vegetable oil for frying

1. Place the cooked sliced veggies and any accompanying sauce in a large bowl. Add the Parmesan and cooked noodles and toss to thoroughly mix. Stir in the eggs and nutmeg and season with salt and pepper.

2. Heat a 9-inch skillet over medium heat and pour in a thin layer of oil. When the oil is shimmering, add the pasta-vegetable mixture and pat down into an even, tightly packed layer.

3. Let cook until the bottom is browned and set, 8 to 10 minutes. Place a large plate over the top and carefully invert the pan, then slide the rösti back into the pan. Brown up on the other side, about 8 to 10 minutes more. Transfer the rösti to a cutting board, sprinkle with the remaining Parmesan, and cut into slices to serve.

LOVE UP YOUR LEFTOVERS
You can mix your spaghetti with cooked, finely sliced, and already sauced vegetables, such as Turnip Latkes (page 159), Brussels Sprouts with Brown Butter (page 174), or Green Cabbage Gratin (page 178).

Louisiana Yaka Mein

A popular Creole dish, especially among the New Orleans African American community, yaka mein is believed to have been introduced by Chinese immigrants in the nineteenth century. Essentially, it's a noodle soup in a light broth, made with bits of vegetable and cheap chunks of braised meat. Which is to say, it's custom-made for using up leftovers, like Mississippi Pot Roast (page 189), Glazed Root Vegetables (page 175), or Collard Green Kimchi (page 161).

SERVES 4 TO 6

1½ pounds leftover meat bones (see Love Up Your Leftovers)

1 (2-pound) whole, uncooked boneless chuck roast or about 3 cups cooked leftover beef, cut into 1-inch pieces

4 cups unsalted beef stock

1 teaspoon Creole seasoning (I like Tony Chachere's)

4 to 6 large eggs (1 egg per serving)

1 tablespoon Worcestershire sauce or ½ teaspoon fish sauce

2 to 3 tablespoons soy sauce

8 ounces ramen noodles or spaghetti, cooked according to package directions

4 scallions, white and green parts, sliced (not too thinly), for garnish

Chopped fresh cilantro and/or parsley, for garnish

1. In a large pot, combine the bones, chuck roast (if you're using the cooked meat, don't add it yet), beef stock, Creole seasoning, and 4 cups of water. Bring to a boil over high heat, then reduce the heat to medium-low and simmer until the meat is tender, 2 to 2½ hours, skimming any fat or foam occasionally. If you're using cooked meat, add it after the bones and stock have simmered for 1 hour, then bring the pot back to a simmer and cook for another 30 minutes, skimming as necessary.

2. Meanwhile, prepare the eggs: Place a medium pot of water over high heat and bring to a boil. Carefully lower the eggs into the boiling water and cook for 6 minutes. Drain the eggs, then transfer to a large bowl of ice water. Let the eggs cool for 10 to 15 minutes. Peel and set aside.

3. When the stock has finished cooking, turn off the heat and use tongs to remove and discard the bones. Strain the stock through a fine-mesh sieve into a smaller pot. If using the chuck roast, let the meat cool a bit, then cut it into bite-size pieces and set them aside in a large bowl.

4. Bring the broth back to a low simmer over medium-low heat. Stir in the Worcestershire sauce. Taste the broth and add soy sauce to taste. (You may also want to add a couple of pinches of salt—it depends on the sodium content of your Creole seasoning.)

5. Divide the cooked noodles among individual serving bowls, add about ½ cup meat to each, and ladle enough broth over the noodles and meat to cover them nicely. Cut the soft-boiled eggs in half and nestle two halves on top of each bowl. Sprinkle with scallions, cilantro, and parsley and enjoy immediately!

LOVE UP YOUR LEFTOVERS
Keep in mind that roasted bones add amazing flavor to this or *any* broth, so never ever throw them away! Make a point of saving and freezing bones of all sorts, such as the carcass of Stout-and-Soy-Roasted Chicken (page 117), cleaned-off Candied Chicken Wings (page 63), and the remainders of Slow-Roasted Harissa Short Ribs (page 192).

Seven-Layer Salad

This dish is a true eighties classic. While the OG version is basically a layered Cobb salad, my mom would constantly switch up the theme, making it Greek (using romaine, olives, cucumbers, feta, etc.), Southern (with chopped-up fried chicken), or chef-style, featuring marinated veggies and leftover cold cuts.

There's really no way to go wrong here, *unless* you neglect to season each layer. Dressing doesn't stand a chance of permeating everything if it's simply poured on top. Whether you season each addition with olive oil, vinegar, and salt or toss with a bit of chopped scallion or dill, putting love into each layer is the difference between a simple *meh* salad and a totally restaurant-worthy creation.

————————————— SERVES 6 —————————————

1 bunch of kale (any kind)

¼ cup toasted sunflower seeds

Kosher salt and freshly ground black pepper

About ½ cup extra-virgin olive oil

About ¼ cup vinegar or lemon juice, or ½ cup Buttermilk Vinaigrette (page 86)

6 hard-boiled eggs, chopped

2 cups cooked green peas

¼ cup chopped fresh dill

3 cups raw broccoli florets, chopped small

1 scallion, white and green parts, finely chopped

2 cups crumbled feta cheese

2 cups diced cucumber

2 cups cherry tomatoes, quartered

½ cup chopped crispy cooked bacon (optional), such as Candied Bacon (page 37)

1. Cut out the stems from the kale, starting where they get thick toward the bottom of the leaves, and discard (the upper part of the stem is tender enough to stay). Cut the leaves in half lengthwise, then cut crosswise into ¼-inch ribbons.

2. In a large serving bowl, combine the kale, sunflower seeds, a pinch of salt and pepper, 2 tablespoons of the oil, and a splash of vinegar or citrus, or 2 tablespoons of the Buttermilk Vinaigrette. Use your hands to gently massage everything into the kale so it's evenly coated and tenderized. Place in the bottom of a large, clear glass bowl.

3. Scatter the eggs in an even layer over the kale. Season with a couple of pinches of salt and pepper.

4. In the mixing bowl, combine the peas, half of the chopped dill, a couple of pinches of salt and pepper, another drizzle of oil, and a splash of vinegar or citrus or a drizzle of the Buttermilk Vinaigrette. Layer on top of the eggs.

5. Place the broccoli and scallion in the mixing bowl. Season with a pinch or two of salt and pepper and drizzle with oil, vinegar, or citrus or Buttermilk Vinaigrette. Toss well, then layer on top of the peas. Wipe out the bowl (the broccoli usually leaves behind a lot of little pieces).

6. Sprinkle the feta in an even layer on top of the broccoli.

7. Place the cucumber, the remaining dill, a couple of pinches of salt and pepper, and a drizzle of oil/vinegar or citrus or Buttermilk Vinaigrette in the mixing bowl. Toss to combine. Layer on top of the feta.

(recipe continues)

8. In the mixing bowl (don't bother to wipe it), combine the tomatoes and bacon, season with a little salt and pepper, and drizzle with oil or vinegar or citrus or Buttermilk Vinaigrette. Layer on top of the cucumbers.

9. Cover and refrigerate the salad until well chilled. Serve with extra oil or Buttermilk Vinaigrette on the side.

LOVE UP YOUR LEFTOVERS

Re-create this salad, or riff to your heart's content. Crunchy Hoppin' John Bhel Puri (page 80), Grilled Skirt Steak (page 124), Hominy Tabbouleh (page 145), Split Pea Salad (page 150), Elote Macque Choux (page 168), Blistered Green Beans (page 166), and Slow-Roasted Pork Shoulder (page 182) would all make great layers, sauced with Mustard-Green Chimichurri (page 94), Turnip-Top Pesto (page 91), or thinned-out Poor Man's Remoulade (page 109).

SUNDAY BEST FINESSE

This salad looks spectacular if layered in a trifle dish.

Green Tomato Chili

Green chili is big in the Southwest, owing to its Native American and Mexican influences. Not to knock the red version, but using green tomatoes and tomatillos adds an extra level of flavor, tang, and nuance to this homey, comforting, and universally popular dish.

SERVES 4 TO 6

2 large green chile peppers, such as poblanos, seeded and finely chopped

2 green bell peppers, seeded and finely chopped

2 to 3 tablespoons vegetable oil

1 teaspoon kosher salt, plus more for seasoning

1 pound ground white or dark meat chicken (or your choice of meat, see Time-Saving Swaps)

1 large Spanish onion, finely chopped

3 garlic cloves, finely chopped

1 tablespoon ground cumin

1 teaspoon ground coriander

1 teaspoon dried oregano

1 teaspoon chili powder

1 cup lager or light beer of your choice

2 to 3 cups roughly chopped green tomatoes, tomatillos, or leftovers (see Love Up Your Leftovers)

2 to 3 cups unsalted chicken stock or water

Freshly ground black pepper

Chopped fresh cilantro, for garnish

1. Heat the broiler to high.

2. In a medium bowl, combine the chile peppers and bell peppers (feel free to add a chopped jalapeño, if you want a little more spice) and toss with a drizzle of oil and a pinch of salt. Spread in a single layer on a baking sheet and broil until charred in places, about 5 minutes.

3. Meanwhile, heat a large pot over medium-high heat. Drizzle with vegetable oil and when the oil is smoking hot, carefully add the ground chicken. Cook, stirring occasionally and breaking up the meat with a wooden spoon, until the meat is just browned and any liquid that's released has mostly evaporated, 8 to 10 minutes.

4. Stir in the salt, along with the onion, garlic, cumin, coriander, oregano, and chili powder. Reduce the heat to medium-low and cook until the onion is tender and the spices are toasted, 3 to 4 minutes. Add the broiled peppers and any accumulated juices to the pot and cook for 5 minutes.

5. Pour in the beer, scraping up any browned bits (otherwise known as fond) on the bottom of the pot with a wooden spoon. Reduce the heat to low and simmer until reduced

by half, 5 to 7 minutes. Add the green tomatoes and stock and bring to a boil over high heat, then reduce the heat to medium-low and simmer, partially covered, stirring occasionally, until the chili achieves a nice stew consistency, 20 to 30 minutes. Taste and adjust the seasoning with salt and pepper.

6. Ladle into individual bowls, garnish with cilantro, and serve.

TIME-SAVING SWAPS
While green chili is traditionally made with cubed pork stew meat, I've gone with ground chicken (you can also use ground pork, beef, or turkey). Leftover meat (such as Stout-and-Soy-Roasted Chicken, page 117; Slow-Roasted Pork Shoulder, page 182; and Mississippi Pot Roast, page 189) that's been shredded or cut into cubes is great too. Just add it after the sauce has been made instead of browning it first, and cook until tender.

LOVE UP YOUR LEFTOVERS
You can use Green Tomato Shakshuka (page 51) or Grilled Green Tomato Salad (page 171) for the tangy tomato element.

Coconut Curry Stew

During her tenure at Kraft, my mom started selling to a Thai restaurant, and it instantly sent her into an obsessive curry-making kick. She would scour stores near and far for lemongrass, fresh curry leaves, and Thai basil. Seriously, there was an extended period when we ended up having Thai curry for dinner at least three times a week—the result being that we came to love and hate it in equal measure. Now I unequivocally adore Thai curry again, and I've also come to realize why it was such a go-to for my mom. As long as you keep a few staples in the pantry (such as curry paste and coconut milk), you can proceed to toss practically anything you have in your fridge into the mix.

SERVES 3 OR 4

3 tablespoons coconut oil

1 (2-inch) piece of lemongrass, tough outer layer removed, interior finely chopped

3 garlic cloves, sliced

2 medium shallots, sliced

1 (½-inch) piece fresh ginger, peeled and minced (or grated with a Microplane)

2 teaspoons coriander seed

2 tablespoons Thai red curry paste

2 cups unsalted chicken or vegetable stock

1 (13.5-ounce) can unsweetened coconut milk

1 cup sliced carrots (from about 1 large or 2 small carrots)

1 red bell pepper, quartered, seeded, and thinly sliced

1 tablespoon dark brown sugar

2 cups cubed cooked chicken, seafood, or other protein and/or quick-cooking raw vegetables, such as spinach or snow peas

1 tablespoon fresh lime juice

Kosher salt

Steamed rice, for serving (about ½ cup per person)

⅓ cup torn fresh cilantro, mint, and/or basil

Crushed peanuts or cashews (roasted and/or salted, if desired), for serving

1. Place the coconut oil, lemongrass, garlic, shallots, ginger, coriander, and curry paste in a small food processor (or in a mortar and pestle), and process (or crush) to a fine paste. (If using a mortar and pestle, the paste won't be completely uniform.)

2. Heat a large pot over medium heat and put in the paste. Sauté, stirring, until the paste is toasted and aromatic, 2 to 3 minutes.

3. Stir in the stock and bring to a boil. Reduce the heat to medium-low and cook at a low boil for 10 minutes. Stir in the coconut milk, carrots, bell pepper, and brown sugar, raise the heat slightly to bring to a simmer, and cook until slightly reduced and thickened, 7 to 8 minutes.

4. Add the cooked protein and/or quick-cooking raw vegetables. Simmer until the protein is heated through and the vegetables are crisp-tender, usually about 5 minutes. Stir in the lime juice and add salt to taste.

5. Serve over steamed rice and garnish with herbs and nuts.

LOVE UP YOUR LEFTOVERS

You can use picked Braised Turkey Necks (page 121) or Roasted Catfish (page 137) as a protein, either supplemented with or replaced by Blistered Green Beans (page 166), Charred Okra (page 167), Glazed Root Vegetables (page 175), or Whole-Roasted Cauliflower (page 177), for a veggie-centric curry.

SUNDAY BEST SHORTCUT

This first step is flexible (even skippable). The idea here is to amp up the flavor and brightness of the curry paste, which will take the dish to new levels. But you can absolutely use prepared curry paste without adding more aromatics.

Anything Can Pickle

Pickles are an integral part of every single culture, and you'll even find hyper-regional variants within the United States. Take Mississippi, for instance, where locals douse theirs in Kool-Aid. Or Chicago, where they're fond of driving peppermint sticks through the middles (yes, this is really a thing).

That's because pickling is *the* way to deliciously preserve anything you don't want to lose. And this can apply to the most pristine heirloom produce or the half-desiccated head of celery forgotten in the bottom of your crisper drawer. Aromatics and add-ins can be totally subject to the contents of your pantry and spice drawer too. The following recipe calls for bay leaf, mustard seed, cloves, and apple cider vinegar, but feel free to swap in cinnamon, thyme, allspice, white distilled vinegar, or whatever you have on hand!

-------------------- MAKES 1 TO 1½ POUNDS OF PICKLES --------------------

1 to 1½ pounds vegetable of your choice (see Love Up Your Leftovers)

1 dried bay leaf

1 teaspoon yellow mustard seeds

2 teaspoons black peppercorns

4 whole cloves (or ⅛ teaspoon ground cloves)

½ cup honey (or sorghum syrup, if you can get your hands on it)

1 cup apple cider vinegar

1 tablespoon kosher salt

1. If using whole root vegetables, peel, halve (if large), and slice them thin. Place the vegetables in a clean glass jar or other heat-safe container with a lid.

2. Place a medium pot over medium heat. Put in the bay leaf, mustard seeds, peppercorns, and cloves and toast lightly, swirling the pot, just until fragrant, 1 to 2 minutes.

3. Add the honey, vinegar, salt, and 1 cup of water and whisk to combine thoroughly. Let the mixture come to a simmer, then carefully pour it over the veggies in the jar.

4. Let cool, then cover tightly. The pickles will be delicious in 24 hours, but only get better. You can refrigerate and enjoy for up to 3 weeks.

LOVE UP YOUR LEFTOVERS
You can use any cruciferous or nonstarchy root vegetable that's been hanging around your refrigerator for too long.

how to "sunday best" leftovers

FRUIT, THERE IT IS: Dehydrate or roast fruit past its peak—think apples, peaches, or berries—for cocktail garnishes and desserts. Just slice it thin, crosswise (a mandoline is helpful if you have it), arrange in a flat layer on a baking sheet lined with an ungreased silicone baking mat or piece of parchment, and bake in a 200°F oven for 2 to 3 hours or until crisp.

INSANE IN THE GRAIN: Keep containers of cooked quinoa, wild rice, fonio, and amaranth in the fridge, and toss them with whatever leftovers or edible scraps you happen to have for instant, nutritious grain bowls.

MAKE INSTANT MOCHA: Infuse spent coffee grounds in milk or heavy cream and strain them out before using the liquid in chocolate cake batter or to make flavored whipped cream.

GET THE MOST FROM COMPOST: Roast scraps of veggies (cauliflower cores, carrot tops) and then mash them to make a vitamin-rich substitute for potatoes and other starches.

FRY, FRY AGAIN: Turn sticky bun dough (page 25), pizza dough (page 218), or any form of store-bought dough into elephant ears, my favorite childhood treat. Tear off bits of dough, flatten them into pucks, deep-fry, then glaze with butter and salt or cinnamon and sugar.

HIT THE (HOT) SAUCE: Who said hot sauce needs to be red? Purée roasted carrots, pumpkin, or sweet potatoes and blend with your choice of aromatics, acid, and as hot a pepper as you can handle.

TRANSFORM TAKEOUT: Who *doesn't* have containers of leftover rice from takeout? Make like poor twenty-year-old sous chef Adrienne: stir-fry it in a pan, top it with an egg and sriracha, and enjoy it with the only other thing you have in your fridge—beer.

WAFFLE AROUND: Tater Tots and challah aren't the only unusual suspects I stick in my mini waffle maker. Anything starchy, like leftover potatoes, can be crisped up in the waffle iron and cut into wedges to make a base for hors d'oeuvres (or enjoyed all on their own as a solo snack).

GOT MILK? GET RICOTTA: If the expiration date on your milk is rapidly approaching, pour 4 cups of it into a saucepan with ½ teaspoon of kosher salt. Heat the milk to 190°F, stirring occasionally, then remove from the heat and stir in 3 tablespoons of lemon juice. Let sit for 5 minutes while you line a colander with a few layers of cheesecloth and set it over a bowl. Pour the milk mixture over the cheesecloth, and allow it to strain for at least 1 hour. Presto—ricotta!

HAM IT UP: A ham bone is the best friend of beans and greens. Whether it comes from a ham hock or a spiral ham, boil your bone in a pot to create a stock, then use your infused liquid to cook anything from black-eyed peas to collards.

Creamy Vegan Pasta

Whether you're vegan or not, we could probably all stand to take an occasional break from dairy. Cooking down cashews is an ingenious way to create cheese-like creaminess, as is puréeing veggies such as parsnips or cauliflower. You can easily convince your kids (or yourself) that this is actually indulgent fettucine alfredo!

─────────── SERVES 3 OR 4 ───────────

½ pound dry pasta of your choice

2 tablespoons extra-virgin olive oil

2 garlic cloves, sliced

1 medium onion, halved and thinly sliced

½ teaspoon kosher salt, plus more as needed

½ teaspoon freshly ground black pepper, plus more for seasoning

½ cup dry white wine

½ cup raw cashews (optional)

2 cups leftover cooked vegetables of any sort, mashed, roasted, or steamed (see Love Up Your Leftovers)

2 tablespoons nutritional yeast or ¼ cup grated Parmesan cheese (not vegan), plus more for serving

2 tablespoons chopped fresh parsley

2 tablespoons chopped fresh chives

1. Bring a pot of lightly salted water to a boil over medium-high heat. Cook the pasta to al dente, about 1 minute less than indicated on the package directions. Scoop out and reserve two cups of the starchy pasta-cooking water, then drain the pasta in a colander. Rinse the pasta under cool water and set aside.

2. Heat a large saucepan over medium-low heat. Put in the oil, garlic, onion, salt, and pepper. Cook, stirring occasionally, until the onion is tender and translucent, 4 to 5 minutes.

3. Pour in the wine, bring to a simmer, and cook until reduced by half, about 5 minutes. Add the cashews (if using) and 1½ cups of the reserved pasta water. Bring to a boil over high heat, reduce to a simmer, and cook until the cashews are tender, or about 7 minutes.

4. If your leftover vegetables are mashed, whisk them into the liquid to fully incorporate, bring to a simmer, then remove the pan from the heat. If your veggies are roasted or steamed (cauliflower florets, turnips, etc.), add them to the liquid and simmer together until warmed through and very tender, adding a few tablespoons of pasta cooking water as needed.

5. Let the mixture cool for a moment, then transfer it to a blender along with the nutritional yeast. Blend to a smooth paste, adjusting the consistency with as much of the remaining pasta water as needed (make sure it's not too thin—you want it to coat the pasta when tossed together).

6. Pour the sauce back into the pot and warm it up over medium-low heat. Taste and adjust the seasoning, if needed. If the pasta has begun to stick together, rinse it again under cool water while gently separating it with your fingers (works every time, without adding additional oil).

7. Add the pasta to the sauce along with half of the parsley and chives and toss to coat. Divide among serving bowls and sprinkle with the remaining parsley and chives and extra nutritional yeast, if you like.

LOVE UP YOUR LEFTOVERS
You can use Mashed Parsnips (page 156) or Whole-Roasted Cauliflower (page 177) for a velvety veggie sauce.

TASTY TRANSFORMATIONS: LEFTOVERS REIMAGINED

my goodies
Sweets and Desserts

Just like making a sauce from scratch, whipping up dessert is something many of us are hesitant to spend energy on, especially if we've cooked the entire dinner too. When you do take the time to make dessert, it's a clear-cut way of showing that you care. Anyone can open a box of cookies at the end of a meal, but what about offering up a ramekin of Buttermilk Brûlée with Pickled Blueberry Compote (page 252)?

That said, preparing a from-scratch sweet isn't a task you need to undertake every single day. Since most of the following recipes yield multiple servings, they can easily last the whole week through. And incidentally, if you shave a bit of time off your nightly routine by reimagining leftovers for dinner (see the Tasty Transformations chapter), you'll have bought yourself an extra 30 minutes or so that could totally be dedicated to throwing together dessert!

I'll also let you in on a professional pastry chef secret: Most restaurant desserts are prepared ahead in various stages, and they're frequently frozen before they're served. Freezing or chilling the dessert makes the structure better for cutting perfect slices or rewarming or baking off right before serving without sacrificing a bit of their original integrity. You can try this trick to great effect with just about anything in the chapter, from the Roasted White Chocolate Crepe Cake with Hazelnuts and Pecans (page 259), to the Chocolate-Bourbon Pecan Pie (254) and the Apple Pie for Uncle George (page 267).

So put your Sunday Best foot forward and devote a bit of effort—or at least make it look like you did—to a truly spectacular dessert!

No-Churn Strawberry Shortcake Ice Cream

I grew up across the street from the Baskin-Robbins where Michelle and Barack Obama went on their first date. The older kids who worked there kindly treated me to deep discounts, so I would buy myself at least a scoop whenever I possibly could.

As much as I love ice cream, though, I've always lacked the money or space for an at-home ice cream maker. That's why I avail myself of a clever hack—using condensed milk. You see, the aim with ice cream is to keep ice crystals from forming, which is what traditional churning methods achieve. Condensed milk is created by removing all excess water, so it helps make ice cream that's smooth and scoopable instead of gritty and icy, even without endless agitating. Just make sure to stay ahead of your cravings, as this particular recipe needs to be started a day in advance.

By the way, you can use this recipe as a jumping-off point for all manner of no-churn ice creams. Any fruit will work, from bananas to blueberries to peaches and cream!

--- SERVES 4 ---

1½ pounds very ripe strawberries, hulled and halved

1 tablespoon sugar

Grated zest of 1 lemon or 1 tablespoon citrus liqueur, such as Grand Marnier

1 (14-ounce) can sweetened condensed milk, chilled

1 cup heavy cream

1 cup broken shortbread cookies, plus more broken cookies for serving

Whipped cream, for serving

1. Set a handful of the halved strawberries aside for garnish, then place the rest in a zip-top bag with the sugar and lemon zest. Shake to distribute the sugar and zest, giving the bag a little massage, if needed. Let sit at room temperature until you see juices accumulating in the bag, about 10 minutes. Freeze overnight, or up to 1 week. While we're at it, chill the condensed milk in the fridge overnight as well.

2. When you're ready to make the ice cream, place the strawberries, condensed milk, and cream in a large food processor. Process until everything is thoroughly incorporated and smooth, about 30 seconds. It will look lumpy and weird at first, but I promise it will come together.

3. Scrape the strawberry mixture into a large bowl and sprinkle the broken shortbread over the top. Using a spatula, gently fold the components together, just 3 or 4 folds, then transfer to a freezer-safe container with a lid. Cover and freeze until firm, at least 4 hours.

4. Scoop and serve with whipped cream, more shortbread cookies, and the reserved strawberries.

PERFECT PAIRING
This is amazing served with Sugared Biscuits, with or without their Chocolate Gravy (page 269).

Sweet Tea Granita

I was never a huge fan of sweet tea until I started spending summers in Tallahassee, Florida, where I stayed on to work during college breaks. That's when I realized that the aggressively saccharine drink was a godsend against the oppressive heat and humidity. I especially enjoyed it when it was freshly brewed and still a little warm, poured over a tall cup of ice chips. And this refreshing granita recipe absolutely reminds me of that!

SERVES 4

3 black tea bags (Lipton and Luzianne are traditional, but not essential)

1 sprig of mint, plus a few leaves for garnish

½ cup sugar

1 tablespoon fresh lemon juice

Lemon wedges, for garnish (optional)

1. Bring 2 cups of water to a boil in a medium saucepan, then turn off the heat and slide the pot off the burner. Add the tea bags (with the strings hanging over the pot lip) and the mint sprig and let steep for 10 minutes.

2. Remove the mint and tea bags (resist the urge to squeeze the liquid out of the tea bags). Stir in the sugar until fully dissolved, followed by the lemon juice. Stir in 2 cups of cold water, then pour the sweet tea into an 8-inch square glass baking dish.

3. Place the baking dish in the freezer and stir the tea with a fork every half hour until mostly frozen but still slushy, about 1½ hours.

4. Scoop the granita into a large bowl and, using a fork, stir well for 10 to 15 seconds, until the crystals are smaller and smoother. Cover and return to the freezer for about 30 minutes.

5. Using an ice cream scoop, divide the granita into glasses. Garnish with mint leaves and lemon wedges (if using) and enjoy the cooldown!

The Best Baked Apples

My mom was very strict about our sugar intake. No matter how hard we tried to negotiate with her, my sister and I were only allowed a maximum of three cookies, three times a week. And once our quota was met, it was met. If we got to indulge in sweets on the other days, it was likely to be apples, which my mom would halve, core, sprinkle with cinnamon and sugar, and microwave. The treat was quick and uncomplicated but inarguably delicious and cemented my love for easy and effortless desserts.

When I started working at Le Bernardin, I was excited to find the restaurant actually had baked apples on the menu. Undoubtedly elegant without being overly fussy, the caramelized fruit cooks down into a beautiful, compact disc that's concentrated in flavor and utterly charming in its simplicity.

SERVES 6

½ cup (100g) light brown sugar

2 tablespoons unsalted butter

1 vanilla bean, split lengthwise and seeds scraped (save the pod for another use, like Yuzu Banana Pudding on page 251!)

⅛ teaspoon kosher salt

⅛ teaspoon ground cardamom

6 crisp apples, such as Honeycrisp or Gala, peeled, quartered, and cored

1. Preheat the oven to 325°F.

2. Put the brown sugar in a large, oven-safe stainless-steel or enameled skillet and melt, stirring, over medium heat. Cook until the sugar is bubbling and has darkened to a medium-amber color, 5 to 6 minutes. Turn off the heat and stir in the butter, vanilla seeds, salt, cardamom, and 2 tablespoons of water.

3. Arrange the apples, cored-side up and tightly spaced, in the pan and cover tightly with aluminum foil. Bake for 30 minutes.

4. Open the foil and, using tongs, turn the apples cored-side down. Cover tightly again and bake for another 30 minutes, or until tender. Carefully vent a corner of the foil to release the steam, then serve the apples with their warm syrup poured over top.

Yuzu Banana Pudding

I debuted this dessert on the finale of *Top Chef* to really drive home my culinary point of view. Needless to say, banana pudding is a big deal in the African American community, and omnipresent at family functions and gatherings. I devised this recipe to honor that, while incorporating the classic techniques and global influences I've acquired throughout my career. Because that's what Sunday Best is about—finding ways to elevate and celebrate every moment and every dish.

SERVES 8 TO 10

1 quart whole milk

1 teaspoon pure vanilla extract (if you have a scraped vanilla bean pod, use that instead!)

4 egg yolks (save the whites for meringue!), at room temperature

1½ cups (300g) sugar

¼ cup (35g) cornstarch

½ teaspoon kosher salt

½ teaspoon ground ginger

4 tablespoons (½ stick) unsalted butter, cut into pieces

½ cup no-sodium bottled yuzu juice (juice of 1 lemon works in a pinch)

1 (11-ounce) box Nilla wafers (shortbread cookies or crushed ice cream cones work too)

3 *just*-ripe bananas (very ripe bananas will turn brown too quickly)

1. Heat the milk and vanilla in a medium saucepan over medium-low heat until bubbles just begin to form at the edges, about 5 minutes.

2. In a large bowl, whisk the egg yolks, sugar, cornstarch, and salt until smooth and lump-free. Gradually whisk ½ cup of the hot milk into the egg yolk mixture to bring the temperature up (this is called "tempering"; it ensures the shock of the heat doesn't curdle and cook the yolks).

3. Whisk the yolk mixture back into the pot. Raise the heat to medium and cook, whisking constantly and making sure to scrape the bottom and edges of the pot, until the custard is thick and smooth, 10 to 12 minutes. Remove the pot from the heat and stir in the ginger, butter, and yuzu juice until fully incorporated. Allow to cool for about 2 minutes, then press a piece of plastic wrap directly onto the surface of the custard.

4. In an 8-inch square baking dish, arrange an even layer of Nilla wafers. Lightly crush a few wafers and sprinkle the pieces over the whole wafers, filling in the gaps.

5. Peel the bananas and slice them about ¼ inch thick. Layer the banana slices over the wafers. Spoon half of the warm custard on top of the banana slices and smooth the top with a spatula, pressing gently to force the custard into the nooks between the bananas.

6. Reserving 6 to 8 wafers for the top, repeat the layering with wafer cookies, banana slices, and the remaining custard. Break up the reserved wafers and sprinkle over the top. Cover with plastic wrap pressed directly on the surface and chill for at least 2 hours before serving.

Buttermilk Brûlée *with* Pickled Blueberry Compote

I've got to tell you, nothing makes me madder than breaking through the crust of a crème brûlée only to find that the custard underneath is only half an inch thick. It's the worst kind of tease. I'm getting worked up just thinking about it.

Since I insist on serving (and eating) an entire ramekin full of custard, I use buttermilk in my base, which acts as a perfect foil for all that rich unctuousness. I've also doubled down on tang with a topping of pickled blueberries, which cuts right through the sugar-on-sugar sweetness.

SERVES 4

PICKLED BLUEBERRY COMPOTE

½ cup white wine vinegar or red wine vinegar

1 teaspoon lemon zest

1 teaspoon fresh lemon juice

⅓ cup (65g) granulated sugar

Small pinch of nutmeg, ground cloves, or ground juniper

2 cups blueberries, fresh or frozen

2 teaspoons cornstarch

BUTTERMILK BRÛLÉE

6 egg yolks

⅓ cup (65g) granulated sugar

1 cup heavy cream

1 cup buttermilk

1 teaspoon pure vanilla extract

⅛ teaspoon kosher salt

¼ cup light brown sugar (50g) or granulated sugar (50g), for the crust

1. Preheat the oven to 300°F.

2. MAKE THE PICKLED BLUEBERRY COMPOTE: In a medium saucepan or sauté pan (wide enough to fit most of the berries in a single layer), combine the vinegar, lemon zest, lemon juice, sugar, and nutmeg. Bring to a bare simmer over medium heat, stirring to dissolve the sugar. Add the blueberries, shaking the pan to coat the berries. Simmer, swirling the pan occasionally (do not stir with a spoon; it will burst the berries), until the berries are warmed and softened but still intact, about 5 minutes.

3. In a small bowl, stir 1 tablespoon of room-temperature water into the cornstarch until it is dissolved, then pour the slurry into the pan while swirling. Continue to simmer, gently stirring, until the liquid thickens, 3 to 4 minutes. Transfer the compote to a glass container and let cool until ready to use.

4. MAKE THE BUTTERMILK BRÛLÉE: Place the egg yolks and granulated sugar in a blender and blend on medium speed until lightened and a little fluffy, 1 minute.

5. Combine the cream, buttermilk, vanilla, and salt in a small saucepan and bring just to a simmer over medium heat. With the blender on low speed, add ¼ cup of the hot cream mixture. Gradually pour in the remaining cream mixture, increasing the speed to just short of medium. The blender should run for 3 to 4 minutes total to ensure the mixture is smooth and lump-free.

6. Select a baking dish that will fit all of your ramekins with about ¼ inch of space between them. Bring a kettle of water to a boil.

7. Divide the custard mixture among four 6-ounce ramekins, filling each almost to the top. Place the ramekins in the baking dish and pour enough boiling water into the dish to reach about halfway up the sides of the ramekins.

8. Place the dish in the oven and bake until the centers are barely set, 30 to 45 minutes (the time is highly dependent on how hot your oven runs; you may need more or less time). Carefully remove the ramekins to a rack and let cool for 30 minutes to 1 hour, then refrigerate until well chilled, at least 3 hours and up to 3 days.

9. When you're ready to serve, grab a kitchen torch or heat your broiler to high. Sprinkle 1 tablespoon of the brown sugar over each ramekin. If using a torch, hold the flame about 2 inches away from the sugar-coated surface, moving it around to evenly melt and caramelize the sugar until it is bubbly and giving off little wafts of sweet smoke. If using the broiler, place ramekins 4 to 5 inches below the heat source and let the sugar melt and bubble. Remove as soon as the sugar turns deep brown in spots, keeping close watch, as all broilers function differently.

10. Dollop a spoonful of compote on one side of each ramekin and serve.

MAKE AHEAD

The Pickled Blueberry Compote can be prepared and refrigerated up to 6 days before serving, and the Buttermilk Brûlée can be prepared and refrigerated up to 3 days before serving.

Chocolate-Bourbon Pecan Pie

During our college years, my sister and I regularly undertook sixteen-hour road trips from Florida to our home back in Chicago. We'd always see billboards for the Jack Daniel Distillery on our drive through Tennessee, so one time, we decided to finally go check it out. Problem was, while the ads made it seem like it was right off the interstate, it was actually an hour-plus drive out of our way. Since it had already messed up our timeline for getting home, we decided to make the most of the journey and eat our way through all the pecan pies that the distillery—and various other eateries on our trip through the South—had to offer.

Unsurprisingly, pecan pie (ideally gussied up with bourbon and chocolate!) became one of our favorite things to serve for Cheatham Soul Food Sundays. And it's one of the first dishes I proudly brought to Saturday family meal at Le Bernardin, baking it on late Friday night, as soon as I got home from work!

──────────── MAKES ONE 9-INCH PIE ────────────

Nonstick cooking spray or vegetable oil

1 (9-inch) piecrust

3 large eggs

¼ cup (20g) unsweetened cocoa powder

1 cup dark corn syrup

¾ cup (150g) sugar

1 tablespoon cornstarch

2 tablespoons bourbon (feel free to substitute room-temperature water)

4 tablespoons (½ stick) unsalted butter or dairy-free butter substitute

1 teaspoon pure vanilla extract

¼ teaspoon kosher salt

⅔ cup semisweet chocolate chips

1 to 1½ cups pecan halves (or 1 cup pecan pieces)

Whipped cream or vanilla ice cream, for serving

1. Preheat the oven to 375°F with a rack in the center position. Line a baking sheet with parchment paper or aluminum foil.

2. Spray a 9-inch deep-dish pie pan with oil and lightly press the rolled-out piecrust into the pan, crimping the top edges. You can also use a 9-inch springform pan: Spray it with oil and press the piecrust into the bottom and edges and halfway up the sides, flattening any folds and making sure the crust is touching the pan. Pinch the top edges so they are even all the way around. Refrigerate until ready to use.

3. In a large bowl, beat the eggs and cocoa powder until just combined. Set aside.

4. Place a small saucepan over medium-low heat and pour in the corn syrup and sugar, stirring to combine until the sugar is completely melted. In a small bowl, combine the cornstarch and bourbon and stir until no lumps remain. Stir the cornstarch slurry into the pot, bring to a boil, and cook for 1 minute. Turn off the heat and stir in the butter, vanilla, and salt with a wooden spoon or a spatula until fully combined and smooth. Let cool for 10 minutes.

5. Sprinkle the chocolate chips evenly over the crust, then arrange the pecan halves in concentric circles on top (or just sprinkle them in—no judgment, just depends on the time you have).

6. Gradually whisk the slightly cooled syrup into the bowl with the eggs and cocoa powder until thoroughly mixed with no visible streaks. Pour the mixture over the pecans, using a rubber spatula to get all that goodness out of the bowl.

7. Place the pie on the prepared baking sheet and bake on the middle rack for 10 minutes. Reduce the oven temperature to 350°F and continue baking until the pie is just set in the center when tapped and the top looks beautifully crusted, about 45 minutes.

8. Let the pie cool completely on a wire rack before slicing, at least 30 minutes. Serve as is or with vanilla ice cream or barely sweetened whipped cream.

MAKE AHEAD
This pie slices beautifully after it has been refrigerated overnight.

EXTRAS
Any leftover syrup can be used to make candied nuts. Boil nuts and syrup together for a few minutes in a pot, spread into a single layer on a parchment-covered baking sheet, and roast at 350°F for about 10 minutes until fragrant and crisp!

Sugar-and-Spice-Dusted Calas

(AKA RICE BEIGNETS)

Everyone has heard of beignets, but I say it's time for a resurgence of their lesser-known cousin, calas. From the West African Nupe word for "fried cake," these little fritters are formed from sweetened and spiced rice. And they were commonly sold by African American vendors in New Orleans's French Quarter, in the mid-1700s. In fact, during the days of slavery, many women were able to buy their freedom with the money they earned selling calas and café au lait on the side.

—————————————————— MAKES ABOUT 2 DOZEN CALAS ——————————————————

Neutral oil, such as canola or grapeseed, for frying

2 cups cooked white rice

1 tablespoon orange zest

½ teaspoon ground cinnamon

½ teaspoon ground allspice

1 cup (140g) all-purpose flour

⅓ cup (65g) granulated sugar

½ teaspoon kosher salt, plus a pinch

2 teaspoons baking powder

3 large eggs

1 teaspoon pure vanilla extract

⅓ cup (40g) confectioners' sugar

1. Fill a wide, shallow pot with oil, about 2 inches deep, for frying. Heat the oil to 360°F over medium-low heat while you make the batter.

2. In a large microwave-safe bowl, combine the rice, orange zest, cinnamon, and allspice. Microwave for 30 seconds or until the rice is a little steamy and the orange zest is aromatic.

3. Mix in the flour, granulated sugar, and salt with a fork so the rice grains separate and get coated in flour. Let the mixture cool slightly, then mix in the baking powder. Set aside.

4. In another medium bowl, whisk the eggs and vanilla for 30 to 45 seconds, or until the eggs are lightened in color and have an airy foam on top. Use a spoon to stir the eggs into the rice mixture until thoroughly combined.

5. Before you start frying, get the following items ready: two spoons to drop the batter into the oil, a slotted spoon to remove the calas from the oil, a paper-towel-lined tray or plate, and a basket strainer or sifter for the powdered sugar.

6. When the oil has reached 360°F, use one spoon to scoop the batter from the bowl. Hold it right above the surface of the oil and use the other spoon to carefully scrape the batter down into the oil (this will not only help shape the calas, but also keep the batter from splashing hot oil on you!). Repeat with as many calas as you can fit without overcrowding in the pot. Work in batches if needed.

7. Use the slotted spoon to flip the calas once they have browned on one side, about 2 minutes per side. Adjust the heat as needed to prevent the temperature from dropping below 360°F.

8. When the calas are GBD (golden brown and delicious) all over, use the slotted spoon to transfer them to your paper-towel-lined tray, and immediately sprinkle them with a layer of confectioners' sugar while piping hot. Repeat with the remaining calas, transfer to a serving plate, and sift any remaining sugar over the full plate of calas to pile it on, French Quarter style.

PRO TIP

If you don't have a deep-frying thermometer, you're looking for the batter to bubble, sizzle, and float as soon as it hits the oil. If the batter sinks without any bubbling, the oil is too cool. If the batter gets dark brown very quickly, the oil is too hot (the outside will brown before the inside is cooked).

Roasted White Chocolate Crepe Cake
with Hazelnuts and Pecans

With its stacked layers of roasted white chocolate, mascarpone cream, and crunchy hazelnuts, this "cake" looks truly spectacular. But there are so many shortcuts you can take in making it, from purchasing packaged precooked crepes to setting aside extras from a batch made for breakfast. You can even prepare the crepe batter or cook the crepes the day before, or construct the entire cake in advance and freeze it!

By the way, if you thought you hated white chocolate (*very* much like me), you need to experience it roasted. The smell is out of this world, and caramelizing all of that milk fat gives it an incredible dulce de leche quality.

— SERVES 12 —

CREPES

5 large eggs

2½ cups whole milk (or nondairy milk)

2½ cups (350g) all-purpose flour

4 tablespoons (½ stick) butter, melted

¼ cup (50g) granulated sugar

¼ teaspoon kosher salt

1 teaspoon pure vanilla extract

Vegetable oil, for greasing

ROASTED WHITE CHOCOLATE FILLING

1½ cups white chocolate chips

1 cup heavy cream

6 tablespoons (¾ stick) unsalted butter, at room temperature

½ cup (60g) confectioners' sugar

8 ounces mascarpone cheese

½ teaspoon kosher salt

1 cup toasted hazelnuts

1 cup toasted pecans

1. MAKE THE CREPES: In a blender, combine the eggs, milk, flour, butter, sugar, salt, and vanilla. Purée on medium speed until completely blended, with no lumps, and a little frothy on top, 1 to 2 minutes. Place the lid on the blender, remove the blender jar from the base, and refrigerate for at least 1 hour and up to 24 hours.

2. To cook the crepes, have ready a spatula, a baking sheet, and a couple of pieces of parchment paper. Heat an 8-inch nonstick skillet over medium-high heat and rub the pan with a little vegetable oil, using a folded paper towel. Reduce the heat to medium-low and lift the pan slightly off the burner. Pour about ¼ cup of batter into the pan while slowly tilting and swirling it so the batter coats the bottom in a thin layer. Set the pan back on the burner and cook for 30 seconds, until firmed up, then carefully flip the crepe with the spatula and cook for 10 to 15 seconds on the second side, until just firmed up. Transfer to the baking sheet.

3. Repeat with the rest of the batter, overlapping the cooked crepes on the baking sheet slightly. When you have a full layer, cover it with parchment paper and start another. The cooled crepes can be stacked and refrigerated for up to 3 days.

4. MAKE THE ROASTED WHITE CHOCOLATE FILLING: Preheat the oven to 325°F.

(recipe continues)

5. Place the white chocolate chips in a large glass baking dish and bake until the edges caramelize, 10 to 12 minutes. Stir and continue baking until the edges are deep brown, about 7 minutes more, checking occasionally and stirring if some edges are browning too quickly.

6. Scrape the roasted white chocolate into a blender with ⅔ cup of the cream. Blend on low to medium speed until smooth, adding 1 or 2 more tablespoons of the cream if needed to keep the mixture moving.

7. Place the butter and confectioners' sugar in a large bowl. Beat with a hand mixer on medium speed until light and fluffy, 3 to 4 minutes (you can also use a stand mixer). Add the mascarpone and salt and beat for another 2 minutes. Scrape in the roasted white chocolate purée and continue beating until fully incorporated. Add the remainder of the heavy cream and beat until just incorporated.

8. Place the hazelnuts in a food processor and pulse 3 or 4 times, then add the pecans and pulse until both are finely chopped. Transfer to a small bowl.

9. ASSEMBLE THE CAKE: Place one crepe on a large serving plate. Spread it evenly with 2 to 3 heaping tablespoons of the filling and sprinkle evenly with 1 to 2 tablespoons of the chopped nuts. Cover with another crepe and repeat until all the crepes and filling are used up, making sure you have a crepe as the final layer. (Don't fret if you have leftover crepes; you can freeze them and save for another use.) Cover with plastic wrap and refrigerate for at least 2 hours and up to overnight to set fully.

10. To serve, slice the cake straight from the refrigerator (keep in mind that the cake slices are *infinitely* more attractive than the whole cake) and garnish with any leftover chopped nuts.

FYI
White chocolate will not melt and brown evenly, so don't expect it to. It will look funny and crumbly but smell and taste amazing!

Salted Vanilla-Coconut Rice Pudding

I hate to say it, but I never enjoyed rice pudding prepared by my mom's side of the family, which was basically just rice cooked in sugared milk. But when it came to pudding from the Mississippi side, thickened with egg yolks to make it more of a custard—well. That was a different story entirely.

As for the salted element of this recipe, that inspiration came from Yasha, the pastry chef I worked under at Sandestin in Florida. He taught me that salt belongs in *each and every dessert*. It enhances and elevates all the other ingredients and helps your tongue pick up distinct flavors.

SERVES 4 TO 6

2 cups whole milk

1½ cups unsweetened coconut milk

1 vanilla bean, split lengthwise, or 1 teaspoon pure vanilla extract

½ cup short-grain rice

2 egg yolks

⅓ cup (65g) sugar

¼ teaspoon kosher salt

¼ teaspoon ground cardamom (optional)

½ cup sliced almonds, toasted

¼ cup toasted shredded coconut (sweetened or unsweetened, your choice)

1. Combine the milk, coconut milk, vanilla bean (if using extract, don't add it yet), and rice in a medium pot and bring to a boil over medium-high heat, stirring occasionally. Reduce the heat to medium-low and simmer, stirring regularly, until the mixture is thickened and the rice is tender, 25 to 30 minutes.

2. In a small bowl, whisk the egg yolks and sugar together. Stir a spoonful of the hot rice into the yolk mixture to temper the yolks, then scrape the yolk mixture into the pot and cook, stirring constantly, for 3 to 4 minutes. Add the salt and cardamom, if using. If using vanilla extract, add it now as well.

3. Continue to cook, stirring frequently, until the pudding is thick enough to coat a spoon. Taste and adjust with a pinch of salt or sugar as needed.

4. Remove the vanilla bean and divide the pudding into serving bowls. Top with toasted almonds and coconut.

MAKE AHEAD
The rice pudding can be prepared up to 2 days ahead. It will thicken when chilled, but you can quickly thin it out by warming it in a pot with a splash of milk or water.

how to "sunday best" desserts

YOU CAN PICKLE THAT: Pickled elements aren't just for savory dishes. A quick dip in vinegar and sugar really makes fruit pop and adds a deliciously unique dimension to desserts—especially when you infuse the pickling brine with spices like juniper or star anise.

SWITCH UP YOUR MILK: There's nothing "vanilla" about desserts made with tangy alternative dairies, like buttermilk, goat's milk, or crème fraîche.

GET TOASTED: Needless to say, whole or crushed toasted nuts contribute terrific taste and texture to sweets of all sorts. But you also can (and should!) lightly toast up to ½ cup of the flour called for in cookie or cake recipes for an intriguingly warm and earthy note.

BE A POD PERSON: If you're going to splurge on vanilla beans, be sure to make the most of the pod as well as the seeds. Once you've scraped it clean, you can store the dried pod in an airtight jar of sugar to infuse the sugar with pure vanilla essence, or pop it in a bottle with cheap vodka to make your own vanilla extract. Incidentally, if you ever come across vanilla paste, buy it! More deeply flavored than extract and chock-full of seeds, it's the next best thing to purchasing super-expensive whole vanilla beans.

TOOL AROUND WITH TEXTURE: Even the simplest and most basic desserts can benefit from a bit of textural contrast. That's why my mom often added granola to the top of her microwaved apples. Look for ways to create balance by sprinkling toasted coconut over pudding, crumbling cookies over ice cream, or dolloping crème fraîche or mascarpone over flaky piecrusts.

BRING THE HEAT: Even if your dessert is meant to be served cold, that doesn't mean you can't roast a few of the elements first. Especially for fruit, from pineapple to peaches to raspberries, roasting concentrates the flavor and draws out the syrupy juices without adding excess sugar.

ENSURE A CLEAN RELEASE: As long as the sides of your pan are well greased, the edges of your cake will reliably pull away. That's not the case for the bottom, however, and even the smallest scratch in your pan can create a stuck-on mess. So make sure to line the base with a small piece of parchment paper every time you bake.

SAVE THE CRUMBS: Even if you've experienced sticking, make the most of your mess! Gather stray cake crumbles (or whatever parts of the cake you may have trimmed) and bake them in a 250 to 300°F oven until crispy to add a compellingly textured garnish to your creation.

THINK OUT OF THE BOX: There's no shame in seeking a shortcut via boxed cake mixes, especially since they're so easy to elevate through a few simple tweaks. Substitute melted butter for oil; add a bit of vanilla extract, fresh vanilla seeds, or vanilla paste; or sprinkle in a bit of nutmeg. There's a reason the underappreciated spice is often stirred into béchamel—it really amps up the flavor of anything creamy and sweet.

ADD FINESSE TO FRUIT PLATES: Fresh herbs are the way to turn even the most average supermarket assortment into an elegant display. Blueberries and rosemary, strawberries and basil, and cherries and thyme are all mind-blowing pairings.

Apple Pie for Uncle George

It wasn't until I was thirteen years old that I found out that Uncle George wasn't my real uncle. I was devastated! My dad's decades-long close friend, Uncle George lived half a block away from us, and the two would often get together to listen to jazz and have a drink.

George was also the family connoisseur of apple pie. He never came across one he wouldn't gladly eat, though he was always quick to give a detailed analysis of how it could be improved. Naturally, it became a long-running mission for my sister and I to develop an apple pie that would bowl over Uncle George.

When he was diagnosed with cancer about ten years ago, it kicked us into high gear. Upon arriving home from college for holiday break, we got to work perfecting apple pie, and eventually brought him our top contenders. Upon taking a bite of one, he exclaimed it was the best he'd ever had in his life, and the search was off to find any better. This is that pie.

MAKES ONE 9-INCH PIE

CRUMBLE TOPPING

¾ cup (105g) all-purpose flour

½ teaspoon kosher salt

½ teaspoon ground cinnamon

¼ teaspoon ground allspice

½ cup (100g) dark brown sugar, packed

6 tablespoons (¾ stick) cold unsalted butter, cubed

¾ cup (75g) old-fashioned oats

APPLE PIE

1 (9-inch) piecrust (homemade is great, but a good store-bought crust will work too)

6 tart apples, such as Granny Smith, halved and cored

½ cup (1 stick) unsalted butter

¼ cup (35g) all-purpose flour

2 tablespoons bourbon, brandy, or cognac (or water in a pinch)

1 tablespoon vanilla

⅓ cup (65g) granulated sugar

½ cup (100g) dark brown sugar, packed

½ teaspoon ground cinnamon

¼ teaspoon freshly grated nutmeg

Pinch of kosher salt

1. MAKE THE CRUMBLE TOPPING: Combine the flour, salt, cinnamon, allspice, brown sugar, and butter in a small food processor. Pulse the ingredients until the butter is broken up and thoroughly incorporated. Pour the mixture into a large bowl and add the oats. Use your hands to work the oats in, squeezing handfuls of the mixture into clumps, then place the bowl in the refrigerator.

2. MAKE THE APPLE PIE: Dust your work surface with flour and roll your piecrust out to ¼ inch thick. Lightly oil an 8-inch springform pan and press your crust into the pan, coming up the sides about 4 inches deep.

3. Preheat the oven to 375°F with a rack in the center position. Line a baking sheet with aluminum foil.

4. Place the apples cut-side down on your cutting board so they're lying flat, then cut ¼-inch-thick *slices* that have even thickness from end to end (not wedges, which are inherently uneven). Shingle the slices in layers in the crust until they reach just below the top of the crust. Place the pan in the refrigerator.

(recipe continues)

5. Melt the butter in a small pot on medium-low heat. Whisk in the flour and let cook for 2 minutes. Whisk in the bourbon, ¼ cup water, vanilla, and the granulated and brown sugars, and let the mixture come to a simmer at the edges.

6. When the edges begin to bubble, whisk constantly in circles for 2 minutes. Lift the whisk and look at the syrup. It should look smooth and glossy and slide off the bottom of the pot when tilted. If it looks grainy and the butter is separating, add another tablespoon of water and whisk for another 1 to 2 minutes, until smooth. Turn off the heat and whisk in the cinnamon, nutmeg, and salt.

7. Remove the apple-filled piecrust from the fridge (don't worry if the apples have browned a little; you can't tell after the pie cooks) and pour the warm syrup over the apples. Let the syrup settle a bit, then take the chilled crumble topping from the refrigerator and crumble it over the top of the pie, covering the entire surface. It will seem like a lot of topping, but trust me, you want it all. Place the pie on the prepared baking sheet and place on the middle rack in the oven.

8. Bake until the syrup is bubbling and the crumble is browned and crisp, 40 to 45 minutes. Set the pie on a wire rack and let cool for at least an hour before slicing, if not longer. If you cut the pie before the filling sets, it will be runny.

9. This pie is even better the next day served cold, since it slices beautifully. Just cover the top with plastic wrap, and store it in the fridge for up to 1 week. If you'd like it warm, pop the slices on a baking sheet in a 350°F oven for 7 to 10 minutes, or microwave for 30 seconds.

MAKE AHEAD
The crumble can be made up to 4 days ahead and refrigerated. And the pie itself gets even better the next day and slices beautifully after chilling.

Sugared Biscuits and Chocolate Gravy

Sweet biscuits and gravy sounds like a gimmick, right? Well, there's documentation of this dish being made as far back as the 1700s. It's a fascinating example of how migration along the Appalachian trading route helped establish Indigenous Mexican influence on Southern cuisine.

Thickened in the traditional French way, warm, spicy, and faintly bitter Mexican chocolate ganache forms the "gravy" for raw-sugar-crusted biscuits. It's great with any biscuit recipe really, though. The relationship of sugared biscuits to plain ones is very similar to that of pâte sucrée (sweet pastry crust) to pâte brisée (savory pie dough).

SERVES 8

SUGARED BISCUITS

2 cups (280g) all-purpose flour, plus more for dusting

¼ cup (30g) confectioners' sugar

1 tablespoon baking powder

1 teaspoon kosher salt

6 tablespoons (¾ stick) unsalted butter

½ cup whole milk (or buttermilk or dairy-free substitute), cold

2 tablespoons Demerara sugar, for topping (regular sugar will do fine)

CHOCOLATE GRAVY

3 tablespoons unsalted butter

3 tablespoons all-purpose flour

⅓ cup (25g) unsweetened cocoa powder

⅔ cup (130g) granulated sugar

½ teaspoon kosher salt

½ teaspoon ground cinnamon

⅛ teaspoon chili powder

Pinch of ground cayenne pepper (kinda optional, although I recommend using)

2 cups whole milk

1 teaspoon pure vanilla extract

Strong black coffee, for serving

1. Preheat the oven to 400°F. Line a baking sheet with parchment paper.

2. MAKE THE SUGARED BISCUITS: In a large bowl, combine the flour, confectioners' sugar, baking powder, and salt. Cut 4 tablespoons of the butter into cubes and use your hands to work them into the dry ingredients until the mixture looks like wet sand.

3. Gradually add the milk, pressing and folding with your hands in the bowl to combine the ingredients and form a dough. Turn the dough out onto a work surface lightly dusted with flour and gently knead it once or twice.

4. Flour your hands and pat the dough into a rectangle a little less than 1 inch thick. Melt the remaining 2 tablespoons butter in a small bowl in the microwave and brush it over the top of the dough. Sprinkle evenly with the Demerara sugar.

5. Cut the dough into 2-inch squares (circles are too wasteful) and place them on the prepared baking sheet. Bake until the biscuits are golden brown, 12 to 15 minutes. Let cool on a wire rack.

(recipe continues)

6. MAKE THE CHOCOLATE GRAVY: Melt the butter in a small saucepan over medium heat. Whisk in the flour. Whisk in the cocoa powder, granulated sugar, salt, cinnamon, chili powder, and cayenne. Whisking constantly, add the milk little by little.

7. Bring to a simmer, whisking frequently, then reduce the heat to medium-low, so the gravy doesn't burn, and continue cooking until thickened, 3 to 5 minutes. Remove from the heat and stir in the vanilla.

8. Arrange the biscuits on serving plates and spoon the gravy over the tops. Serve immediately with strong black coffee.

SUNDAY BEST FINESSE
Garnish with candied orange, satsuma, or kumquat peels for an upscale look and a citrusy kick.

life lessons in
yasha's kitchen

After college ended, I took on an internship at Sandestin Golf and Beach Resort in Florida, where a chef named Yasha Becker had ruled the pastry department for years (and still does!). He was entirely self-taught but would invariably have some sous chef just out of culinary school who thought they knew everything and would try to change his recipes or techniques. He was always so cool and laid-back about it, saying that if they could teach him something new, he'd be happy to learn. But they were always wrong. Yasha showed me that you just don't deviate when it comes to technique. The reason someone developed a way of doing something is because it works. These early lessons blew my mind.

He also kept an assortment of three-ring binders filled with recipes, each of them credited to other chefs he'd worked with, such as "Bill's Pastry Cream." On the last day of my internship, besides gifting me with a collection of all the tools I'd need to start my career, he offered to let me Xerox any recipes I wanted from the binders (this was pre-internet, remember), as long as I promised to always give those chefs credit.

And there's a memory that I prize just as much as those recipes. One early morning when I was between double shifts, Yasha told me to grab a cup of coffee and join him just outside the pastry kitchen, which looked over the Gulf of Mexico. The sun was rising and the dolphins were jumping. He told me, "No matter how hard you're working, take a moment to appreciate what's going on around you. No matter where you are, just remember to enjoy life."

Roasted Pineapple Cornmeal Cake

The base cake in this recipe may well become your go-to, since it's endlessly versatile. You can simply top with sifted powdered sugar and orange zest or dollop with whipped cream and berries, but I love making pineapple upside-down cake with it—a staple of buffet tables at Southern Baptist church rectories.

My great-grandmother's house was on Farish Street in Jackson, Mississippi, which was essentially the epicenter of Black life in town. The church was a stone's throw away from her place, as was Big Apple Inn, renowned for its pig ear sandwiches. So that was summer in Mississippi for me—Grandma Lula's house, pig ear sandwiches, and pineapple upside-down cake in the basement of a Baptist church.

MAKES ONE 12-INCH CAKE

6 cups fresh pineapple chunks (from 1 large ripe pineapple)

¼ cup dark rum

1½ cups (210g) all-purpose flour

½ cup (70g) fine yellow cornmeal

¾ cup (150g) granulated sugar

1 tablespoon baking powder

½ teaspoon kosher salt

Zest of ½ orange

½ cup coconut oil, melted

1 cup whole milk, coconut milk, or nondairy creamer

2 large eggs

1 teaspoon pure vanilla extract

½ cup (1 stick) unsalted butter

½ cup (100g) dark brown sugar, packed

1. Preheat the oven to 425°F.

2. Spread the pineapple chunks in a single layer on a baking sheet. Roast until the edges begin to caramelize and turn dark brown, 10 to 15 minutes. Give the pineapple a stir and continue cooking until the juices in the pan have reduced and started to brown. Remove from the oven and pour the rum around the pineapple, stirring to dissolve all the caramelized juice. Let cool. Reduce the oven temperature to 350°F.

3. In a large bowl, combine the flour, cornmeal, granulated sugar, baking powder, salt, and orange zest. In a separate medium bowl, whisk together the coconut oil, milk, eggs, and vanilla. Stirring with a wooden spoon, gradually pour the liquid mixture into the dry ingredients; stir until the batter is smooth.

4. Scrape the roasted pineapple and all the liquid from the baking sheet into a food processor and pulse until the pineapple is finely chopped.

5. Line a baking sheet with parchment paper or aluminum foil.

6. Heat a 10-inch cast-iron skillet over medium heat and put in the butter and brown sugar. Cook, stirring occasionally, until the sugar is bubbling and darkens slightly, about 5 minutes. Remove the pan from the heat and let cool for a couple of minutes.

(recipe continues)

7. Carefully spoon the roasted pineapple over the caramelized sugar, and use a spatula to spread it into an even layer, almost to the edges of the pan. Pour the cake batter over the pineapple and spread it into an even layer. Place the skillet on the prepared baking sheet and transfer to the oven.

8. Bake until a cake tester or toothpick inserted in the center comes out clean, about 45 minutes. Place the skillet on a rack (or a cool burner grate) and let cool for 10 minutes.

9. Place a large serving plate upside down over the skillet and invert the cake onto the plate. Spoon any pineapple remaining in the pan over the cake. Let cool for a few more minutes, then serve warm.

SUNDAY BEST FINESSE
Serve slices of warm cake with coconut ice cream.

Acknowledgments

Writing a cookbook was a pipe dream of mine. Something I've always wanted, but never really thought I'd get the opportunity to do. I'd jot down a few recipes and a couple of paragraphs of what could be an introduction when I would get home late at night from the restaurants I worked in. But inevitably, the present, pressing needs of those restaurants would always end up pushing my visions of a cookbook onto the back burner.

That was, until I met Sarah Zorn at *Cherry Bombe* magazine's annual jubilee in New York City shortly after my season of *Top Chef* aired. She introduced me to Sarah Smith at the David Black Agency and we got to work.

During the process, I saw how many people it takes to bring such a book to life, and I am so fortunate to have so many people who have helped and supported me along the way in this project. First is Stephen Bailey, my husband, who never misses an opportunity to cheer me on, keep me motivated, troubleshoot ideas, and nudge me and make sure I know how much he loves me no matter what. My mother, Susan, has provided me with countless hours of advice and guidance throughout my life and career in restaurants and is always there to offer encouragement or a swift kick in the behind if I'm slacking. Without her, none of this would have been possible. My sister and best friend, Jacqueline, has supported me in more ways than she could ever know; from answering calls at 1 a.m. so I could vent about the sexist or racist antics of my coworkers to hopping a red-eye flight to New York if I was moving and needed help. The help they all provided when I was writing recipes, looking for photos, or asking hundreds of questions about family traditions and foodways has been invaluable.

Big Sister (Mrs. Ruby Cannon-Cheatham), my great-aunt, who I love dearly, has been one of my closest friends since I was in college at FAMU. She has given me more family history, stories, and recipes as the years go on. She is soon to be ninety-six but has slowed down only a little and still tells me she hopes to see me on *Rachael Ray* someday. My father, Jack, made sure that Jacqui and I had a solid foundation and relationships with our family both in Chicago and in Mississippi. He taught us the history of our family, of ourselves, and made sure that we saw the beauty in both. Chelsea Harvey, my sister-cousin, is the patron saint of chefs and restaurants in Chicago. Ceola, Aunt Cookie, and Aunt Giselle have provided stories and food that nourished our hearts and minds, and were always happy to walk us through how to cook something, even over the phone . . . because recipes are never written down in our family.

My thanks go to Chef Eric Ripert for the years of mentorship, support, encouragement, and honest conversations. Chef Geoff for first throwing me on

the line in Orlando, whether I was ready or not. Chef Yasha for taking time to teach me technique and share his understanding of ingredients and never taking anything too seriously. Chef Marcus Samuelsson for pushing me to get outside of my comfort zone, and for supporting me once I got there.

Nicole Albano and Crystal Wang at Bolster Media have supported my career in so many ways and introduced me to countless wonderful people to help further my career and led to this book. One of those people was Sarah Zorn, who brought this book to life by listening, talking, asking questions, becoming a friend, and making sense of my crazy stories and memories. Her ability to take our interviews and discussions and help craft a narrative and tell a cohesive story is a true talent, and I could not have done this without her. Sarah Smith has been the advocate I never knew I needed, and I am so grateful that I have her on my side. Jasmine Moy has fine-tuned and reviewed contracts, sometimes with little turnaround time, but is always there for her chefs. My friend Rita Jammet, New York's doyenne of dining and Champagne, is quick to offer a glass of bubbles and help me talk through any culinary issue. IzzyE gave me the space to fulfill this dream and offered quiet mazel tovs and encouragement along the way.

Thank you to the team at Clarkson Potter: Jennifer Sit for enthusiastically jumping in as editor, bringing genuine excitement about the *Sunday Best* concept, and highlighting the connections that cultures share through food. Also for encouraging me to bring more historical context to the stories to push the dialogue forward. Amanda Englander for believing in this project enough to fight for it. Stephanie Huntwork for her creative direction, La Tricia Watford for crafting visuals that really reflect the sentiment of this book, and Robert Diaz for his design support.

On the design end, Kelly Marshall, a phenomenal woman and photographer who helped hone the vision and bring out the beauty and depth in every frame.

Thank you for pushing me to define the tone and for helping me bring it to life. Maeve Sheridan for creating environments that I can genuinely see and feel in the images, that remind me of eating with family and spending time with friends. Micah Morton for the thorough food styling, understanding the food and bringing out the nuance and beauty in these dishes. Julia Choi, another talented food stylist, for helping us finish strong and creating dishes that look and taste amazing. Also Gerri Noack and Veronica Martinez for all of your assistance with team food. Khalil Hasty for working with me on your days off to recipe-test in the final stretch and prep for food styling as only a chef of your professionalism and talents can.

Doris LeBlanc, my mother-in-law, who has graciously plied me with too much food and chicory coffee at all hours of the day in New Orleans, and generously regaled me with the history and food customs of her hometown and family. Brooke, Franklin, and Marivic Bailey, for sharing your love and food memories that helped provide modern-day context for the food of NOLA. Lisa Wooley-Laws; Suheily Natal; Sarah Schlessinger; Leslie Grooms, Amy Feuer, Jaya Lindbergh; Jiae Lee; Melissa and Mama Gettis; Ebonique Welton; Joanne, Glen, and Shelley Fondren; and all the people I grew up with who invited me to your homes and fed me, sparking my interest and curiosity in the food of different regions and cultures. The meals we shared as kids and lunches we swapped from paper bags made me see that no matter how different our families or cultures were, we have more that bonds us than separates us.

I would also like to thank the community of friends in the industry who have taken time to talk with me, meet for a (virtual) drink, offer support and advice, and share information so that we can all succeed together: Melba Wilson, Toni Tipton-Martin, Cheryl Day, Alexander Smalls, Nicole A. Taylor, Thérèse Nelson, Osayi Endolyn, Clay Williams, Jerrelle Guy, Yewande Komolafe, Nyesha Arrington, Chris Scott, and so many others.

The team at the Institute of Culinary Education—Rick Smilow, Brian Aronowitz, Ashley Day, Stephanie Fraiman, Cory Sale, Andrea Tutunjian—for lending any and all resources to help me along in my career from work-study student, to commis, line cook, sous chef, exec sous, exec chef, chef-instructor, private chef, occasional TV personality, and now cookbook author. Having such a strong institution rooting me on to succeed at every step has had a profound impact along the way. Thank you.

Team 740, Tanya, Natalia, Sylvia, and Ewa, thank you for always jumping in and being so supportive throughout this process and lending a hand whenever I needed it most.

There are undoubtedly several people who I have left off either here or in the body of the book. Please know that it was not intentional.

Index

Abyssinia, 77
Ali, Fatima, 80
almonds
    Barley Grits with Roasted Grapes and
        Almonds, 147
    in Salted Vanilla-Coconut Rice
        Pudding, 261
Anchovy Dip, Fried Olives with, 71
andouille sausage
    in Controversial Gumbo, 204
    Cornbread Toad-in-the-Hole with
        Crab and Andouille, 45
    in Grandma Lydia's Shrimp Creole,
        202
Anything Can Pickle, 235
appetizers. See snacks
apples
    Apple Pie for Uncle George, 267
    The Best Baked Apples, 248
Apple-Beer Jus, 100
    in Slow-Cooked Ham Hocks, 134
Apple Pie for Uncle George, 267
Arancini, Overnight Grits, 217
artichokes, in Big Easy Eggs Sardou, 47

bacon
    Bacon-Miso Sauce, 102
    in Grand Slam Breakfast Tarts, 52
    in Seven-Layer Salad, 231
    Tater Tot Waffles with Candied
        Bacon, 37
    Warm Bacon-Sherry Vinaigrette, Split
        Pea Salad with, 150
Bacon-Miso Sauce, 102
    Sweet Potato Gnocchi with, 152
Baked Apples, The Best, 248
baked goods, reviving tip, 40

Banana Pudding, Yuzu, 251
Barley Grits with Roasted Grapes and
    Almonds, 147
basil
    in Cornbread (or Biscuit) Panzanella,
        214
    in Turnip-Top Pesto, 91
BBQ Quail, Red Miso, 123
BBQ Sauce, Red Miso, 98
beans
    Butter Bean Hummus, 60
    Pilsen Red Beans and Rice, 141
Becker, Yasha, 261, 272
beef
    Cheerwine-Braised Oxtail, 127
    Grilled Skirt Steak with Mustard-
        Green Chimichurri, 124
    Louisiana Yaka Mein, 227
    Mississippi Pot Roast, 189
    Roger's Park Meat and Potatoes, 190
    Slow-Roasted Harissa Short Ribs, 192
Beer-Apple Jus, 100
    in Slow-Cooked Ham Hocks, 134
Beet and Red Cabbage Slaw, 165
Beignets, Rice (Sugar-and-Spice-Dusted
    Calas), 256
Berbere-Spiced Mini Lamb Meatballs, 77
Best Baked Apples, The, 248
Best-Ever Hush Puppies, 74
Bhel Puri, Crunchy Hoppin' John, 80
Big Easy Eggs Sardou, 47
biscuits
    Biscuit Panzanella, 214
    Flaky Layered Biscuits with Sausage
        Gravy, 23
    Sugared Biscuits and Chocolate
        Gravy, 269

Biscuit Panzanella, 214
black-eyed peas, in Crunchy Hoppin'
    John Bhel Puri, 80
Black Garlic Roasted Leg of Lamb, 183
blanching tip, 149
Blistered Green Beans with Crushed
    Peanuts and Soy, 166
Blueberry Compote, Buttermilk Brûlée
    with Pickled, 252
Boudin-Stuffed Calamari, 208
Bourbon-and-Brown-Sugar-Glazed Root
    Vegetables, 175
Braised Turkey Necks, 121
bread crumbs, 56
breakfast
    about, 21
    Big Easy Eggs Sardou, 47
    Buttermilk and Corn Flour Pancakes
        with Warm Peach Compote, 29
    Challah French Toast Waffles, 31
    Cornbread Toad-in-the-Hole with
        Crab and Andouille, 45
    Flaky Layered Biscuits with Sausage
        Gravy, 23
    Grand Slam Breakfast Tarts, 52
    Green Tomato Shakshuka, 51
    how to "Sunday Best," 40–41
    Kick the Can Salmon Croquettes, 38
    as most important meal of the day,
        32
    Overnight Grits with Fried Eggs and
        Mushroom Ragout, 33
    Pecan Five-Spice Sticky Buns, 25
    Tater Tot Waffles with Candied
        Bacon, 37
    Toasted American Cheese
        "Parachutes," 42

breakfast sandwiches, 40
Brioche-Crusted Salmon, 114
broccoli, in Seven-Layer Salad, 231
Brown Butter and Hazelnuts, Brussels
    Sprouts with, 174
Brussels Sprouts with Brown Butter and
    Hazelnuts, 174
Butter Bean Hummus, 60
buttermilk, making your own, 41
Buttermilk and Corn Flour Pancakes
    with Warm Peach Compote, 29
Buttermilk Brûlée with Pickled
    Blueberry Compote, 252
Buttermilk Vinaigrette, 86
    Grilled Green Tomato Salad with
        Pepitas and, 171

cabbage
    Green Cabbage Gratin, 178
    Red Cabbage and Beet Slaw, 165
cacao nibs, 40
cakes
    Roasted Pineapple Cornmeal Cake,
        273
    Roasted White Chocolate Crepe
        Cake with Hazelnuts and Pecans,
        259
Calamari, Boudin-Stuffed, 208
Calas, Sugar-and-Spice-Dusted (aka
    Rice Beignets), 256
Candied Bacon, Tater Tot Waffles with,
    37
carrots
    Bourbon-and-Brown-Sugar-Glazed
        Root Vegetables, 175
    in Cheerwine-Braised Oxtail, 127
    in Slow-Roasted Harissa Short Ribs,
        192
Cast-Iron Deep-Dish Pizza, 219
Catfish, Roasted, with Herby Yogurt,
    137
Cauliflower, Spicy and Crispy Whole-
    Roasted, 177
Celery, Pimento Cheese-Stuffed, 61
Cha-Cha (Tabletop Pepper Sauce), 88
Cha-Cha's Cousin (Fermented Pepper
    Sauce), 92
Challah French Toast Waffles, 31
Charred Green Onion Relish, 96
Charred Okra with Roasted Tomatoes,
    167
cheddar cheese
    in Hanky-Pankies (Cheesy Porky
        Caraway Bites), 56
    Pimento Cheese-Stuffed Celery, 61

Cheerwine-Braised Oxtail, 127
Cheesy Porky Caraway (Bites Hanky-
    Pankies), 56
chicken
    Chicken and Cornbread Dumplings,
        195
    in Coconut Curry Stew, 234
    cutting tips, 120
    in Green Tomato Chili, 233
    Humboldt Park Fried Chicken, 118
    Red Miso BBQ Chicken, 123
    Spicy-Sweet-Crispy Candied Chicken
        Wings, 63
    Stout-and-Soy-Roasted Chicken, 117
Chicken and Cornbread Dumplings,
    195
chicken livers, in Boudin-Stuffed
    Calamari, 208
chile peppers
    Cha-Cha (Tabletop Pepper Sauce), 88
    Fermented Pepper Sauce (Cha-Cha's
        Cousin), 92
Chili, Green Tomato, 233
Chimichurri, Mustard-Green, 94
    Grilled Skirt Steak with, 124
Chocolate-Bourbon Pecan Pie, 254
chorizo, in Pilsen Red Beans and Rice,
    141
chuck roast
    in Louisiana Yaka Mein, 227
    Mississippi Pot Roast, 189
Coconut Curry Stew, 234
collard greens
    Collard Green Kimchi, 161
    Collard Green Salad with Sesame
        Vinaigrette, 172
    in Hominy Tabbouleh, 145
Collard Green Kimchi, 161
Collard Green Salad with Sesame
    Vinaigrette, 172
compote, 40
    Corn Flour and Buttermilk Pancakes
        with Warm Peach Compote, 29
compound butters, about, 105
Controversial Gumbo, 204
corn, in Elote Macque Choux, 168
Cornbread, Sour Cream, 144
Cornbread Dumplings, Chicken and,
    195
Cornbread Gougères, 70
Cornbread Panzanella, 214
Cornbread Toad-in-the-Hole with Crab
    and Andouille, 45
Corn Flour and Buttermilk Pancakes
    with Warm Peach Compote, 29

Cornmeal Cake, Roasted Pineapple,
    273
Country Gravy (aka the Southern
    Mother Sauce), 108
crab
    in Controversial Gumbo, 204
    Cornbread Toad-in-the-Hole with
        Crab and Andouille, 45
cracked pepper, about, 19
Creamed Spinach, in Big Easy Eggs
    Sardou, 47
Creamy Vegan Pasta, 241
Creole, Grandma Lydia's Shrimp, 202
Crepe Cake, Roasted White Chocolate,
    with Hazelnuts and Pecans, 259
Croquettes, Kick the Can Salmon, 38
Crunchy Hoppin' John Bhel Puri, 80
Crustless Kitchen-Sink Quiche, 223
Curry Stew, Coconut, 234

dashi
    about, 103
    in Bacon-Miso Sauce, 102
Deep-Dish Pizza, Cast-Iron, 219
deglazing, about, 105
desserts. See also cakes; pies; pudding
    about, 243
    The Best Baked Apples, 248
    Buttermilk Brûlée with Pickled
        Blueberry Compote, 252
    how to "Sunday Best," 262–63
    No-Churn Strawberry Shortcake Ice
        Cream, 244
    Sugar-and-Spice-Dusted Calas, 256
    Sugared Biscuits and Chocolate
        Gravy, 269
    Sweet Tea Granita, 247
dips
    Anchovy Dip, Fried Olives with, 71
    Butter Bean Hummus, 60
    Poor Man's Remoulade, 109
    Turnip-Top Pesto, 91
DIY dinners, 200

eggs
    Big Easy Eggs Sardou, 47
    in Cornbread Toad-in-the-Hole with
        Crab and Andouille, 45
    in Crustless Kitchen-Sink Quiche, 223
    in Green Tomato Shakshuka, 51
    omelets, cooking tips, 40
    Overnight Grits with Fried Eggs and
        Mushroom Ragout, 33
    poaching tips, 41, 48
    in Seven-Layer Salad, 231

Elephant Ears, 21, 238
Elote Macque Choux, 168
Escabeche, Pickled Shrimp, 66

family-style feasts
    about, 181
    Black Garlic Roasted Leg of Lamb,
        183
    Boudin-Stuffed Calamari, 208
    Chicken and Cornbread Dumplings,
        195
    Controversial Gumbo, 204
    Grandma Lydia's Shrimp Creole, 202
    how to "Sunday Best," 200–201
    Mississippi Pot Roast, 189
    Mom's Stuffed Shells with Smoky Red
        Gravy, 197
    Pecan-Crusted Pork Rib Roast, 187
    Roger's Park Meat and Potatoes, 190
    Slow-Roasted Harissa Short Ribs, 192
    Slow-Roasted Pork Shoulder (Pernil),
        182
Fermented Pepper Sauce (Cha-Cha's
    Cousin), 92
feta cheese
    in Berbere-Spiced Mini Lamb
        Meatballs, 77
    in Cornbread (or Biscuit) Panzanella,
        214
    in Green Tomato Shakshuka, 51
    in Seven-Layer Salad, 231
fish and seafood. See also shrimp
    Boudin-Stuffed Calamari, 208
    in Coconut Curry Stew, 234
    Controversial Gumbo, 204
    Roasted Catfish with Herby Yogurt, 137
Flaky Layered Biscuits with Sausage
    Gravy, 23
Franklin, Aretha, 86
French Toast Waffles, Challah, 31
Fried Chicken, Humboldt Park, 118
Fried Eggs and Mushroom Ragout,
    Overnight Grits with, 33
Fried Olives with Anchovy Dip, 71

garnishes, about, 19, 76, 200
Gazpacho Shooters, Mango Tajín, 73
Gnocchi, Sweet Potato, with Bacon-
    Miso Sauce, 152
Gougères, Cornbread, 70
Grandma Lydia's Shrimp Creole, 202
Grand Slam Breakfast Tarts, 52
Granita, Sweet Tea, 247
Grapes, Barley Grits with Roasted
    Almonds and, 147

Gras, Laurent, 114
Gratin, Green Cabbage, 178
Green Beans, Blistered, with Crushed
    Peanuts and Soy, 166
Green Cabbage Gratin, 178
Green Onion Relish, Charred, 96
Green Tomato Chili, 233
Green Tomato Salad, Grilled, with
    Buttermilk Vinaigrette and Pepitas,
    171
Green Tomato Shakshuka, 51
Grilled Green Tomato Salad with
    Buttermilk Vinaigrette and Pepitas,
    171
Grilled Skirt Steak with Mustard-Green
    Chimichurri, 124
grits
    Barley Grits with Roasted Grapes and
        Almonds, 147
    Overnight Grits Arancini, 217
    Overnight Grits with Fried Eggs and
        Mushroom Ragout, 33
Gruyère cheese
    in Cornbread Gougères, 70
    in Grand Slam Breakfast Tarts, 52
    in Green Cabbage Gratin, 178
Gumbo, Controversial, 204

ham hocks, 239
    Slow-Cooked Ham Hocks, 134
Hanky-Pankies (Cheesy Porky Caraway
    Bites), 56
Harissa Short Ribs, Slow-Roasted, 192
Herb-and-Mustard-Slathered Veal
    Chops, 133
high heat, using, 18, 149
Hollandaise, in Big Easy Eggs Sardou, 47
Hominy Tabbouleh, 145
Hoppin' John Bhel Puri, Crunchy, 80
hors d'oeuvres. See snacks
hot sauces, 238
    Cha-Cha (Tabletop Pepper Sauce), 88
    Fermented Pepper Sauce (Cha-Cha's
        Cousin), 92
Humboldt Park Fried Chicken, 118
Hummus, Butter Bean, 60
Hush Puppies, Best-Ever, 74

Ice Cream, No-Churn Strawberry
    Shortcake, 244
instant mocha, 238
Institute of Culinary Education, 14, 157

Jus, Beer-Apple, 100
    in Slow-Cooked Ham Hocks, 134

kale, in Seven-Layer Salad, 231
Kick the Can Salmon Croquettes, 38
Kimchi, Collard Green, 161

lamb
    Berbere-Spiced Mini Lamb Meatballs,
        77
    Black Garlic Roasted Leg of Lamb,
        183
    Roger's Park Meat and Potatoes,
        190
Latkes, Turnip, 159
Le Bernardin, 14–16, 38, 73, 85, 86, 95,
    102, 152, 248
    family meals, 52, 182, 254
leftovers reimagined
    about, 213
    Anything Can Pickle, 235
    Cast-Iron Deep-Dish Pizza, 219
    Coconut Curry Stew, 234
    Cornbread (or Biscuit) Panzanella,
        214
    Creamy Vegan Pasta, 241
    Crustless Kitchen-Sink Quiche, 223
    Green Tomato Chili, 233
    how to "Sunday Best," 238–39
    Louisiana Yaka Mein, 227
    Overnight Grits Arancini, 217
    Pan-Fried Spaghetti Rösti, 226
    Seven-Layer Salad, 231
Louisiana Yaka Mein, 227

Macque Choux, Elote, 168
Mango Tajín Gazpacho Shooters, 73
Mashed Parsnips, 156
Meatballs, Berbere-Spiced Mini Lamb,
    77
miso
    about, 98
    Bacon-Miso Sauce, 102
    Red Miso BBQ Quail, 123
    Red Miso BBQ Sauce, 98
Mississippi Pot Roast, 189
Mom's Stuffed Shells with Smoky Red
    Gravy, 197
mozzarella cheese
    in Cast-Iron Deep-Dish Pizza, 219
    in Cornbread (or Biscuit) Panzanella,
        214
    in Mom's Stuffed Shells with Smoky
        Red Gravy, 197
Mushroom Ragout
    in Overnight Grits Arancini, 217
    Overnight Grits with Fried Eggs and,
        33

Mustard-Green Chimichurri, 94
   Grilled Skirt Steak with, 124

Nash, Helen, 159
natural emulsifiers, about, 104
Nilla wafers, in Yuzu Banana Pudding, 251
No-Churn Strawberry Shortcake Ice Cream, 244

Obama, Michelle and Barack, 244
okra
   Charred Okra with Roasted Tomatoes, 167
   Oven-Fried Okra Chips, 67
Olives, Fried, with Anchovy Dip, 71
omelets, 40
Oven-Fried Okra Chips, 67
Overnight Grits Arancini, 217
Overnight Grits with Fried Eggs and Mushroom Ragout, 33
Oxtail, Cheerwine-Braised, 127

Pancakes, Buttermilk and Corn Flour, with Warm Peach Compote, 29
Pan-Fried Spaghetti Rösti, 226
Panzanella, Cornbread (or Biscuit), 214
Parmesan cheese
   in Cornbread Gougères, 70
   in Grand Slam Breakfast Tarts, 52
   in Green Cabbage Gratin, 178
   in Mom's Stuffed Shells with Smoky Red Gravy, 197
   in Overnight Grits Arancini, 217
   in Turnip-Top Pesto, 91
parsnips
   Bourbon-and-Brown-Sugar-Glazed Root Vegetables, 175
   Mashed Parsnips, 156
pasta
   cooking tip, 148
   Creamy Vegan Pasta, 241
   Mom's Stuffed Shells with Smoky Red Gravy, 197
   Pan-Fried Spaghetti Rösti, 226
   Sweet Potato Gnocchi with Bacon-Miso Sauce, 152
Peach Compote, Buttermilk and Corn Flour Pancakes with Warm, 29
pecans
   Chocolate-Bourbon Pecan Pie, 254
   Pecan-Crusted Pork Rib Roast, 187
   Pecan Five-Spice Sticky Buns, 25
   Roasted White Chocolate Crepe Cake with Hazelnuts and Pecans, 259

Pecan-Crusted Pork Rib Roast, 187
Pecan Five-Spice Sticky Buns, 25
Pernil (Slow-Roasted Pork Shoulder), 182
Pesto, Turnip-Top, 91
Pickled Blueberry Compote, Buttermilk Brûlée with, 252
Pickled Shrimp Escabeche, 66
pickles, 262
   Anything Can Pickle, 235
   Collard Green Kimchi, 161
pies
   Apple Pie for Uncle George, 267
   Chocolate-Bourbon Pecan Pie, 254
Pilsen Red Beans and Rice, 141
Pimento Cheese-Stuffed Celery, 61
Pineapple Cornmeal Cake, Roasted, 273
Pizza, Cast-Iron Deep-Dish, 219
Poor Man's Remoulade, 109
Popovers, Sky-High, 140
pork. See also bacon
   Flaky Layered Biscuits with Sausage Gravy, 23
   Hanky-Pankies (Cheesy Porky Caraway Bites), 56
   Pecan-Crusted Pork Rib Roast, 187
   Slow-Cooked Ham Hocks, 134
   Slow-Roasted Pork Shoulder (Pernil), 182
   Smothered Pork Chops with Smoky Red Gravy, 130
potatoes
   Bourbon-and-Brown-Sugar-Glazed Root Vegetables, 175
   in Grand Slam Breakfast Tarts, 52
   Roger's Park Meat and Potatoes, 190
   in Smothered Pork Chops with Smoky Red Gravy, 130
   Tater Tot Waffles with Candied Bacon, 37
Pot Roast, Mississippi, 189
preheating pans, 19
"protein, starch, and veg"
   about, 111, 126
   how to "Sunday Best," 148–49
   learning how to cook like a grown-up, 126
pudding
   Salted Vanilla-Coconut Rice Pudding, 261
   Yuzu Banana Pudding, 251

Quail, Red Miso BBQ, 123
Quiche, Crustless Kitchen-Sink, 223

ramen noodles, in Louisiana Yaka Mein, 227
recycling scraps, 105, 227
Red Beans and Rice, Pilsen, 141
Red Cabbage and Beet Slaw, 165
Red Gravy. See Smoky Red Gravy
Red Miso BBQ Quail, 123
Red Miso BBQ Sauce, 98
Red Rooster, 15–16, 144
Remoulade, Poor Man's, 109
Rice, Pilsen Red Beans and, 141
Rice Beignets (Sugar-and-Spice-Dusted Calas), 256
Rice Pilaf. See Trinity Rice Pilaf
Rice Pudding, Salted Vanilla-Coconut, 261
ricotta, 239
Ripert, Eric, 15–16
risotto, 148, 217
Roasted Catfish with Herby Yogurt, 137
Roasted Chicken, Stout-and-Soy, 117
Roasted Leg of Lamb, Black Garlic, 183
Roasted Pineapple Cornmeal Cake, 273
Roasted Tomatoes, Charred Okra with, 167
Roasted White Chocolate Crepe Cake with Hazelnuts and Pecans, 259
Roger's Park Meat and Potatoes, 190
Root Vegetables, Bourbon-and-Brown-Sugar-Glazed, 175
Rösti, Pan-Fried Spaghetti, 226
rule of three, 76

sage, about, 41
salads
   Collard Green Salad with Sesame Vinaigrette, 172
   Cornbread (or Biscuit) Panzanella, 214
   Grilled Green Tomato Salad with Buttermilk Vinaigrette and Pepitas, 171
   Hominy Tabbouleh, 145
   Seven-Layer Salad, 231
   Split Pea Salad with Warm Bacon-Sherry Vinaigrette, 150
salmon
   Brioche-Crusted Salmon, 114
   Kick the Can Salmon Croquettes, 38
salt-crusted whole fish, 200
Salted Vanilla-Coconut Rice Pudding, 261
Samuelsson, Marcus, 15–16, 45, 77
Sandestin Golf and Beach Resort, 261, 272

sauces. *See also* hot sauces
    about, 85
    Bacon-Miso Sauce, 102
    Beer-Apple Jus, 100
    building bridges with, 95
    Buttermilk Vinaigrette, 86
    Charred Green Onion Relish, 96
    Country Gravy, 108
    how to "Sunday Best," 104–5
    Mustard-Green Chimichurri, 94
    Poor Man's Remoulade, 109
    Red Miso BBQ Sauce, 98
    Smoky Red Gravy, 99
    Turnip-Top Pesto, 91
Sausage Gravy, Flaky Layered Biscuits
    with, 23
seasoning tips, 18, 19, 148, 187
Sesame Vinaigrette, Collard Green
    Salad with, 172
Seven-Layer Salad, 231
Shakshuka, Green Tomato, 51
Shepherd's Pie (Roger's Park Meat and
    Potatoes), 190
Short Ribs, Slow-Roasted Harissa, 192
shrimp
    Grandma Lydia's Shrimp Creole,
        202
    Pickled Shrimp Escabeche, 66
    Third Coast Shrimp Toast, 83
Skirt Steak, Grilled, with Mustard-Green
    Chimichurri, 124
Sky-High Popovers, 140
Slaw, Red Cabbage and Beet, 165
Slow-Cooked Ham Hocks, 134
Slow-Roasted Harissa Short Ribs, 192
Slow-Roasted Pork Shoulder (Pernil),
    182
slow-roasting, about, 148
Smoky Red Gravy, 99
    Mom's Stuffed Shells with, 197
    Smothered Pork Chops with, 130
Smothered Pork Chops with Smoky Red
    Gravy, 130
snacks
    about, 55
    appetizers for dinner, 64
    Berbere-Spiced Mini Lamb Meatballs,
        77
    Best-Ever Hush Puppies, 74
    Butter Bean Hummus, 60
    Cornbread Gougères, 70

Crunchy Hoppin' John Bhel Puri,
    80
Fried Olives with Anchovy Dip, 71
Hanky-Pankies, 56
how to "Sunday Best," 76, 200
Mango Tajín Gazpacho Shooters, 73
Oven-Fried Okra Chips, 67
Pickled Shrimp Escabeche, 66
Pimento Cheese-Stuffed Celery, 61
Spicy-Sweet-Crispy Candied Chicken
    Wings, 63
Third Coast Shrimp Toast, 83
sofrito, 96
    Trinity Sofrito, 141, 157
Sour Cream Cornbread, 144
Southern Mother Sauce (Country
    Gravy), 108
spaghetti, in Louisiana Yaka Mein,
    227
Spaghetti Rösti, Pan-Fried, 226
Spicy and Crispy Whole-Roasted
    Cauliflower, 177
Spicy-Sweet-Crispy Candied Chicken
    Wings, 63
spinach
    in Big Easy Eggs Sardou, 47
    in Mom's Stuffed Shells with Smoky
        Red Gravy, 197
Split Pea Salad with Warm Bacon-
    Sherry Vinaigrette, 150
Sticky Buns, Pecan Five-Spice, 25
Stout-and-Soy-Roasted Chicken, 117
Strawberry Shortcake Ice Cream,
    No-Churn, 244
Streetbird, 45
Stuffed Shells with Smoky Red Gravy,
    Mom's, 197
Sugar-and-Spice-Dusted Calas (aka Rice
    Beignets), 256
Sugared Biscuits and Chocolate Gravy,
    269
"Sunday Best," how to
    breakfast, 40–41
    desserts, 262–63
    every day, 18–19
    family-style feasts, 200–201
    leftovers reimagined, 238–39
    protein, starch, and veg, 148–49
    sauces, 104–5
    snacks, 76
supermarket swap, 19

Sweet Potato Gnocchi with Bacon-Miso
    Sauce, 152
Sweet Tea Granita, 247

Tabbouleh, Hominy, 145
Tarts, Grand Slam Breakfast, 52
Tater Tot Waffles with Candied Bacon, 37
Third Coast Shrimp Toast, 83
Toad-in-the-Hole with Crab and
    Andouille, Cornbread, 45
Toast, Third Coast Shrimp, 83
Toasted American Cheese
    "Parachutes," 42
toasted nuts, 262
tomatillos
    in Green Tomato Chili, 233
    in Green Tomato Shakshuka, 51
tomatoes
    Charred Okra with Roasted
        Tomatoes, 167
    cherry, about, 40
    Green Tomato Chili, 233
    Green Tomato Shakshuka, 51
    Grilled Green Tomato Salad with
        Buttermilk Vinaigrette and Pepitas,
        171
Top Chef (TV show), 16–17, 251
Trinity Rice Pilaf, 157
    in Grandma Lydia's Shrimp Creole, 202
    in Pilsen Red Beans and Rice, 141
Trinity Sofrito, 141, 157
Turkey Necks, Braised, 121
Turnip Latkes, 159
Turnip-Top Pesto, 91

Vanessa's Dumpling House, 96
vanilla beans, about, 262
Veal Chops, Herb-and-Mustard-
    Slathered, 133
Vegan Pasta, Creamy, 241

waffles, 238
    Challah French Toast Waffles, 31
    Tater Tot Waffles with Candied
        Bacon, 37
Warm Bacon-Sherry Vinaigrette, Split
    Pea Salad with, 150
Wondra, about, 24

Yaka Mein, Louisiana, 227
Yuzu Banana Pudding, 251

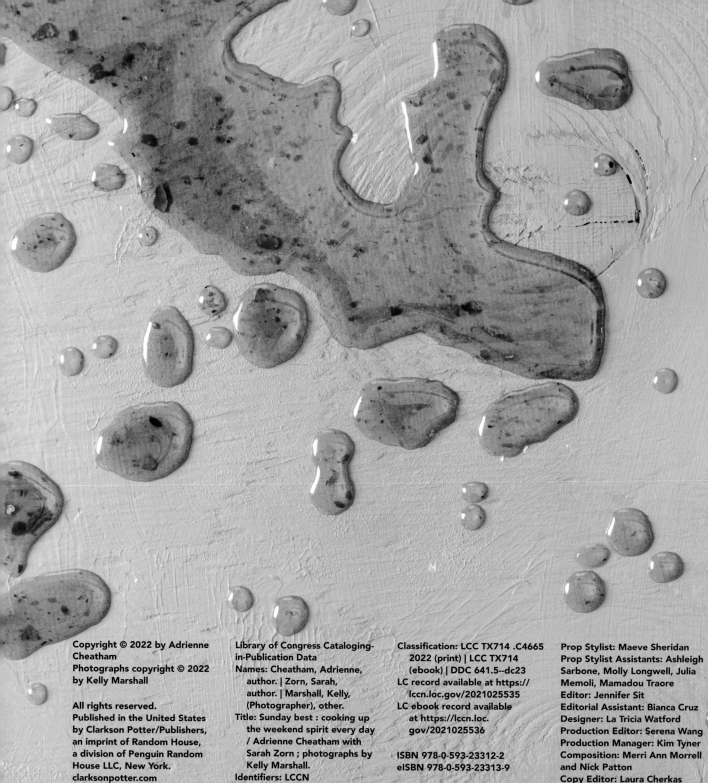

Library of Congress Cataloging-in-Publication Data
Names: Cheatham, Adrienne, author. | Zorn, Sarah, author. | Marshall, Kelly, (Photographer), other.
Title: Sunday best : cooking up the weekend spirit every day / Adrienne Cheatham with Sarah Zorn ; photographs by Kelly Marshall.
Identifiers: LCCN 2021025535 (print) | LCCN 2021025536 (ebook) | ISBN 9780593233122 (hardcover) | ISBN 9780593233139 (ebook)
Subjects: LCSH: Cooking. | LCGFT: Cookbooks.
Classification: LCC TX714 .C4665 2022 (print) | LCC TX714 (ebook) | DDC 641.5--dc23
LC record available at https://lccn.loc.gov/2021025535
LC ebook record available at https://lccn.loc.gov/2021025536

ISBN 978-0-593-23312-2
eISBN 978-0-593-23313-9

Photographer: Kelly Marshall
Photography Assistants: Jamie Ellington, Michael Oliver, Tatum Mangus
Food Stylists: Micah Morton, Julia Choi
Food Stylist Assistants: Khalil Hasty, Gerri Noack, Veronica Martinez
Prop Stylist: Maeve Sheridan
Prop Stylist Assistants: Ashleigh Sarbone, Molly Longwell, Julia Memoli, Mamadou Traore
Editor: Jennifer Sit
Editorial Assistant: Bianca Cruz
Designer: La Tricia Watford
Production Editor: Serena Wang
Production Manager: Kim Tyner
Composition: Merri Ann Morrell and Nick Patton
Copy Editor: Laura Cherkas
Indexer: Stephen Callahan
Marketer: Monica Stanton
Publicist: Erica Gelbard

Printed in China

10 9 8 7 6 5 4 3 2 1

First Edition